THEOLOGY OF JESUS

Dr. Maxwell Shimba

TABLE OF CONTENTS

INTRODUCTION

Overview of Jesus Christ's Significance in Christian Theology

Jesus Christ stands as the central figure in Christian theology, embodying the fulcrum upon which the entire Christian faith balances. His life, teachings, death, and resurrection form the foundation of Christian belief and practice, making Him not merely a historical figure but the cornerstone of a profound theological narrative that spans over two millennia.

At the heart of Christian theology is the belief in Jesus as the Son of God, whose Incarnation represents the divine becoming human to effectuate salvation. This concept of

Jesus' dual nature—fully divine and fully human—is not just a theological abstraction but a core tenet that shapes Christian understanding of God's interaction with humanity. The belief that Jesus is both true God and true man is central to the doctrine of the Trinity, which posits that God exists as three distinct persons—Father, Son, and Holy Spirit—in one essence. This theological framework provides the basis for understanding Jesus' role in the divine economy of salvation.

Jesus' teachings, recorded in the New Testament, are foundational to Christian ethics and spirituality. His parables, sermons, and interactions with people reflect a radical reorientation of the human relationship with God. The Sermon on the Mount, for instance, offers profound insights into the nature of the Kingdom of God and the ethical implications of living in accordance with God's will. His message of love, forgiveness, and reconciliation challenges believers to live out these values in their own lives, setting a standard for moral and spiritual conduct.

The crucifixion and resurrection of Jesus are pivotal events in Christian theology. The Cross is not merely a historical fact but a symbol of Jesus' sacrificial love and the means by which believers are reconciled with God. The resurrection, celebrated as the ultimate victory over sin and death, is the cornerstone of Christian hope, affirming the promise of eternal life and the assurance of Christ's ongoing presence in the lives of believers. The resurrection also validates Jesus' claims to divinity and underscores the transformative power of His work.

Jesus' role as the Messiah, as foretold in the Old Testament, is crucial for understanding His significance. Christians believe that Jesus fulfilled the Messianic prophecies, which spoke of a Savior who would deliver God's people and establish His reign. This Messianic expectation, however, was redefined by Jesus' life and ministry, challenging traditional notions of a political or military leader and instead presenting a vision of a Savior who brings redemption through suffering and self-sacrifice.

In the realm of contemporary theology, Jesus continues to be a subject of deep reflection and diverse interpretations. Modern theological discourse often explores Jesus' teachings in the context of social justice, liberation theology, and interfaith dialogue. These perspectives seek to understand and apply Jesus' message in a rapidly changing world, highlighting His relevance beyond the confines of traditional doctrinal debates.

This book aims to delve into the rich theological landscape surrounding Jesus Christ, exploring His significance from multiple angles. By examining the historical context, core teachings, theological implications, and contemporary interpretations of Jesus, this study seeks to provide a comprehensive understanding of why Jesus remains central to Christian faith and practice. Through this exploration, readers will gain insights into the profound impact of Jesus' life and teachings on the Christian tradition and their enduring relevance in today's world.

The Importance of Studying Jesus' Life, Teachings, and Divine Nature

1.1. Introduction to Jesus' Centrality in Christianity

Jesus Christ is undeniably the central figure in Christianity, and understanding His life, teachings, and divine nature is crucial for grasping the essence of Christian faith. The significance of studying Jesus extends beyond mere historical inquiry; it encompasses a deep exploration of theological, ethical, and spiritual dimensions that shape Christian doctrine and practice. This chapter will illuminate why the study of Jesus' life, teachings, and divine nature is vital for both individual believers and the Christian community as a whole.

1.2. Historical Significance

Jesus of Nazareth, a figure whose existence is well-documented within and outside Christian texts, stands at the crossroads of history and divinity. His life and ministry occurred in a specific historical context—first-century Judea—marked by Roman occupation and Jewish expectations of a Messiah. Studying Jesus' historical context helps to understand the profound impact He had on His contemporaries and the world that followed. His revolutionary teachings and the manner in which He engaged with the social and religious norms of His time are key to understanding the origins of Christianity and its subsequent spread.

The historical study of Jesus also sheds light on the authenticity of the Gospel accounts and their development. By examining historical sources, scholars can assess the credibility of the events described and better appreciate the transformative nature of Jesus' message.

1.3. Theological Importance

Theological inquiry into Jesus' life and teachings is foundational to Christian belief. Jesus is regarded as the Son of God, a core tenet that emphasizes His divine nature and His role in the Trinity. Understanding His divine nature is essential for comprehending the concept of the Incarnation—God becoming human to fulfill the divine plan of salvation.

Jesus' teachings are not just ethical guidelines but revelations of divine truth. The Sermon on the Mount, parables, and other teachings reveal the nature of God's Kingdom and the transformative power of living according to divine principles. They offer insights into the nature of God's love, justice, and mercy, which are central to Christian ethics and spirituality.

Theological exploration also involves understanding Jesus' role in the atonement and salvation. His sacrificial death and resurrection are seen as the means by which humanity is reconciled with God. This doctrine of atonement is central to Christian faith, and a thorough understanding of it requires a deep dive into the theological implications of Jesus' sacrificial act.

1.4. Ethical and Spiritual Implications

Jesus' teachings provide a moral framework that has influenced Christian ethics for centuries. His emphasis on love, forgiveness, and humility challenges believers to embody these virtues in their daily lives. The ethical teachings of Jesus offer guidance on issues such as justice, compassion, and reconciliation, encouraging followers to live out their faith in tangible and transformative ways.

Spiritually, the study of Jesus' life offers insights into the nature of discipleship and the path to spiritual growth. His example of devotion, prayer, and relationship with God serves as a model for Christians seeking to deepen their spiritual lives. By following His teachings and example, believers can cultivate a closer relationship with God and a more profound understanding of their own spiritual journey.

1.5. Contemporary Relevance

The relevance of studying Jesus extends into contemporary issues and challenges. In an increasingly pluralistic and diverse world, the teachings of Jesus continue to offer guidance on how to navigate complex moral and ethical dilemmas. The principles of love, justice, and reconciliation are as applicable today as they were in the first century, providing a timeless framework for addressing modern concerns.

Furthermore, the study of Jesus' life and teachings fosters interfaith dialogue and mutual understanding. Recognizing Jesus' significance from various perspectives—whether within Christian, Jewish, or Islamic contexts—can promote respect and collaboration among different faith communities.

1.6. Conclusion

The study of Jesus Christ's life, teachings, and divine nature is of paramount importance for understanding the Christian faith. His historical impact, theological significance, ethical teachings, and contemporary relevance underscore the need for a comprehensive exploration of His role in both historical and modern contexts. Engaging deeply with the figure of Jesus enriches not only one's personal faith but also contributes to the broader discourse on spirituality, ethics, and interfaith relations. Through this study, believers and scholars alike can gain a deeper appreciation of the profound influence Jesus continues to have on the world.

1.1. Understanding the Centrality of Jesus in Christian Faith

Jesus Christ occupies a unique and unparalleled position in Christian theology. He is not just a historical figure or a religious leader; He is the very foundation upon which Christianity is built. The importance of studying Jesus' life, teachings, and divine nature cannot be overstated, as these elements are the bedrock of Christian belief and practice. For Christians, Jesus is the ultimate revelation of God, the Savior of humanity, and the model for living a life that aligns with God's will.

The study of Jesus Christ encompasses several dimensions—historical, theological, ethical, and spiritual. Each of these aspects offers profound insights that are essential for a comprehensive understanding of the Christian faith. This introduction will explore why studying the life, teachings, and divine nature of Jesus is crucial for anyone seeking to understand and live out the principles of Christianity.

1.2. The Historical Importance of Jesus

Jesus of Nazareth lived over 2,000 years ago, yet His life and influence continue to be of immense importance. Understanding the historical context in which Jesus lived helps to situate His teachings and actions within the broader narrative of human history. First-century Judea was a land under Roman occupation, with a Jewish population longing for the promised Messiah. This context shaped much of Jesus' ministry and provides insight into why His message was so revolutionary and, at the same time, so contentious.

The historical study of Jesus also involves examining the reliability of the Gospel accounts and other historical sources. These texts provide a window into the life of Jesus and the early Christian community. By studying these documents, believers and scholars alike can gain a deeper appreciation of how Jesus' life and message have been understood and transmitted through the ages.

1.3. Theological Significance of Jesus' Divine Nature

In Christian theology, Jesus is not merely a prophet or teacher; He is the Son of God, fully divine and fully human. This dual nature of Christ is a cornerstone of Christian doctrine, encapsulating the mystery of the Incarnation—God becoming man to redeem humanity. Understanding Jesus' divine nature is essential for grasping the broader Christian narrative of salvation.

Theological study of Jesus involves exploring doctrines such as the Trinity, the Atonement, and the Resurrection. These are not abstract concepts but vital truths that shape the Christian understanding of God's relationship with humanity. The Incarnation, for example, reveals God's profound love and commitment to His creation, while the Resurrection affirms the victory over sin and death. By studying these doctrines, believers can deepen their understanding of God's plan for humanity and their place within it.

1.4. The Ethical and Moral Teachings of Jesus

Jesus' teachings are foundational to Christian ethics and morality. His message of love, forgiveness, compassion, and justice challenges believers to live in ways that reflect the character of God. The Sermon on the Mount, one of the most famous discourses of Jesus, encapsulates the ethical teachings that have guided Christians for centuries. In it, Jesus calls for a radical way of living that goes beyond mere adherence to the law, emphasizing the importance of inner transformation and a heart aligned with God's will.

Studying Jesus' teachings is essential for anyone seeking to live a life that honors God. His teachings address every aspect of human life—relationships, wealth, power, and spirituality. By engaging with these teachings, believers can develop a moral compass that guides them through the complexities of modern life, ensuring that their actions reflect their faith.

1.5. The Spiritual Implications of Following Jesus

Beyond historical and theological study, following Jesus is a deeply spiritual endeavor. Jesus calls His followers to a life of discipleship, characterized by a personal relationship with Him. This relationship is not just about adhering to a set of rules or doctrines; it is about a transformative journey that shapes the believer's entire being.

Studying Jesus' life and teachings leads to spiritual growth, as believers are invited to model their lives after His example. Jesus demonstrated perfect obedience to the Father, compassion for the marginalized, and unwavering commitment to truth and righteousness. In following Him, believers are not only learning about God but are also being transformed into the likeness of Christ. This transformation is the essence of Christian spirituality, as believers are called to embody the love, grace, and truth of Jesus in their daily lives.

1.6. The Relevance of Jesus in Contemporary Society

In a world that is increasingly complex and diverse, the teachings and example of Jesus remain profoundly relevant. The issues of justice, peace, and ethical living that Jesus addressed are as pertinent today as they were in the first century. Studying Jesus provides insights into how Christians can engage with the world around them in ways that promote healing, reconciliation, and hope.

Furthermore, the study of Jesus fosters dialogue and understanding across different faith traditions. Jesus is a figure of significance not only in Christianity but also in other major religions, including Islam and Judaism. By studying Jesus, believers can engage in meaningful conversations with people of other faiths, building bridges of understanding and respect.

1.7. Conclusion

The study of Jesus' life, teachings, and divine nature is not merely an academic exercise; it is a journey into the heart of Christian faith. It is through this study that believers come to understand who Jesus is, what He has done, and what He continues to do in the world today. By engaging deeply with the person of Jesus, Christians are equipped to live out their faith with conviction, compassion, and purpose.

As we embark on this exploration of Jesus' life, teachings, and divine nature, we open ourselves to a deeper understanding of God's love and His plan for humanity. This study will not only enrich our knowledge but will also transform our hearts and lives, drawing us closer to the One who is the way, the truth, and the life.

Objectives and Structure of the Book

1.1. The Purpose of This Study

The life, teachings, and divine nature of Jesus Christ have been subjects of profound interest and study for centuries, shaping not only religious thought but also influencing culture, ethics, and human history. This book aims to delve deeply into these aspects of Jesus Christ, offering a comprehensive exploration that seeks to illuminate His significance from multiple perspectives. The primary objective of this study is to provide readers with a thorough understanding of who Jesus is, what He taught, and why He is considered central to Christian theology.

The objectives of this book are manifold:

1. To Understand the Historical Jesus: The book seeks to place Jesus within the historical context of first-century Judea, examining the social, political, and religious factors that influenced His life and ministry. Understanding the historical Jesus is crucial for appreciating the impact of His teachings and actions.

2. To Explore the Theological Significance of Jesus: Central to this study is an exploration of the theological implications of Jesus' life, death, and resurrection. The book will delve into doctrines such as the Incarnation, the Trinity, and the Atonement, seeking to explain how these concepts shape Christian beliefs about God, salvation, and the nature of humanity.

3. To Analyze Jesus' Teachings: Jesus' teachings, as recorded in the Gospels, are foundational to Christian ethics and spirituality. This book aims to unpack these teachings, exploring their meaning, relevance, and application in both ancient and modern contexts.

4. To Reflect on the Divine Nature of Jesus: Understanding Jesus' divine nature is key to grasping the Christian understanding of God. The book will examine the biblical and theological basis for the belief in Jesus as the Son of God, and what this belief means for the Christian faith.

5. To Assess the Contemporary Relevance of Jesus' Life and Teachings: The book will explore how Jesus' teachings and example continue to influence contemporary issues, including ethics, social justice, and interfaith dialogue. It will seek to demonstrate that the study of Jesus is not merely historical or doctrinal but also profoundly relevant to modern life.

6. To Engage in Interdisciplinary Dialogue: While rooted in theology, this study will also engage with other disciplines, including history, philosophy, and ethics, to provide a well-rounded understanding of Jesus. This interdisciplinary approach will help readers see the broad

impact of Jesus' life and teachings across various fields of study.

1.2. The Structure of the Book

To achieve these objectives, the book is structured in a way that systematically explores each aspect of Jesus' life, teachings, and divine nature. The following is an outline of the book's structure, designed to guide readers through a comprehensive study of Jesus Christ:

Chapter 1: The Historical Context of Jesus

- This chapter sets the stage by providing a detailed look at the historical and cultural context in which Jesus lived. It will explore the political, social, and religious landscape of first-century Judea, offering insights into how these factors shaped Jesus' ministry.

Chapter 2: The Person of Jesus Christ

- This chapter will delve into the identity of Jesus, exploring the mystery of the Incarnation and the theological implications of Jesus being both fully God and fully man. It will also address key Christological debates that have shaped Christian understanding of who Jesus is.

Chapter 3: The Teachings of Jesus

- Focusing on Jesus' teachings, this chapter will analyze key themes such as the Kingdom of God, love, forgiveness, and justice. It will examine how these teachings were revolutionary in their time and how they continue to influence Christian ethics today.

Chapter 4: The Death and Resurrection of Jesus

- This chapter will explore the significance of Jesus' crucifixion and resurrection, examining their theological implications for salvation, atonement, and eternal life. It will also discuss the resurrection as a cornerstone of Christian faith and its role in the hope of believers.

Chapter 5: Jesus as the Fulfillment of Prophecy

- In this chapter, the book will explore how Jesus is seen as the fulfillment of Old Testament prophecies, particularly the Messianic prophecies. It will look at the ways in which Jesus redefined Jewish expectations of the Messiah.

Chapter 6: The Role of the Holy Spirit in Jesus' Ministry

- This chapter will focus on the role of the Holy Spirit in Jesus' life and ministry, as well as in the lives of believers.

It will explore the significance of Pentecost and the ongoing work of the Holy Spirit in the Church.

Chapter 7: Christological Controversies and Their Impact

- This chapter will address the early Church's debates over the nature of Christ, including key controversies such as Arianism and Nestorianism. It will explore how these debates were resolved and their lasting impact on Christian doctrine.

Chapter 8: Jesus and Salvation

- A thorough examination of Jesus' role in the salvation of humanity, this chapter will explore different theories of atonement and the significance of Jesus' sacrifice. It will discuss how the concept of salvation has evolved and its central place in Christian theology.

Chapter 9: The New Testament Witness to Jesus

- This chapter will analyze how Jesus is portrayed in the New Testament, particularly in the Gospels and the writings of Paul. It will offer a comparative study of the Synoptic Gospels and the Gospel of John, as well as an exploration of how the New Testament as a whole testifies to Jesus' identity and mission.

Chapter 10: Jesus in Early Christian Thought

- This chapter will explore how early Christian writers and theologians understood and interpreted Jesus' life and teachings. It will examine the development of Christology in the early Church and the influence of these early interpretations on subsequent Christian thought.

Chapter 11: Contemporary Perspectives on Jesus

- This chapter will engage with modern theological perspectives on Jesus, including liberation theology, feminist theology, and post-colonial interpretations. It will explore how contemporary issues and challenges are addressed through the lens of Jesus' life and teachings.

Chapter 12: Jesus in Interfaith Dialogue

- The final chapter will consider how Jesus is viewed in other major world religions, such as Islam and Judaism, and the implications for interfaith dialogue. It will explore the potential for Jesus to be a bridge in conversations between different faith communities.

1.3. Conclusion

The structure of this book is designed to guide readers through a comprehensive and in-depth study of Jesus Christ. Each chapter builds upon the previous one, offering a cohesive narrative that encompasses the historical, theological, ethical, and spiritual dimensions of Jesus' life and teachings. By the end of this book, readers should have a well-rounded understanding of why Jesus is central to Christian faith and how His life and message continue to shape the world.

This study is not just an academic exercise but a journey into the heart of Christian belief. It invites readers to engage with the person of Jesus in a way that is both intellectually rigorous and spiritually enriching. Through this exploration, it is hoped that readers will come to a deeper appreciation of who Jesus is, what He taught, and why He remains a transformative figure in the lives of millions around the world.

This introduction outlines the book's objectives and structure, setting the stage for a detailed and comprehensive exploration of Jesus Christ. It emphasizes the importance of each chapter in contributing to the overall understanding of Jesus' life, teachings, and divine nature.

DR. MAXWELL SHIMBA

CHAPTER 01

HISTORICAL AND CULTURAL CONTEXT

1.1. Historical Background of Jesus' Time

The historical background of Jesus' time is essential to understanding His life and ministry. The world in which Jesus lived was complex, shaped by a variety of cultural, political, and religious influences that all contributed to the environment in which His teachings were received. This chapter will provide an overview of the key historical elements of the first century, particularly in the region of Judea, that influenced the life and work of Jesus.

1.2. The Roman Empire and Its Influence

By the time of Jesus' birth, the Roman Empire was the dominant political force in the Mediterranean world. Rome had extended its reach into Judea, transforming it into a province under its control. The Roman occupation of Judea was marked by significant political and social tension, as many Jews resented Roman rule and the imposition of taxes, laws, and foreign customs.

The Roman Empire brought with it the Pax Romana, a period of relative peace and stability across its vast territories. While this provided certain economic and infrastructural benefits, such as roads and a common language (Latin and Greek), it also meant that the local population was subject to the whims of Roman governors and soldiers. The presence of Roman authority in Judea, epitomized by figures such as Herod the Great and Pontius Pilate, was a constant source of friction and discontent among the Jewish people.

The Roman practice of appointing client kings or governors to manage regions like Judea was intended to maintain order while extracting resources and ensuring loyalty to Rome. Herod the Great, who ruled from 37 to 4 BCE, was one such ruler. Though he was a Jewish king, Herod was seen by many as a puppet of Rome, and his reign was characterized by significant building projects, including the expansion of the Second Temple in Jerusalem, as well as by brutality and paranoia. His death shortly before Jesus' birth led to the division of his kingdom among his sons and eventually to more direct Roman oversight.

1.3. Jewish Religious and Social Context

The Jewish people of the first century were deeply religious, and their faith was centered on the worship of Yahweh, adherence to the Torah, and the observance of religious practices rooted in their covenantal relationship with God. This period was marked by a strong expectation of the coming Messiah—a divinely appointed leader who would liberate Israel from foreign oppression and restore the nation to its former glory.

Judea was home to several religious sects, each with its interpretation of Jewish law and expectations for the Messiah:

- The Pharisees: The Pharisees were a prominent religious group known for their strict adherence to the Torah and the oral traditions. They believed in the resurrection of the dead, the existence of angels, and divine judgment. The Pharisees were influential in the synagogues and among the common people, often clashing with Jesus over interpretations of the law and ritual purity.

- The Sadducees: The Sadducees were a more aristocratic and conservative group, closely associated with the Temple priesthood and the wealthy elite. They rejected the oral traditions upheld by the Pharisees and did not believe in the resurrection, angels, or an afterlife. The Sadducees held significant power in the Sanhedrin, the Jewish ruling council, and were often seen as collaborators with the Roman authorities.

- The Essenes: The Essenes were a separatist group that withdrew from mainstream Jewish society to live in communal, ascetic communities, most famously at Qumran near the Dead Sea. They believed that the existing religious establishment was corrupt and awaited a coming apocalypse that would vindicate their way of life. Some scholars suggest that John the Baptist may have been influenced by Essene teachings.

- The Zealots: The Zealots were a radical political group committed to the violent overthrow of Roman rule. They were driven by a fierce desire for Jewish independence and were willing to use force to achieve their goals. The Zealots' actions eventually contributed to the outbreak of the Jewish-Roman War (66–73 CE), which culminated in the destruction of the Second Temple.

This religious diversity contributed to a vibrant but fractured Jewish society, where debates over the interpretation of Scripture, the role of the Temple, and the coming of the Messiah were common. The religious landscape of Judea was one of anticipation and tension, as many Jews looked for signs of divine intervention in the face of Roman oppression.

1.4. The Role of the Temple in Jerusalem

The Temple in Jerusalem was the religious heart of Judaism during Jesus' time. As the center of worship, sacrifice, and pilgrimage, the Temple played a crucial role in the spiritual life of the Jewish people. The Second Temple, originally built after the return from Babylonian exile and later expanded by Herod the Great, was one of the most magnificent structures of the ancient world.

The Temple was where Jews made sacrifices to atone for sins, offered prayers, and celebrated religious festivals such as Passover, Pentecost, and Sukkot. It was also a place of teaching, where rabbis and scholars discussed the Torah and other religious texts. The high priest, who oversaw the Temple's operations, was a significant religious and political figure, often collaborating with Roman authorities to maintain order.

For many Jews, the Temple symbolized God's presence among His people and His covenant with Israel. However, it was also a focal point of controversy, particularly regarding the corruption and collaboration of the priesthood with Roman rulers. This tension is evident in Jesus' own ministry, particularly in His cleansing of the Temple, where He challenged the practices of the money changers and those selling sacrificial animals, accusing them of turning the house of prayer into a "den of robbers" (Matthew 21:12-13).

The Temple's centrality in Jewish life cannot be overstated, and its destruction in 70 CE by the Romans marked a profound turning point in Jewish history, leading to significant changes in religious practice and identity.

1.5. Messianic Expectations and Prophecies

The first century was a time of heightened Messianic expectations among the Jewish people. The concept of the Messiah—a divinely anointed king who would deliver Israel from its enemies and establish God's kingdom on earth—was rooted in various Old Testament prophecies. Books such as Isaiah, Daniel, and Micah spoke of a coming figure who would bring justice, peace, and restoration to Israel.

These Messianic hopes were varied and sometimes conflicting. Some Jews expected a warrior king like David who would overthrow Roman rule, while others anticipated a more spiritual leader who would purify the people and restore true worship. The Dead Sea Scrolls, discovered at Qumran, reflect some of these diverse expectations, including the belief in a priestly Messiah and a royal Messiah.

Jesus' ministry must be understood against this backdrop of Messianic anticipation. His actions and teachings often provoked questions about His identity as the Messiah. However, Jesus' approach to Messianic fulfillment was radically different from popular expectations. Rather than leading a political revolt, Jesus preached about the Kingdom of God in spiritual terms, emphasizing repentance, forgiveness, and love, and ultimately fulfilling the role of the Suffering Servant described in Isaiah 53.

1.6. The Socio-Economic Landscape

The socio-economic conditions of first-century Judea were marked by stark contrasts between the wealthy elite and the impoverished masses. Roman taxation, combined with the demands of the Temple, placed significant financial burdens on the people, leading to widespread poverty and economic disparity. Land ownership was concentrated in the hands of a few, and many small farmers were driven into debt or forced to sell their land, becoming tenant farmers or day laborers.

This economic hardship contributed to social unrest and fueled resentment against both the Roman authorities and the Jewish leaders who were perceived as complicit in the exploitation of the poor. Jesus' teachings on wealth, poverty, and social justice resonated deeply with the oppressed and marginalized, challenging the status quo and offering a vision of a more equitable society under God's rule.

Jesus' parables often addressed economic themes, using the everyday experiences of His listeners to convey deeper spiritual truths. His concern for the poor, His criticism of the wealthy who exploited others, and His call for generosity and compassion reflected a deep awareness of the socio-economic realities of His time.

1.7. Conclusion

The historical background of Jesus' time is a tapestry woven with the threads of Roman political power, Jewish religious diversity, socio-economic challenges, and Messianic hope. Understanding this context is essential for grasping the significance of Jesus' life and ministry. The complex interplay of these factors created a world ripe for the message of the Kingdom of God that Jesus proclaimed—a message that both challenged and fulfilled the expectations of His time.

By situating Jesus within this historical context, we can better appreciate the radical nature of His teachings, the significance of His actions, and the profound impact He had on His contemporaries and the world that followed. This understanding serves as the foundation for the deeper theological exploration of Jesus' life, teachings, and divine nature that will be undertaken in the chapters that follow.

The Political, Social, and Religious Environment of 1st-Century Judea

1.1. Introduction

The world in which Jesus lived and taught was shaped by a complex and dynamic interplay of political, social, and religious factors. First-century Judea was a land of tension and expectation, marked by the presence of the powerful Roman Empire, deep social divisions, and a rich religious tradition steeped in centuries of history. Understanding the environment of 1st-century Judea is crucial for comprehending the context in which Jesus' ministry took place, as well as the challenges and opportunities He encountered.

1.2. The Political Landscape of 1st-Century Judea

By the time of Jesus' birth, Judea was under the dominion of the Roman Empire, one of the most powerful empires in history. The Roman occupation of Judea began in 63 BCE when General Pompey captured Jerusalem, effectively bringing the region under Roman control. The Romans implemented a system of governance that sought to maintain order and maximize tax revenue while allowing a degree of local autonomy.

1.2.1. Roman Rule and Administration

Rome governed Judea through a combination of direct rule and client kingship. Herod the Great, who reigned from 37 to 4 BCE, was a client king appointed by Rome. Although Herod was of Jewish descent, he was viewed by many Jews as a puppet of the Romans due to his close ties with the Empire and his willingness to impose Roman practices. Herod's rule was marked by grand building projects, including the expansion of the Second Temple in Jerusalem, but also by tyranny, including the execution of members of his own family and the infamous massacre of infants in Bethlehem, as recorded in the Gospel of Matthew.

After Herod's death, his kingdom was divided among his sons, and Judea eventually came under direct Roman administration. By the time of Jesus' ministry, Judea was governed by a Roman prefect, Pontius Pilate (ruled 26-36 CE), who was responsible for maintaining order, collecting taxes, and overseeing legal matters, including capital punishment. Pilate's harsh governance and insensitivity to Jewish customs often led to tension and unrest, exemplified by his controversial decision to use Temple funds to build an aqueduct and his brutal suppression of Jewish protests.

1.2.2. The Role of the Sanhedrin

The Sanhedrin was the Jewish ruling council, composed of leading priests, scribes, and elders. It had significant authority over religious and some civil matters within Judea, although its power was limited by the overarching authority of the Roman governor. The Sanhedrin played a crucial role in maintaining Jewish law and tradition, and its members were often at odds with Roman authorities, as well as with various Jewish sects that challenged the religious status quo.

The high priest, who presided over the Sanhedrin, was a particularly influential figure, often serving as a mediator between the Jewish population and the Roman authorities. However, the position of high priest was also subject to Roman approval, leading to accusations of corruption and collaboration with the occupiers. The tension between upholding Jewish law and navigating Roman demands created a fraught political environment in which religious leaders had to operate.

1.2.3. Jewish Revolts and Resistance

The Roman occupation was deeply resented by many Jews, leading to various forms of resistance. Some groups, like the Zealots, advocated for violent rebellion against Roman rule, believing that armed resistance was the only way to achieve Jewish independence. The Zealots were particularly active in the decades following Jesus' death, eventually leading to the First Jewish-Roman War (66-73 CE), which resulted in the destruction of the Second Temple in 70 CE.

Other Jews, while not necessarily advocating for outright rebellion, expressed their opposition to Roman rule through more passive forms of resistance, such as avoiding paying taxes or engaging in subtle acts of defiance against Roman authority. This pervasive sense of dissatisfaction contributed to an atmosphere of unrest and anticipation of a divinely ordained deliverer, or Messiah, who would liberate Israel from foreign domination.

1.3. The Social Environment of 1st-Century Judea

The social structure of 1st-century Judea was characterized by significant divisions, both within Jewish society and between the Jewish population and the Roman authorities. Understanding these social dynamics is crucial for comprehending the various groups and movements that emerged during this period, as well as the social challenges that Jesus addressed in His teachings.

1.3.1. Social Stratification and Economic Disparity

Judean society was highly stratified, with a small elite class at the top, including the priestly aristocracy, wealthy landowners, and merchants, while the majority of the population consisted of peasants, artisans, and laborers. Economic disparity was widespread, with the elite controlling most of the land and wealth, while the lower classes struggled to survive under the burden of heavy taxation and economic exploitation.

The Roman taxation system was a significant source of hardship for the common people. Taxes were collected by local tax collectors, who were often seen as corrupt and oppressive. These tax collectors, or "publicans," were despised by the Jewish population, not only because they represented Roman authority but also because they often enriched themselves at the expense of their fellow Jews. This economic oppression contributed to a growing sense of injustice and a longing for social and economic reform.

Jesus' teachings frequently addressed issues of wealth, poverty, and social justice, resonating with the experiences of the marginalized and oppressed. His message of the Kingdom of God often included a reversal of social norms, where the poor and meek were blessed, and the rich and powerful were warned of impending judgment.

1.3.2. Religious and Sectarian Divisions

Religious identity was central to Jewish life in 1st-century Judea, but it was not monolithic. Several sects within Judaism had different interpretations of the Torah and varying expectations for the future of Israel. These groups often found themselves in conflict with each other, contributing to the social and religious complexity of the time.

- The Pharisees: The Pharisees were a prominent religious group that emphasized strict adherence to the Torah and the oral traditions. They believed in the resurrection of the dead, angels, and divine judgment. The Pharisees were influential among the common people and were often seen as the defenders of Jewish law and tradition against both Roman and Hellenistic influences. They frequently clashed with Jesus over issues of legal interpretation and ritual purity.

- The Sadducees: The Sadducees were a more conservative group, closely associated with the priestly aristocracy and the Temple establishment. They rejected the oral traditions upheld by the Pharisees and did not believe in the resurrection, angels, or an afterlife. The Sadducees held significant power in the Sanhedrin and were often seen as collaborators with the Roman authorities, given their interest in maintaining the status quo.

- The Essenes: The Essenes were a separatist group that lived in isolated communities, such as the one at Qumran near the Dead Sea. They believed that the religious establishment in Jerusalem had become corrupt and awaited a divine intervention that would purify Israel. The Essenes practiced a strict communal lifestyle, emphasizing ritual purity and apocalyptic expectations.

- The Zealots: The Zealots were a radical political movement that sought to overthrow Roman rule through armed rebellion. They were driven by a fervent belief in Jewish independence and were willing to use violence to achieve their goals. The Zealots played a significant role in the Jewish-Roman conflicts that ultimately led to the destruction of the Second Temple.

These sects, along with other smaller groups, contributed to a highly diverse and often contentious religious landscape. Jesus' teachings and actions were often interpreted differently by these groups, leading to both support and opposition from various quarters. His critiques of religious hypocrisy, emphasis on inner purity over ritual observance, and reinterpretation of the law challenged the prevailing religious authorities, particularly the Pharisees and Sadducees.

1.3.3. The Role of the Family and Community

Family and community life were central to Jewish society in 1st-century Judea. The family was the primary social unit, responsible for religious instruction, economic support, and social stability. Marriages were often arranged, and extended families lived together or in close proximity, providing a network of support and mutual obligation.

Communal worship and religious observance were also vital aspects of social life. The synagogue was not only a place of worship but also a center for education and community gatherings. Here, the Torah was read and interpreted, and religious festivals and rituals were celebrated. The communal aspect of Jewish worship reinforced social bonds and a shared sense of identity, particularly in the face of external pressures from Roman rule and Hellenistic culture.

Jesus' teachings often addressed the dynamics of family and community, challenging traditional structures and calling for a redefinition of relationships in light of the Kingdom of God. His statements about leaving family for the sake of the Gospel (e.g., Matthew 10:37) and His inclusive approach to community, welcoming sinners and outcasts, were radical in the context of 1st-century social norms.

1.4. The Religious Environment of 1st-Century Judea

Religion was the lifeblood of Jewish society in 1st-century Judea. The Jewish people were bound by their covenantal relationship with God, expressed through the

Torah, Temple worship, and various religious practices. This section explores the religious environment of the time, highlighting the key institutions, practices, and expectations that shaped the spiritual life of the Jewish people.

1.4.1. The Centrality of the Temple

The Temple in Jerusalem was the focal point of Jewish religious life. It was the site of sacrificial worship, where offerings were made to atone for sins, express gratitude, and fulfill religious obligations. The Temple also played a crucial role during major religious festivals, such as Passover, Pentecost, and Sukkot, when Jews from all over the region would make pilgrimages to Jerusalem.

The Temple was seen as the dwelling place of God on earth, and its rituals and sacrifices were central to maintaining the covenantal relationship between God and Israel. The high priest, who presided over the Temple's activities, held a position of great authority, both religiously and politically. However, the Temple was also a site of controversy, particularly regarding issues of corruption and collaboration with Roman authorities.

Jesus' relationship with the Temple was complex. He participated in Temple worship but also critiqued the practices He saw as corrupt. His act of cleansing the Temple (Mark 11:15-17), where He drove out the money changers and those selling sacrificial animals, was a symbolic act of judgment against what He perceived as the commercialization of religion and the exploitation of worshipers. This event was one of the key actions that led to His arrest and crucifixion.

1.4.2. The Role of the Synagogue

While the Temple was central to Jewish worship, the synagogue played a crucial role in the daily religious life of the Jewish people, particularly in rural areas and the diaspora. Synagogues were local centers of worship, education, and community life. In the synagogue, Jews gathered to read and interpret the Torah, pray, and discuss religious matters.

The synagogue was also where rabbis and teachers, such as Jesus, would expound on the Scriptures and engage in theological debate. Jesus frequently taught in synagogues, where He attracted large crowds and often faced opposition from religious leaders. The synagogue was a place where His teachings could reach the broader community and where He could engage directly with the religious debates of His time.

1.4.3. The Expectation of the Messiah

Messianic expectations were a significant aspect of the religious environment in 1st-century Judea. The Jewish people, suffering under Roman occupation and longing for deliverance, looked to the Scriptures for hope. Various prophecies in the Hebrew Bible (Old Testament) spoke of a coming Messiah—an anointed one—who would restore Israel, bring justice, and establish God's kingdom on earth.

These expectations were diverse and often conflicting. Some anticipated a warrior king like David who would lead a military revolt against Rome, while others looked for a priestly figure who would purify the Temple and restore true worship. The Dead Sea Scrolls, for example, reflect the belief in both a royal and a priestly Messiah.

Jesus' ministry was marked by questions and debates about His identity as the Messiah. His actions, such as healing the sick, casting out demons, and proclaiming the coming of God's kingdom, were seen by many as signs of Messianic authority. However, Jesus' interpretation of His role as the Messiah was unique and often challenged prevailing expectations. Rather than a political liberator, Jesus presented Himself as a suffering servant, fulfilling prophecies like those in Isaiah 53, where the Messiah is depicted as one who bears the sins of many and brings salvation through suffering and sacrifice.

1.4.4. The Influence of Hellenistic Culture

While the Jewish people maintained a strong sense of religious identity, they were also influenced by the broader Hellenistic culture that had spread throughout the Mediterranean world following the conquests of Alexander the Great. Hellenistic culture, characterized by Greek language, philosophy, and customs, permeated many aspects of life in 1st-century Judea.

This cultural influence was particularly strong in cities like Jerusalem and Caesarea, where Greek ideas and practices coexisted with Jewish traditions. Some Jews, especially those of the upper classes and those living in the diaspora, adopted elements of Hellenistic culture, leading to tensions between those who embraced these influences and those who sought to preserve traditional Jewish customs.

Jesus' teachings were often framed within the context of Jewish tradition, but He also engaged with broader cultural ideas. His use of parables, for instance, was a method of teaching that resonated with both Jewish and Hellenistic audiences, making His message accessible to a wide range of people. However, His emphasis on the distinctiveness of God's kingdom often stood in contrast to the prevailing values of the Hellenistic world.

1.5. Conclusion

The political, social, and religious environment of 1st-century Judea was a complex and volatile landscape, shaped by the interplay of Roman authority, Jewish tradition, social divisions, and Messianic expectations. This environment provided the backdrop for Jesus' ministry, influencing how His message was received and understood by His contemporaries.

Understanding the context in which Jesus lived is essential for grasping the full significance of His life and teachings. The political tensions, social dynamics, and religious fervor of the time all contributed to the challenges and opportunities Jesus encountered as He proclaimed the coming of God's kingdom. By situating Jesus within this historical and cultural framework, we can better appreciate the radical nature of His message and the profound impact He had on the world.

This chapter sets the stage for the deeper exploration of Jesus' life, teachings, and divine nature that will follow in subsequent chapters. As we move forward, we will delve into the specific aspects of Jesus' ministry, examining how He navigated the complexities of His environment to bring about a transformative and enduring message.

Key Jewish Expectations of the Messiah and How Jesus' Ministry Fulfilled or Challenged These

1.1. Introduction

The concept of the Messiah is central to Jewish eschatology and theology. During the first century, many Jews in Judea and beyond were living under Roman occupation, and their hopes for a divinely appointed deliverer were intense and varied. The Messiah, or "anointed one," was expected to fulfill numerous roles that would restore Israel's fortunes, vindicate the Jewish people, and establish God's kingdom on earth. However, these expectations were not monolithic; different Jewish groups held differing views about who the Messiah would be and what He would accomplish.

Jesus of Nazareth's ministry both fulfilled and challenged these diverse Messianic expectations, presenting a reinterpretation of the role of the Messiah that redefined Jewish religious understanding and laid the foundation for

Christian theology. This chapter will explore the key Jewish expectations of the Messiah during the first century and analyze how Jesus' life, teachings, and actions corresponded to or diverged from these expectations.

1.2. The Expectation of a Davidic King

One of the most dominant Messianic expectations was the anticipation of a king from the line of David who would restore the kingdom of Israel. This expectation was rooted in the covenant God made with David, promising that his descendants would rule over Israel forever (2 Samuel 7:12-16). Prophetic writings, such as those found in Isaiah and Jeremiah, reinforced the belief that a righteous king would arise to establish justice, defeat Israel's enemies, and reign over a renewed kingdom.

1.2.1. Biblical Foundations

The expectation of a Davidic Messiah is strongly linked to passages like Isaiah 9:6-7, where the prophet speaks of a child born to rule with justice and righteousness, and Jeremiah 23:5-6, which foretells a righteous Branch from David's line who will reign wisely. These texts inspired hope that the Messiah would be a political and military leader who would overthrow the Roman oppressors and restore Israel to its former glory.

1.2.2. Jesus' Fulfillment and Challenge

Jesus' genealogy, as recorded in the Gospels of Matthew and Luke, traces His lineage back to David, thus fulfilling the expectation that the Messiah would be of Davidic descent. However, Jesus' approach to kingship differed significantly from the political and military expectations held by many Jews.

Jesus proclaimed the Kingdom of God, but He emphasized that this kingdom was not of this world (John 18:36). Instead of leading a rebellion against Roman rule, Jesus preached a message of love, peace, and forgiveness. His entry into Jerusalem on a donkey (Matthew 21:1-11) was a symbolic act that fulfilled the prophecy of Zechariah 9:9, which speaks of a humble king coming to Jerusalem. This act challenged the traditional expectation of a conquering hero by presenting a Messiah who was meek and lowly.

While some saw in Jesus the fulfillment of the Davidic promise, others were disappointed by His refusal to take up arms against Rome. This divergence from popular expectation contributed to the misunderstanding and rejection of Jesus by many of His contemporaries, who could not reconcile their vision of the Messiah with the suffering servant portrayed by Jesus.

1.3. The Expectation of a Priestly Messiah

Another expectation among certain Jewish groups, particularly the Essenes, was the coming of a priestly Messiah who would purify the Temple and restore proper worship. This expectation was rooted in the belief that the existing priesthood had become corrupt and that a new, divinely appointed priest would lead the people back to true worship.

1.3.1. Biblical and Apocryphal Foundations

The expectation of a priestly Messiah is found in texts such as Zechariah 6:12-13, which speaks of a figure called "The Branch" who will build the Temple of the Lord and sit as both priest and king. The Dead Sea Scrolls, particularly the writings of the Essenes, reflect the belief in two Messiahs: one royal and one priestly. The priestly Messiah was expected to lead the people in righteousness and purity, cleansing the Temple and reestablishing the proper sacrificial system.

1.3.2. Jesus' Fulfillment and Challenge

Jesus' actions in the Temple, particularly His cleansing of the Temple (Matthew 21:12-13), can be seen as fulfilling the expectation of a Messiah who would purify the house of God. By driving out the money changers and those selling animals for sacrifice, Jesus demonstrated His authority over the Temple and His concern for true worship. He declared that the Temple was meant to be a house of prayer, not a den of robbers, echoing the prophetic calls for purity in worship.

However, Jesus also challenged the traditional understanding of the Temple's role. He spoke of His own body as the true Temple (John 2:19-21) and predicted the destruction of the physical Temple in Jerusalem (Mark 13:1-2). This shift from a focus on the physical Temple to a spiritual understanding of God's presence and worship was a radical departure from the expectations of a priestly Messiah who would restore the Temple rituals.

Moreover, Jesus' ultimate sacrifice on the cross redefined the concept of priesthood and atonement. The Letter to the Hebrews in the New Testament presents Jesus as the ultimate High Priest who offers Himself as the perfect and final sacrifice for the sins of humanity, thus fulfilling and surpassing the role of any earthly priestly Messiah.

1.4. The Expectation of a Prophetic Messiah

Many Jews also expected the Messiah to be a great prophet, akin to Moses or Elijah, who would reveal God's will, perform signs and wonders, and lead the people in righteousness. This expectation was rooted in the promise of a prophet like Moses (Deuteronomy 18:15-19) who would speak God's words to the people.

1.4.1. Biblical Foundations

The expectation of a prophetic Messiah is drawn from passages such as Deuteronomy 18:15, where Moses tells the Israelites that God will raise up a prophet like him from among their brothers. This figure was expected to have a special relationship with God, receiving and conveying divine revelations to guide the people.

1.4.2. Jesus' Fulfillment and Challenge

Jesus was often recognized as a prophet by His contemporaries. The Gospels record that many people regarded Him as a prophet because of His authoritative teaching and His miraculous deeds, such as healing the sick, raising the dead, and feeding the multitudes (Matthew 21:11; Luke 7:16).

Jesus' prophetic role was evident in His teachings, which often echoed and fulfilled the words of the Old

Testament prophets. He called for repentance, warned of impending judgment, and offered hope for those who would turn to God. His Sermon on the Mount (Matthew 5-7) is a prime example of His prophetic teaching, where He reinterpreted the Law and the Prophets in a way that emphasized the spirit rather than the letter of the law.

However, Jesus also challenged the expectations of a purely prophetic Messiah. Unlike the prophets of old, Jesus claimed a unique authority, identifying Himself as the Son of God and the fulfillment of the Scriptures. He did not merely point to God's will; He embodied it. This claim to divine authority was a profound departure from the traditional role of a prophet and led to significant conflict with the religious leaders of His time.

Furthermore, Jesus' prophecy of His own death and resurrection (Mark 8:31) was a direct challenge to the expectations of a triumphant prophetic Messiah. While some recognized Him as the prophet foretold by Moses, His ultimate fulfillment of the prophetic role was in His suffering, death, and resurrection, which redefined the nature of Messianic prophecy.

1.5. The Expectation of a Suffering Servant

While many Jews expected a triumphant and powerful Messiah, there was also a strand of Messianic expectation rooted in the idea of a suffering servant. This expectation, however, was less prominent and often overlooked in favor of more politically appealing visions of the Messiah.

1.5.1. Biblical Foundations

The concept of a suffering servant is most clearly articulated in the book of Isaiah, particularly in the "Servant Songs" (Isaiah 42, 49, 50, 52-53). Isaiah 53 describes a figure who is "despised and rejected by men," who "bears our griefs" and "carries our sorrows," and who is "wounded for our transgressions" and "bruised for our iniquities." This servant suffers not for his own sins but for the sins of others, bringing healing and redemption through his suffering.

1.5.2. Jesus' Fulfillment

Jesus' life and ministry are a direct fulfillment of the suffering servant prophecies. Throughout His ministry, Jesus identified with the marginalized and the suffering. He healed the sick, forgave sins, and ultimately took upon Himself the sins of the world through His crucifixion. His death on the cross was the ultimate act of self-sacrifice, bearing the weight of humanity's sin and offering redemption to all.

The New Testament writers, particularly in the Gospels and the epistles of Paul, explicitly connect Jesus' suffering and death with the imagery of the suffering servant in Isaiah. Jesus' willingness to endure suffering and death for the sake of others was a radical departure from the more common expectations of a powerful and victorious Messiah. Instead of conquering through force, Jesus conquered through love, humility, and sacrifice.

This aspect of Jesus' fulfillment of Messianic prophecy was not immediately understood or accepted by all His followers. Even His closest disciples struggled to comprehend how the Messiah could suffer and die (Mark 8:31-33). It was only after His resurrection that they fully grasped the significance of His suffering in the context of God's plan for salvation.

1.6. The Expectation of a Cosmic Redeemer

Some Jewish apocalyptic literature, such as the Book of Daniel and various pseudepigraphal writings, anticipated a cosmic figure who would bring about the end of the present age, defeat evil forces, and establish God's eternal kingdom. This expectation involved a Messiah who was more than just a human leader; He would be a divine or semi-divine figure who played a central role in the final judgment and the restoration of creation.

1.6.1. Biblical Foundations

In Daniel 7:13-14, the prophet describes a vision of "one like a son of man" who comes with the clouds of heaven and is given dominion, glory, and a kingdom that will never be destroyed. This "Son of Man" was interpreted by some as a Messianic figure who would bring about the ultimate redemption of Israel and the world.

1.6.2. Jesus' Fulfillment and Challenge

Jesus frequently referred to Himself as the "Son of Man," a title that both connected Him to the apocalyptic expectations in Daniel and emphasized His identification with humanity. However, Jesus used the title in ways that both fulfilled and reinterpreted these expectations.

In His teachings, Jesus spoke of the coming of the Kingdom of God as both a present reality and a future hope. He performed miracles that demonstrated His authority over creation, such as calming the storm and walking on water, which were signs of His cosmic power. Yet, He also spoke of His role as the Son of Man in terms of suffering and sacrifice, predicting His death and resurrection as necessary steps in the fulfillment of God's redemptive plan.

Jesus' resurrection and ascension, as described in the New Testament, further emphasized His role as the cosmic redeemer. His resurrection was seen as the defeat of death and the first step toward the ultimate renewal of creation. His ascension to the right hand of God was interpreted as the fulfillment of the vision in Daniel, where the Son of Man is exalted to a position of divine authority.

While Jesus fulfilled the expectation of a cosmic redeemer, His approach challenged the apocalyptic visions that emphasized immediate judgment and the overthrow of worldly powers. Instead of leading a cataclysmic revolt, Jesus' ministry initiated a new era of grace, where the Kingdom of God was inaugurated but not yet fully consummated. This inaugurated eschatology—where the Kingdom is "already" present but "not yet" fully realized—was a significant departure from the expectations of an immediate, cataclysmic end to the present age.

1.7. Conclusion

The key Jewish expectations of the Messiah in the first century were diverse and often conflicting, encompassing hopes for a Davidic king, a priestly reformer, a prophetic leader, a suffering servant, and a cosmic redeemer. Jesus of Nazareth's ministry both fulfilled and challenged these expectations in profound ways.

Jesus fulfilled the Messianic prophecies by embodying each of these roles, yet He also redefined them, offering a new understanding of what it meant to be the Messiah. Rather than a political or military leader, Jesus presented Himself as a spiritual savior whose kingdom was not of this world but was instead a divine reality breaking into human history.

His life, death, and resurrection fulfilled the prophetic scriptures in ways that were often unexpected and, at times, difficult for His contemporaries to accept. However, it is this very redefinition of the Messiah's role that has had a lasting impact, shaping the foundation of Christian theology and continuing to inspire and challenge believers throughout the centuries.

In understanding how Jesus fulfilled and challenged these expectations, we gain deeper insight into the nature of His mission and the transformative power of His life and teachings. This exploration sets the stage for the further study of Jesus' divine nature, His teachings, and His enduring significance in the chapters that follow.

CHAPTER 02

THE PERSON OF JESUS CHRIST

2.1. Examination of Jesus' Identity as the Son of God

The identity of Jesus Christ as the Son of God is a cornerstone of Christian theology, central to the understanding of His divine nature and His role in the salvation of humanity. This chapter will explore the biblical and theological foundations of Jesus' identity as the Son of God, examining how this title reveals His relationship with God the Father, His divine nature, and the implications of this identity for Christian faith and doctrine.

2.2. Biblical Foundations for Jesus as the Son of God

The New Testament is replete with references to Jesus as the Son of God, a title that carries profound theological significance. This section will examine key biblical passages that affirm Jesus' divine sonship and explore how this identity is portrayed in the Gospels and the epistles.

2.2.1. The Baptism of Jesus

One of the clearest affirmations of Jesus' identity as the Son of God is found in the accounts of His baptism. All four Gospels record this event, where a voice from heaven declares, "This is my beloved Son, with whom I am well pleased" (Matthew 3:17; Mark 1:11; Luke 3:22). This divine proclamation identifies Jesus as the Son of God, affirming His unique relationship with the Father and His divine mission.

The baptism of Jesus not only marks the beginning of His public ministry but also serves as a public declaration of His divine identity. The descent of the Holy Spirit in the form of a dove further emphasizes the Trinitarian nature of God, with the Father, Son, and Holy Spirit all present and active in this moment of divine revelation.

2.2.2. The Transfiguration

The Transfiguration is another key event that highlights Jesus' identity as the Son of God. In this episode, recorded in the Synoptic Gospels (Matthew 17:1-9; Mark 9:2-8; Luke 9:28-36), Jesus is transformed before His disciples, and His appearance becomes dazzlingly bright. Moses and Elijah appear with Him, representing the Law and the Prophets, and a voice from heaven once again declares, "This is my beloved Son; listen to him" (Mark 9:7).

The Transfiguration reinforces Jesus' divine sonship and His unique role as the fulfillment of the Law and the Prophets. It also serves as a foretaste of His glorification in the resurrection, affirming His divine nature and His authority as the Son of God.

2.2.3. Peter's Confession

Another significant moment in the New Testament where Jesus is identified as the Son of God occurs during Peter's confession at Caesarea Philippi. When Jesus asks His disciples who they believe He is, Peter responds, "You are the Christ, the Son of the living God" (Matthew 16:16). Jesus commends Peter for this confession, stating that this revelation came from God the Father.

Peter's confession is a pivotal moment in the Gospels, as it publicly acknowledges Jesus' divine identity. This acknowledgment is not merely a recognition of Jesus as the Messiah but also an affirmation of His unique relationship with God as His Son.

2.2.4. The Trial Before the Sanhedrin

During His trial before the Sanhedrin, Jesus' identity as the Son of God becomes the central issue. When the high priest asks Jesus directly if He is the Christ, the Son of God, Jesus responds affirmatively, declaring, "You have said so. But I tell you, from now on you will see the Son of Man seated at the right hand of Power and coming on the clouds of heaven" (Matthew 26:64).

This response, which echoes the Messianic prophecy from Daniel 7:13-14, affirms Jesus' divine identity and His eschatological role. It is this claim to divine sonship that ultimately leads to His condemnation by the Jewish authorities and His crucifixion, as they consider it blasphemy for a human to claim equality with God.

2.2.5. The Resurrection

The resurrection of Jesus is the ultimate vindication of His identity as the Son of God. In his epistle to the Romans,

Paul writes that Jesus "was declared to be the Son of God in power according to the Spirit of holiness by his resurrection from the dead" (Romans 1:4). The resurrection demonstrates Jesus' victory over sin and death and affirms His divine nature as the Son of God.

The resurrection is also central to the early Christian proclamation, as it confirms that Jesus is not merely a prophet or teacher but the incarnate Son of God who has triumphed over death and offers eternal life to all who believe in Him.

2.3. Theological Implications of Jesus as the Son of God

The title "Son of God" carries deep theological meaning, revealing Jesus' unique relationship with God the Father and His divine nature. This section will explore the theological implications of Jesus' identity as the Son of God, focusing on His relationship within the Trinity, His role in salvation, and the significance of His sonship for Christian believers.

2.3.1. The Relationship Between the Father and the Son

The identity of Jesus as the Son of God points to a unique and eternal relationship within the Godhead, which is foundational to the doctrine of the Trinity. In the Trinitarian understanding, the Father, Son, and Holy Spirit are distinct persons but share one divine essence. The Son is eternally begotten of the Father, meaning that there has never been a time when the Son did not exist. This relationship is characterized by mutual love, submission, and glory.

Jesus often spoke of His relationship with the Father in intimate and profound terms. He described Himself as being "one" with the Father (John 10:30) and stated that He came to do the will of the Father who sent Him (John 6:38). This relationship is also evident in Jesus' prayers, particularly in the High Priestly Prayer in John 17, where Jesus prays for His followers and expresses His desire for them to be united with Him and the Father.

The concept of eternal sonship underscores the uniqueness of Jesus as the Son of God. Unlike believers who are adopted into God's family through faith, Jesus' sonship is eternal and uncreated. This distinction highlights His divinity and His unique role in the divine plan of salvation.

2.3.2. The Incarnation: The Son of God Becoming Man

The doctrine of the Incarnation holds that the eternal Son of God took on human nature, becoming fully God and fully man in the person of Jesus Christ. This is a central tenet of Christian faith, as it reveals God's willingness to enter into human history to redeem humanity.

In the prologue of John's Gospel, we read, "And the Word became flesh and dwelt among us, and we have seen his glory, glory as of the only Son from the Father, full of grace and truth" (John 1:14). This passage emphasizes the reality of the Incarnation: the eternal Son of God became human while retaining His divine nature. The Incarnation is a mystery that lies at the heart of the Christian understanding of Jesus' identity as the Son of God.

The significance of the Incarnation is manifold. It reveals God's love for humanity, as He sent His Son to live among us, experience our struggles, and ultimately offer Himself as a sacrifice for our sins. The Incarnation also affirms the goodness of creation, as God Himself takes on human flesh, thereby sanctifying it.

Through the Incarnation, the Son of God becomes the perfect mediator between God and humanity. As both fully divine and fully human, Jesus bridges the gap between God and mankind, making reconciliation possible. This mediatorial role is emphasized in passages like 1 Timothy 2:5, which states, "For there is one God, and there is one mediator between God and men, the man Christ Jesus."

2.3.3. The Son of God and the Atonement

Jesus' identity as the Son of God is central to the Christian understanding of atonement. As the divine Son, Jesus alone was qualified to offer the perfect sacrifice that could atone for the sins of humanity. His divine nature ensured that His sacrifice had infinite value, capable of covering the sins of all who would believe in Him.

The New Testament presents Jesus as the Lamb of God who takes away the sin of the world (John 1:29). His death on the cross is seen as a substitutionary atonement, where He takes upon Himself the punishment that humanity deserves. In doing so, He satisfies the justice of God while also demonstrating God's love and mercy.

The resurrection further confirms Jesus' role in the atonement, as it is the ultimate demonstration of His victory over sin and death. Through His resurrection, Jesus secures eternal life for those who believe in Him, confirming that He is indeed the Son of God with the power to save.

2.3.4. The Son of God and the Believer's Adoption

The identity of Jesus as the Son of God has profound implications for believers, particularly in the concept of adoption. Through faith in Christ, believers are adopted into God's family and become children of God. This adoption is made possible because of Jesus' sonship, as He enables us to share in His relationship with the Father.

Paul speaks of this adoption in Romans 8:15-17, where he writes, "For you did not receive the spirit of slavery to fall back into fear, but you have received the Spirit of adoption as sons, by whom we cry, 'Abba! Father!' The Spirit himself bears witness with our spirit that we are children of God, and if children, then heirs—heirs of God and fellow heirs with Christ."

This passage highlights the intimate relationship that believers can have with God through Christ. Because Jesus is the Son of God, believers are granted the privilege of calling God "Father" and are made co-heirs with Christ, sharing in His inheritance. This adoption is a profound expression of God's grace and love, as it brings believers into the very life of the Trinity.

2.4. The Son of God in Early Christian Creeds

The early Christian creeds, such as the Apostles' Creed and the Nicene Creed, emphasize the identity of Jesus as the Son of God, underscoring its centrality in Christian doctrine. These creeds were formulated to express the core beliefs of the Christian faith and to address various heresies that arose in the early Church.

2.4.1. The Apostles' Creed

The Apostles' Creed, one of the earliest and most widely recognized Christian creeds, begins with the affirmation, "I believe in God, the Father Almighty, Creator of heaven and earth, and in Jesus Christ, His only Son, our Lord." This statement affirms the unique sonship of Jesus and His lordship, encapsulating the early Church's belief in Jesus as the divine Son of God.

The creed goes on to affirm key aspects of Jesus' life, including His conception by the Holy Spirit, His suffering under Pontius Pilate, His crucifixion, death, and resurrection. These events are seen as integral to His identity as the Son of God and His work of salvation.

2.4.2. The Nicene Creed

The Nicene Creed, formulated at the Council of Nicaea in 325 CE, was a response to the Arian controversy, which denied the full divinity of Jesus. The creed affirms that Jesus is "the only-begotten Son of God, begotten of the Father before all worlds, Light of Light, very God of very God, begotten, not made, being of one substance with the Father, by whom all things were made."

This creed is a profound affirmation of Jesus' divine nature and His eternal relationship with the Father. It rejects the notion that Jesus was a created being and instead affirms that He is co-eternal and co-equal with the Father. The Nicene Creed has been foundational in defining orthodox Christian belief and remains a central expression of faith in the Son of God.

2.5. Challenges to the Identity of Jesus as the Son of God

Throughout history, the identity of Jesus as the Son of God has faced various challenges, both from within and outside the Christian tradition. This section will briefly explore some of these challenges and how they have been addressed by the Church.

2.5.1. Arianism

One of the earliest and most significant challenges to the doctrine of Jesus' divine sonship was Arianism, a theological position that emerged in the early 4th century. Arius, a priest from Alexandria, argued that Jesus, while exalted, was a created being and not co-eternal with the Father. According to Arianism, there was a time when the Son did not exist, making Him subordinate to the Father.

The Council of Nicaea was convened in 325 CE to address this controversy. The Nicene Creed, which was formulated at this council, explicitly rejected Arianism by affirming that Jesus is "begotten, not made, being of one substance with the Father." This affirmation upheld the full divinity of Jesus and His eternal sonship.

2.5.2. Modern Challenges

In the modern era, the identity of Jesus as the Son of God has been questioned by various scholars and religious movements. Some modern theologians and historians have sought to reinterpret the New Testament's portrayal of Jesus, emphasizing His humanity while downplaying or denying His divinity.

These challenges often arise from historical-critical methods that question the reliability of the Gospel accounts or from theological perspectives that seek to reinterpret traditional doctrines in light of contemporary thought.

However, orthodox Christianity continues to affirm the full divinity of Jesus and His unique identity as the Son of God, based on the witness of Scripture and the historic creeds of the Church.

2.6. Conclusion

The identity of Jesus as the Son of God is central to Christian faith and theology. This identity reveals Jesus' unique relationship with God the Father, His divine nature, and His role in the salvation of humanity. Through His life, death, and resurrection, Jesus fulfilled the Messianic prophecies and demonstrated that He is indeed the eternal Son of God, fully divine and fully human.

This chapter has explored the biblical foundations, theological implications, and historical affirmations of Jesus' divine sonship. Understanding Jesus as the Son of God is essential for comprehending the Christian doctrine of the Trinity, the significance of the Incarnation, and the nature of salvation. It also provides the foundation for the believer's relationship with God, as it is through Jesus, the Son of God, that we are adopted into God's family and made co-heirs with Christ.

The Dual Nature of Christ: Fully Divine and Fully Human

2.1. Introduction

One of the most profound and central doctrines of Christianity is the belief that Jesus Christ possesses two natures—He is both fully divine and fully human. This doctrine, known as the hypostatic union, asserts that Jesus is one person with two distinct yet inseparable natures. This concept is foundational to Christian theology and has been the subject of significant reflection, debate, and definition throughout the history of the Church. In this chapter, we will explore the biblical foundations, historical development, theological implications, and significance of the doctrine of the dual nature of Christ.

2.2. Biblical Foundations for the Dual Nature of Christ

The New Testament provides the primary source for understanding the dual nature of Christ. Various passages highlight both His divinity and His humanity, affirming that Jesus is fully God and fully man. This section will examine key scriptural texts that form the basis of this doctrine.

2.2.1. Jesus' Divinity in Scripture

The New Testament repeatedly affirms the divinity of Jesus, presenting Him as the eternal Son of God, co-equal with the Father, and the agent of creation and redemption.

- John 1:1-14: The opening verses of the Gospel of John are among the clearest affirmations of Jesus' divinity. John declares, "In the beginning was the Word, and the Word was with God, and the Word was God" (John 1:1). The "Word" (Logos) is identified as Jesus, who "became flesh and dwelt among us" (John 1:14). This passage affirms that Jesus is not only with God but is God Himself, emphasizing His preexistence and divine nature.

- Colossians 1:15-20: In his letter to the Colossians, Paul describes Jesus as "the image of the invisible God" and "the firstborn of all creation" (Colossians 1:15). He goes on to state that "in him all the fullness of God was pleased to dwell" (Colossians 1:19). This passage highlights Jesus' role in creation and His divine status as the fullness of God.

- Hebrews 1:1-3: The author of Hebrews emphasizes Jesus' divinity by stating that He is "the radiance of the glory of God and the exact imprint of his nature" (Hebrews 1:3). This verse underscores the belief that Jesus perfectly reflects God's nature and is fully divine.

2.2.2. Jesus' Humanity in Scripture

Alongside affirmations of His divinity, the New Testament also clearly presents Jesus as fully human. He was born, lived, suffered, and died as a man, experiencing the full range of human emotions and experiences.

- Luke 2:1-7: The birth narrative in Luke's Gospel emphasizes Jesus' humanity. He was born of a woman, Mary, in humble circumstances, and His birth was attended by the ordinary experiences of human life, such as being wrapped in swaddling cloths and laid in a manger.

- Philippians 2:5-8: In his letter to the Philippians, Paul speaks of Jesus "who, though he was in the form of God, did not count equality with God a thing to be grasped, but emptied himself, by taking the form of a servant, being born in the likeness of men. And being found in human form, he humbled himself by becoming obedient to the point of death, even death on a cross" (Philippians 2:6-8). This passage highlights Jesus' voluntary assumption of human nature, including the capacity for suffering and death.

- Hebrews 4:15: The humanity of Jesus is also emphasized in Hebrews, where the author writes, "For we do not have a high priest who is unable to sympathize with our weaknesses, but one who in every respect has been tempted as we are, yet without sin" (Hebrews 4:15). This verse affirms that Jesus experienced the same trials and temptations as all humans, yet He remained sinless.

2.2.3. The Unity of the Two Natures

The New Testament presents Jesus as fully divine and fully human, but it does so without suggesting any division or confusion between these two natures. Rather, the divine and human natures are united in the one person of Jesus Christ.

- John 1:14: The Word (Logos) became flesh and dwelt among us, indicating that the divine nature took on human nature without losing its divinity. This verse encapsulates the mystery of the Incarnation—God becoming man.

- Romans 1:3-4: Paul speaks of Jesus as "descended from David according to the flesh" and "declared to be the Son of God in power according to the Spirit of holiness by his resurrection from the dead" (Romans 1:3-4). Here, Paul acknowledges both Jesus' human lineage and His divine sonship, united in one person.

The biblical testimony affirms that Jesus is both fully God and fully man, a truth that the early Church sought to articulate more clearly as it developed its doctrine of the hypostatic union.

2.3. The Historical Development of the Doctrine of the Hypostatic Union

The doctrine of the hypostatic union, which asserts that Jesus Christ is one person with two distinct natures, fully divine and fully human, was not fully formulated until the early ecumenical councils. This section will trace the historical development of this doctrine, highlighting key debates and councils that shaped the Church's understanding of the dual nature of Christ.

2.3.1. Early Christological Debates

In the early centuries of the Church, various heresies arose that challenged the orthodox understanding of Jesus' nature. Two major heresies that necessitated the clarification of Christology were:

- Docetism: This heresy taught that Jesus only appeared to be human but was not truly human. Docetists believed that Jesus' physical body was an illusion, and that His sufferings and death were not real. This view was rejected by the early Church because it denied the reality of the Incarnation and the genuine humanity of Jesus.

- Ebionitism: The Ebionites were an early Jewish-Christian sect that denied the divinity of Jesus, viewing Him as a mere human prophet who was adopted by God at His baptism. This view was also rejected by the Church, as it denied Jesus' preexistence and divine nature.

These early heresies prompted the Church to more clearly articulate the belief that Jesus is both fully divine and fully human.

2.3.2. The Council of Nicaea (325 CE)

The Council of Nicaea was convened in 325 CE to address the Arian controversy, which challenged the divinity of Jesus. Arius, a priest from Alexandria, taught that Jesus was a created being and not co-eternal with the Father. The council rejected Arianism and affirmed the full divinity of Jesus, declaring that He is "of one substance with the Father" (homoousios). This was a crucial step in the development of Christology, as it established that Jesus is fully divine, equal to the Father in essence.

2.3.3. The Council of Ephesus (431 CE)

The Council of Ephesus was convened to address the teachings of Nestorius, who argued that Jesus' divine and human natures were separate and that Mary should not be called Theotokos ("God-bearer") but Christotokos ("Christ-bearer"). The council rejected Nestorianism and affirmed that Jesus is one person with two natures, fully united. It also upheld the title Theotokos for Mary, affirming that she gave birth to God in the person of Jesus Christ.

2.3.4. The Council of Chalcedon (451 CE)

The Council of Chalcedon is perhaps the most significant in the development of the doctrine of the hypostatic union. This council produced the Chalcedonian Definition, which declared that Jesus is "one and the same Christ, Son, Lord, only-begotten, acknowledged in two natures unconfusedly, unchangeably, indivisibly, inseparably." The council affirmed that the two natures of Christ, divine and human, are distinct yet united in one person, without confusion or separation.

The Chalcedonian Definition became the standard of orthodox Christology, rejecting both Nestorianism (which overly separated the two natures) and Eutychianism (which blended the two natures into one). It provided a clear articulation of the belief that Jesus is fully divine and fully human, a belief that remains central to Christian theology.

2.4. Theological Implications of the Dual Nature of Christ

The doctrine of the dual nature of Christ has profound theological implications for understanding the person and work of Jesus, as well as for Christian faith and practice. This section will explore these implications in greater detail.

2.4.1. The Mediatorial Role of Christ

One of the key implications of the dual nature of Christ is His unique role as the mediator between God and humanity. As both fully divine and fully human, Jesus bridges the gap between God and mankind, making reconciliation possible. His divinity ensures that He has the authority and power to accomplish salvation, while His humanity enables Him to represent humanity and to experience human suffering and temptation.

The Apostle Paul emphasizes this mediatorial role in 1 Timothy 2:5, where he writes, "For there is one God, and there is one mediator between God and men, the man Christ Jesus." Jesus' dual nature is essential for His role as mediator, as it allows

Him to fully represent both parties in the covenant of salvation.

2.4.2. The Atonement

The dual nature of Christ is also central to the doctrine of the atonement. Only as fully divine could Jesus offer a sacrifice of infinite value, sufficient to atone for the sins of all humanity. At the same time, only as fully human could He truly represent humanity and bear the punishment for human sin.

The author of Hebrews emphasizes the importance of Jesus' humanity in the context of the atonement: "Since therefore the children share in flesh and blood, he himself likewise partook of the same things, that through death he might destroy the one who has the power of death, that is, the devil" (Hebrews 2:14). Jesus' death on the cross, as both God and man, fulfills the requirements of divine justice and makes possible the forgiveness of sins.

2.4.3. The Resurrection and Ascension

The resurrection of Jesus is a profound demonstration of His dual nature. As a human, He truly died, experiencing the full reality of death. As divine, He conquered death and rose again, demonstrating His power over life and death. The resurrection is the vindication of Jesus' divine identity and the confirmation of His victory over sin and death.

The ascension of Jesus further emphasizes His dual nature. He ascended to heaven in His glorified human body, where He now sits at the right hand of the Father, interceding for believers. This ongoing intercession is possible because Jesus retains His human nature even in His glorified state, making Him the perfect high priest who continuously mediates on behalf of His people.

2.4.4. The Importance of Christ's Humanity for Christian Living

The humanity of Christ is not only essential for salvation but also serves as a model for Christian living. Jesus, in His humanity, experienced the same challenges, temptations, and sufferings that all humans face. Yet, He lived a sinless life, demonstrating perfect obedience to the Father.

Christians are called to follow the example of Jesus, striving to live in accordance with His teachings and to emulate His humility, love, and service. The fact that Jesus was fully human assures believers that they, too, can overcome sin and live lives that are pleasing to God, empowered by the same Spirit that was at work in Jesus.

As the Apostle Peter writes, "For to this you have been called, because Christ also suffered for you, leaving you an example, so that you might follow in his steps" (1 Peter 2:21). Jesus' humanity provides a tangible model for discipleship, encouraging believers to live out their faith in the context of their own human experience.

2.5. The Significance of the Hypostatic Union in Christian Worship

The dual nature of Christ also has significant implications for Christian worship. In worship, believers recognize and celebrate both the divinity and humanity of Jesus, acknowledging Him as both Lord and Savior. This section will explore how the hypostatic union informs Christian worship practices and theology.

2.5.1. Worship of Christ as God

Because Jesus is fully divine, He is worthy of worship and adoration. Throughout the New Testament, Jesus is worshiped by His followers, who recognize His divine identity. For example, after His resurrection, Thomas declares to Jesus, "My Lord and my God!" (John 20:28). This acknowledgment of Jesus' divinity is foundational to Christian worship, as believers honor Him as God incarnate.

The worship of Christ as God is reflected in Christian liturgy, hymns, and prayers. The Nicene Creed, recited in many Christian worship services, affirms the divinity of Jesus and His consubstantiality with the Father. Hymns such as "O Come, All Ye Faithful" (which includes the line "Word of the Father, now in flesh appearing") celebrate the Incarnation and the mystery of the hypostatic union.

2.5.2. The Eucharist

The doctrine of the dual nature of Christ is also central to the Christian understanding of the Eucharist (or Holy Communion). In the Eucharist, believers partake of the body and blood of Christ, receiving the grace that flows from His sacrificial death. The belief that Jesus is fully present in the Eucharist, both in His divinity and humanity, is rooted in the doctrine of the hypostatic union.

The Eucharist is seen as a means of participating in the life of Christ, uniting believers with Him in His death and resurrection. As the Apostle Paul writes, "The cup of blessing that we bless, is it not a participation in the blood of Christ? The bread that we break, is it not a participation in the body of Christ?" (1 Corinthians 10:16). The Eucharist is a profound expression of the mystery of the Incarnation, where the divine and human natures of Christ are made present to the faithful.

2.5.3. The Incarnation in Christian Art and Devotion

The dual nature of Christ has also been a central theme in Christian art and devotion. The depiction of Jesus in icons, paintings, and sculptures often emphasizes both His divinity and humanity. For example, icons of Christ Pantocrator (Ruler of All) depict Him with a halo, symbolizing His divinity, while also showing the wounds of His crucifixion, highlighting His humanity.

Christian devotion often reflects on the mystery of the Incarnation, with prayers and meditations focusing on the humility of God in becoming man. The liturgical seasons of Advent and Christmas, in particular, are times when Christians contemplate the significance of the Word becoming flesh and dwelling among us.

2.6. Conclusion

The doctrine of the dual nature of Christ—His being fully divine and fully human—is a central tenet of Christian faith that has profound implications for theology, worship, and Christian living. Rooted in Scripture and articulated by the early Church councils, this doctrine affirms that Jesus Christ is one person with two distinct yet united natures.

The hypostatic union is essential for understanding the person and work of Christ. It explains how Jesus can be the perfect mediator between God and humanity, how He can offer an atoning sacrifice of infinite value, and how He can serve as both Lord and exemplar for believers.

As we continue to explore the person of Jesus Christ in the chapters that follow, the dual nature of Christ will remain a foundational concept, shaping our understanding of His teachings, His role in salvation history, and His ongoing presence in the life of the Church. This doctrine invites believers to marvel at the mystery of the Incarnation and to live in response to the incredible truth that God has become man in the person of Jesus Christ.

The Theological Implications of the Incarnation

2.1. Introduction

The Incarnation is one of the most profound and mysterious doctrines in Christian theology. It asserts that the eternal Son of God, the second person of the Trinity, took on human flesh and became fully human in the person of Jesus Christ. This doctrine is not just a theological abstraction but a central truth that has deep implications for understanding God, salvation, the nature of humanity, and the Christian life. In this chapter, we will explore the theological implications of the Incarnation, considering how it shapes our understanding of God's relationship with the world, the nature of salvation, and the Christian experience of grace, redemption, and sanctification.

2.2. The Incarnation and the Nature of God

The Incarnation reveals profound truths about the nature of God, particularly His love, humility, and commitment to His creation. This section will explore how the doctrine of the Incarnation impacts our understanding of God's character and His relationship with humanity.

2.2.1. God's Love and Commitment to Creation

The Incarnation is the ultimate expression of God's love for His creation. In becoming human, God enters into the fullness of human experience, including suffering and death, to redeem and restore humanity. The Gospel of John encapsulates this truth with the famous verse, "For God so loved the world that he gave his only Son, that whoever believes in him should not perish but have eternal life" (John 3:16). The Incarnation demonstrates that God is not distant or detached from His creation but is deeply invested in its redemption.

This divine love is not an abstract concept but is made tangible in the person of Jesus Christ. Through the Incarnation, God identifies with human weakness, pain, and sorrow, showing that His love is not conditional or limited but is willing to go to the utmost lengths to bring about the salvation of His people.

2.2.2. The Humility of God

The Incarnation also reveals the humility of God. The Apostle Paul emphasizes this aspect in his letter to the Philippians, where he describes how Christ, "though he was in the form of God, did not count equality with God a thing to be grasped, but emptied himself, by taking the form of a servant, being born in the likeness of men" (Philippians 2:6-7). This "self-emptying" (kenosis) of Christ is a profound demonstration of divine humility, as God willingly sets aside His divine privileges to become fully human and to serve His creation.

This humility challenges human conceptions of power and greatness. In the Incarnation, God does not come as a conquering king or a distant ruler but as a humble servant, born in a manger, living among the poor and the marginalized. This redefines the nature of divine power, showing that true greatness is found in humility, service, and self-sacrificial love.

2.2.3. The Revelation of God's Nature

The Incarnation is also the definitive revelation of God's nature. In Jesus Christ, God is fully revealed to humanity. As the author of Hebrews states, "He is the radiance of the glory of God and the exact imprint of his nature" (Hebrews 1:3). Jesus Himself declared, "Whoever has seen me has seen the Father" (John 14:9). Through the Incarnation, God makes Himself known in a way that is accessible and comprehensible to human beings.

This revelation is not just informational but relational. God reveals Himself in the context of a personal relationship with humanity, inviting people to know Him not merely as a concept but as a loving Father, a compassionate Savior, and a guiding Spirit. The Incarnation shows that God's nature is one of intimacy, communion, and relationship, inviting humans into a deep, personal connection with the divine.

2.3. The Incarnation and the Doctrine of Salvation

The Incarnation is central to the Christian understanding of salvation. Without the Incarnation, the entire framework of redemption—Christ's life, death, resurrection, and ascension—would be incomprehensible. This section will explore how the Incarnation underpins the doctrine of salvation and its implications for the Christian understanding of redemption, atonement, and sanctification.

2.3.1. The Necessity of the Incarnation for Atonement

The Incarnation is essential for the atonement—the reconciliation of humanity with God. Only by becoming fully human could Jesus represent humanity and offer Himself as a perfect sacrifice for sin. The author of Hebrews explains, "Since therefore the children share in flesh and blood, he himself likewise partook of the same things, that through death he might destroy the one who has the power of death, that is, the devil" (Hebrews 2:14). Jesus' full humanity was necessary for Him to fully bear the penalty of sin on behalf of humanity.

At the same time, Jesus' divinity ensured that His sacrifice had infinite value. As fully divine, Jesus' death on the cross was sufficient to atone for the sins of the entire world. The Incarnation, therefore, makes the atonement possible by uniting the divine and human natures in the person of Christ, enabling Him to be the perfect mediator between God and humanity.

2.3.2. The Recapitulation of Humanity

The doctrine of the Incarnation is also closely tied to the idea of recapitulation, as articulated by early Church Fathers such as Irenaeus of Lyons. Recapitulation (anakephalaiosis) refers to the concept that Christ, through His life, death, and resurrection, sums up and redeems the entirety of human history. By becoming human, Jesus "recapitulates" or "re-heads" humanity, reversing the disobedience of Adam and restoring the human race to its intended relationship with God.

Irenaeus explains that just as humanity fell through the disobedience of the first Adam, it is redeemed through the obedience of Christ, the "second Adam" (Romans 5:12-21). The Incarnation is thus seen as a crucial moment in the redemption of humanity, where Christ takes on human nature and renews it from within, leading to the possibility of eternal life for all who are united with Him.

2.3.3. The Union of Divinity and Humanity

The Incarnation also establishes the foundation for the union of divinity and humanity, not only in the person of Christ but also in the salvation of believers. Through the Incarnation, Christ sanctifies human nature, making it possible for humans to share in the divine life. The Eastern Orthodox tradition refers to this process as theosis or deification, where believers become "partakers of the divine nature" (2 Peter 1:4) through their union with Christ.

The Incarnation, therefore, is not just a historical event but a present reality that continues to shape the Christian experience of salvation. Through the sacraments, prayer, and participation in the life of the Church, believers are continually united with Christ, growing in holiness and being transformed into His likeness. The Incarnation makes this transformative union possible, as it bridges the gap between the divine and the human, allowing believers to enter into the life of God.

2.4. The Incarnation and the Dignity of Human Nature

The Incarnation has profound implications for the Christian understanding of human nature and dignity. By taking on human flesh, God affirms the goodness and worth of human beings, elevating humanity to a place of unique honor in creation. This section will explore how the Incarnation impacts the Christian view of human dignity, the body, and the material world.

2.4.1. The Affirmation of Human Dignity

The Incarnation affirms the inherent dignity of every human being. In becoming human, God sanctifies human nature and declares it to be of immense value. This has profound implications for Christian ethics and the way believers view themselves and others. Every person, regardless of their status, race, or abilities, is seen as possessing intrinsic worth because they are made in the image of God and because God Himself took on their nature.

This understanding of human dignity has shaped Christian approaches to social justice, human rights, and the sanctity of life. It underscores the belief that all human life is sacred and must be treated with respect and compassion. The Incarnation teaches that every person is loved by God and is capable of being redeemed and transformed by His grace.

2.4.2. The Sanctification of the Body

The Incarnation also has significant implications for the Christian view of the body. By taking on human flesh, Jesus affirms the goodness of the physical body, challenging any notion that the body is inherently inferior or evil. This stands in contrast to various dualistic philosophies that devalue the material world in favor of the spiritual.

The Christian doctrine of the resurrection further emphasizes the value of the body. Just as Christ was raised from the dead in a glorified body, so too will believers be raised to new life, with their bodies transformed and glorified (1 Corinthians 15:42-44). The Incarnation, therefore, encourages a holistic view of human beings, recognizing the unity of body and soul and the importance of caring for both.

This understanding impacts Christian practices related to the body, including the sacraments, which often involve physical elements (such as water, bread, and wine) as means of grace. It also informs ethical considerations regarding health, sexuality, and the treatment of the body, emphasizing that the body is a temple of the Holy Spirit and should be treated with honor and care.

2.4.3. The Redemption of the Material World

The Incarnation also has broader implications for the material world as a whole. By entering into the created order, God affirms the goodness of creation and sets the stage for its redemption. The Incarnation is a promise that the material world is not destined for destruction but for renewal.

This has implications for Christian attitudes toward the environment and the stewardship of creation. The belief that God became part of the material world encourages Christians to value and care for the earth, recognizing that it is part of God's good creation and that it will ultimately be restored in the new heavens and new earth (Revelation 21:1).

The Incarnation challenges any form of escapism that seeks to reject the material world in favor of a purely spiritual existence. Instead, it calls Christians to engage with the world, to care for creation, and to work toward the redemption of all things in Christ.

2.5. The Incarnation and the Christian Life

The incarnation not only has theological implications but also practical ones for the Christian life. It shapes the way believers understand their relationship with God, their calling to discipleship, and their mission in the world. This section will explore how the Incarnation informs Christian spirituality, ethics, and mission.

2.5.1. The Imitation of Christ

The Incarnation serves as the ultimate model for Christian living. Jesus, in His humanity, provides a perfect example of how to live in accordance with God's will. Believers are called to imitate Christ, to follow His teachings, and to embody His love, humility, and service in their own lives.

The Apostle Paul encourages this imitation of Christ in his letter to the Philippians: "Have this mind among yourselves, which is yours in Christ Jesus, who, though he was in the form of God, did not count equality with God a thing to be grasped, but emptied himself, by taking the form of a servant" (Philippians 2:5-7). This call to imitate Christ's humility and self-sacrifice is central to Christian discipleship.

The Incarnation also informs the Christian practice of love and service to others. Just as Christ came "not to be served but to serve" (Matthew 20:28), so too are Christians called to serve others, especially the poor, the marginalized, and the suffering. The Incarnation provides the foundation for a life of compassion, justice, and self-giving love.

2.5.2. Participation in the Divine Life

The Incarnation also invites believers to participate in the divine life. Through union with Christ, Christians are drawn into the life of the Trinity, experiencing the love and communion that exists between the Father, Son, and Holy Spirit. This participation is often referred to as "theosis" or "deification," where believers become "partakers of the divine nature" (2 Peter 1:4).

This concept of participation has deep implications for Christian spirituality. It means that the Christian life is not merely about following rules or adhering to moral principles but about entering into a transformative relationship with God, where the believer's life is increasingly conformed to the image of Christ.

The sacraments, particularly the Eucharist, play a key role in this participation. In the Eucharist, believers receive the body and blood of Christ, experiencing a deep union with Him and being nourished by His life. The Incarnation makes this sacramental participation possible, as it is through Christ's physical humanity that believers are drawn into the divine life.

2.5.3. The Mission of the Church

The Incarnation also has significant implications for the mission of the Church. Just as Christ was sent into the world to reveal God's love and bring about redemption, so too is the Church sent into the world to continue this mission. The Church, as the body of Christ, is called to incarnate the presence of Christ in the world, bearing witness to the Gospel through word and deed.

This mission is not limited to preaching and teaching but encompasses all aspects of life. The Church is called to be a community of love, justice, and service, reflecting the character of Christ in its relationships and actions. The Incarnation provides the model for this mission, as it demonstrates that God's love is not abstract but concrete, lived out in the reality of human life.

The Incarnation also challenges the Church to engage with the world in all its complexity, to enter into the lives of others, especially those who are suffering or marginalized, and to bring the light of Christ into the darkest places. This incarnational mission is a call to be the hands and feet of Christ in the world, continuing His work of healing, reconciliation, and redemption.

2.6. The Incarnation and Eschatology

The Incarnation also has eschatological implications, shaping the Christian understanding of the end times and the ultimate destiny of creation. This section will explore how the Incarnation informs the Christian hope for the future and the belief in the resurrection of the body and the renewal of creation.

2.6.1. The Resurrection of the Body

The Incarnation affirms the goodness of the body and the material world, and this has direct implications for the Christian belief in the resurrection of the body. Just as Christ was raised from the dead in a glorified body, so too will believers be raised to new life in their own glorified bodies. This resurrection is not a mere spiritual continuation but a physical and bodily renewal, rooted in the reality of the Incarnation.

The Apostle Paul speaks of this resurrection hope in 1 Corinthians 15, where he describes how the perishable body will put on imperishability, and the mortal body will put on immortality (1 Corinthians 15:53). The Incarnation assures believers that their bodies, along with all of creation, will be redeemed and transformed in the new creation.

2.6.2. The Renewal of Creation

The Incarnation also points to the ultimate renewal of all creation. In becoming part of the material world, God affirms its goodness and sets the stage for its redemption. The Christian hope is not for an escape from the material world but for its transformation and renewal.

This hope is expressed in the vision of the new heavens and the new earth in Revelation 21, where God dwells with His people, and all things are made new. The Incarnation assures believers that God's redemptive work encompasses the entire cosmos, bringing healing, restoration, and eternal life to all creation.

This eschatological vision impacts how Christians live in the present, encouraging them to work toward the renewal of the world, to care for creation, and to live in anticipation of the coming Kingdom. The Incarnation provides the foundation for this hope, as it shows that God is committed to the redemption of the entire created order.

2.7. Conclusion

The theological implications of the Incarnation are vast and profound, touching every aspect of Christian doctrine, spirituality, and practice. The Incarnation reveals the nature of God as loving, humble, and committed to His creation. It is the foundation of the Christian understanding of salvation, where God becomes human to redeem humanity and restore it to communion with Himself.

The Incarnation also affirms the dignity of human nature and the material world, showing that they are not to be despised or rejected but valued and sanctified. It shapes the Christian life, calling believers to imitate Christ, to participate in the divine life, and to engage in the mission of the Church with love and humility.

Finally, the Incarnation points to the ultimate hope of the Christian faith—the resurrection of the body and the renewal of all creation. It assures believers that God's redemptive work is not limited to the spiritual realm but encompasses the entire cosmos, bringing everything to its fulfillment in Christ.

As we continue to explore the person and work of Jesus Christ in the chapters that follow, the doctrine of the Incarnation will remain central, providing a lens through which to understand the depth of God's love, the mystery of salvation, and the hope of eternal life. The Incarnation is not just a theological concept but the heart of the Christian faith, a mystery that invites believers to worship, to wonder, and to live in the light of God's amazing grace.

CHAPTER 03

THE TEACHING OF JESUS

3.1. Introduction

The teachings of Jesus Christ form the foundation of Christian ethics, spirituality, and understanding of the Kingdom of God. Through His teachings, Jesus conveyed deep spiritual truths, ethical principles, and the nature of God's relationship with humanity. His teachings were often delivered through parables—simple stories with profound meanings that challenged His listeners to see the world through the lens of God's Kingdom. This chapter provides an overview of Jesus' core teachings and parables, highlighting their significance and the central themes that underpin them.

3.2. The Kingdom of God

One of the most central themes in Jesus' teachings is the Kingdom of God. This concept is foundational to understanding Jesus' mission and message. The Kingdom of God, also referred to as the Kingdom of Heaven in the Gospel of Matthew, is the reign of God over all creation, bringing about justice, peace, and restoration.

3.2.1. The Nature of the Kingdom

Jesus taught that the Kingdom of God is both a present reality and a future hope. In Mark 1:15, Jesus begins His public ministry by proclaiming, "The time is fulfilled, and the kingdom of God is at hand; repent and believe in the gospel." This statement reveals that the Kingdom of God had begun to manifest in Jesus' own ministry, yet it also pointed toward a future fulfillment when God's reign would be fully realized.

The Kingdom of God is not a geographical or political entity but a spiritual reality that transcends earthly powers. Jesus described the Kingdom as something that grows from small beginnings, as seen in the parables of the mustard seed and the yeast (Matthew 13:31-33). These parables illustrate that the Kingdom may start small and unnoticed, but it will eventually grow and transform everything it touches.

3.2.2. The Ethics of the Kingdom

Jesus' teachings also emphasized the ethical demands of living in the Kingdom of God. The Sermon on the Mount, recorded in Matthew chapters 5 through 7, is a key passage where Jesus outlines the values and behaviors expected of those who belong to the Kingdom. He teaches about the importance of humility, mercy, peacemaking, and righteousness, contrasting the ways of the Kingdom with the values of the world.

In the Beatitudes (Matthew 5:3-12), Jesus blesses those who are poor in spirit, mournful, meek, and persecuted, indicating that the values of the Kingdom often stand in opposition to worldly notions of power and success. The ethics of the Kingdom call for a radical transformation of the heart, where love, forgiveness, and justice prevail.

3.2.3. The Parables of the Kingdom

Jesus frequently used parables to teach about the Kingdom of God. Parables are simple, often allegorical stories that use everyday experiences to convey spiritual truths.

Through these parables, Jesus invited His listeners to see the world from a divine perspective and to understand the nature of God's reign.

Some of the most well-known parables of the Kingdom include:

- The Parable of the Sower (Matthew 13:1-23): This parable illustrates the different responses people have to the message of the Kingdom. The seed represents the word of God, and the various types of soil represent the conditions of human hearts. The parable teaches that while many may hear the word, only those with receptive hearts will truly understand and bear fruit.

- The Parable of the Wheat and the Tares (Matthew 13:24-30): In this parable, Jesus compares the Kingdom of God to a field where both wheat and tares (weeds) grow together until the harvest. The parable highlights the coexistence of good and evil in the world and the ultimate judgment that will separate the righteous from the wicked.

- The Parable of the Hidden Treasure and the Pearl of Great Price (Matthew 13:44-46): These parables illustrate the immense value of the Kingdom of God. In both stories, the characters sell everything they have to obtain something of incomparable worth, symbolizing the total commitment required to enter the Kingdom.

- The Parable of the Prodigal Son (Luke 15:11-32): Although often focused on repentance and forgiveness, this parable also reveals the nature of God's Kingdom as a place of grace and reconciliation. The father in the story represents God, who welcomes the repentant sinner with open arms, demonstrating the boundless love and mercy that characterize the Kingdom of God.

Through these parables, Jesus communicated the mystery and the transformative power of the Kingdom, challenging His listeners to reconsider their priorities and align their lives with God's will.

3.3. The Great Commandment: Love of God and Neighbor

Central to Jesus' teachings is the commandment to love—both love for God and love for neighbor. When asked about the greatest commandment, Jesus responded by summarizing the Law with two commandments: "You shall love the Lord your God with all your heart and with all your soul and with all your mind. This is the great and first commandment. And a second is like it: You shall love your neighbor as yourself" (Matthew 22:37-39).

3.3.1. Love of God

The command to love God with all one's heart, soul, and mind is rooted in the Shema, a central prayer in Jewish tradition (Deuteronomy 6:4-5). Jesus emphasizes that love for God is the foundation of all other commandments. This love is not merely an emotional feeling but a total commitment to God's will, involving every aspect of one's life.

Loving God requires obedience, worship, and devotion. Jesus taught that this love is demonstrated through keeping His commandments (John 14:15). It is a love that seeks to honor God in every thought, word, and deed, prioritizing His kingdom and righteousness above all else.

3.3.2. Love of Neighbor

The command to love one's neighbor as oneself extends the love of God into human relationships. Jesus radically expanded the definition of "neighbor" to include not only fellow Israelites but all people, including enemies and those who are marginalized.

This teaching is powerfully illustrated in the Parable of the Good Samaritan (Luke 10:25-37). In this parable, a Samaritan—a member of a group despised by Jews—shows compassion to a wounded man, while a priest and a Levite pass by without helping. Jesus uses this story to challenge social and ethnic boundaries, teaching that true love of neighbor transcends prejudice and extends to all people, regardless of their background or status.

Jesus' command to love one's neighbor is a call to active compassion and justice. It demands that believers not only refrain from harming others but also seek their well-being, advocating for those who are oppressed and caring for those in need.

3.3.3. The New Commandment

In addition to the Great Commandment, Jesus gave His disciples a "new commandment" at the Last Supper: "A new commandment I give to you, that you love one another: just as I have loved you, you also are to love one another" (John 13:34). This commandment emphasizes the self-sacrificial love that Jesus demonstrated through His life and death. It calls His followers to love one another with the same unconditional and self-giving love that He showed.

The love that Jesus commands is a reflection of divine love. It is a love that is willing to lay down one's life for others (John 15:13), and it is the defining mark of a true disciple of Christ: "By this all people will know that you are my disciples, if you have love for one another" (John 13:35).

3.4. The Teachings on Forgiveness and Mercy

Forgiveness and mercy are central themes in Jesus' teachings, reflecting the heart of the Gospel message. Jesus emphasized the importance of forgiveness both in receiving and extending it, linking it directly to the nature of God's mercy.

3.4.1. Forgiveness in the Lord's Prayer

In the Lord's Prayer, Jesus taught His disciples to pray, "Forgive us our debts, as we also have forgiven our debtors" (Matthew 6:12). This prayer highlights the reciprocal nature of forgiveness in the Kingdom of God. Jesus goes on to emphasize this point by stating, "For if you forgive others their trespasses, your heavenly Father will also forgive you, but if you do not forgive others their trespasses, neither will your Father forgive your trespasses" (Matthew 6:14-15).

Forgiveness is presented not as an option but as a requirement for those who seek God's forgiveness. It is a reflection of the mercy that believers have received from God and are therefore called to extend to others.

3.4.2. The Parable of the Unforgiving Servant

The Parable of the Unforgiving Servant (Matthew 18:21-35) vividly illustrates the necessity of forgiveness. In this parable, a servant who owes an enormous debt to his master is forgiven when he pleads for mercy. However, this same servant refuses to forgive a fellow servant who owes him a small amount. When the master hears of this, he is enraged and revokes his forgiveness, throwing the unforgiving servant into prison.

The parable underscores the principle that those who have received God's mercy are obligated to show mercy to others. It warns of the dire consequences of an unforgiving heart and teaches that true forgiveness must be generous and unconditional, mirroring the forgiveness that God offers.

3.4.3. The Call to Mercy

Jesus' teachings also emphasize the importance of showing mercy to others. In the Beatitudes, He declares, "Blessed are the merciful, for they shall receive mercy" (Matthew 5:

7). Mercy, in this context, involves compassion for those who are suffering, as well as a willingness to forgive those who have wronged us.

Jesus demonstrated mercy throughout His ministry, healing the sick, forgiving sinners, and reaching out to those who were marginalized by society. He called His followers to do likewise, instructing them to "be merciful, even as your Father is merciful" (Luke 6:36). This call to mercy is a reflection of God's own character and a central aspect of living in the Kingdom of God.

3.5. The Teachings on Faith and Prayer

Faith and prayer are foundational to Jesus' teachings, serving as the means by which believers connect with God and participate in His Kingdom. Jesus taught extensively on the nature of faith, the power of prayer, and the importance of trust in God's provision.

3.5.1. The Nature of Faith

Jesus emphasized that faith is essential for experiencing the power and presence of God. In many of His healings and miracles, Jesus highlighted the role of faith, often stating that it was the individual's faith that made them whole (e.g., Mark 5:34, Luke 17:19).

Faith, according to Jesus, is not merely intellectual assent but a deep trust in God's goodness and power. He famously taught, "Truly, I say to you, if you have faith like a grain of mustard seed, you will say to this mountain, 'Move from here to there,' and it will move, and nothing will be impossible for you" (Matthew 17:20). This teaching underscores the transformative power of even a small amount of genuine faith.

3.5.2. The Power of Prayer

Jesus also taught that prayer is a vital expression of faith and a means of communicating with God. He provided a model for prayer in the Lord's Prayer (Matthew 6:9-13), which includes elements of worship, petition, confession, and intercession. This prayer emphasizes the importance of aligning one's will with God's will and trusting in His provision.

Jesus encouraged persistent and bold prayer, as seen in the Parable of the Persistent Widow (Luke 18:1-8) and the Parable of the Friend at Midnight (Luke 11:5-13). These parables teach that believers should approach God with confidence and perseverance, trusting that He hears and answers their prayers.

Prayer, according to Jesus, is not just about asking for things but about cultivating a relationship with God. He frequently withdrew to solitary places to pray (Mark 1:35), modeling the importance of regular, intimate communion with the Father.

3.5.3. Trust in God's Provision

Jesus taught that faith involves trusting in God's provision for all of life's needs. In the Sermon on the Mount, He instructed His followers not to worry about their material needs, saying, "Therefore do not be anxious, saying, 'What shall we eat?' or 'What shall we drink?' or 'What shall we wear?' For the Gentiles seek after all these things, and your heavenly Father knows that you need them all. But seek first the kingdom of God and his righteousness, and all these things will be added to you" (Matthew 6:31-33).

This teaching calls believers to a radical trust in God's care and to prioritize the pursuit of His Kingdom above all else. Jesus used the example of the birds of the air and the lilies of the field, which are provided for by God, to illustrate that God is fully aware of and responsive to the needs of His people.

3.6. The Teachings on Judgment and Grace

Jesus' teachings often addressed the themes of judgment and grace, emphasizing the reality of divine judgment and the abundant grace that God offers to those who repent and believe.

3.6.1. The Reality of Judgment

Jesus spoke frequently about the coming judgment, warning His listeners of the consequences of rejecting God's Kingdom. He used vivid imagery to describe the final judgment, including the separation of the righteous from the wicked, as seen in the Parable of the Sheep and the Goats (Matthew 25:31-46). In this parable, Jesus teaches that the basis of judgment will be how individuals have responded to the needs of others, particularly the "least of these."

Jesus also warned of the reality of hell, describing it as a place of eternal punishment for those who reject God (Matthew 10:28, Matthew 25:46). These teachings underscore the seriousness of sin and the importance of repentance.

3.6.2. The Offer of Grace

Alongside His teachings on judgment, Jesus emphasized the abundant grace that God offers to all who turn to Him. The Parable of the Prodigal Son (Luke 15:11-32) is a powerful illustration of God's grace. In this parable, a wayward son who has squandered his inheritance returns to his father in repentance, and the father, representing God, welcomes him back with open arms and a celebration.

Jesus' interactions with sinners, tax collectors, and those considered unclean demonstrate the inclusivity of God's grace. He often sought out those who were marginalized, offering forgiveness and a new beginning. In the story of the woman caught in adultery (John 8:1-11), Jesus famously says, "Neither do I condemn you; go, and from now on sin no more," demonstrating both His mercy and His call to transformation.

3.6.3. The Call to Repentance

Jesus' message of grace was always accompanied by a call to repentance. He began His public ministry with the proclamation, "Repent, for the kingdom of heaven is at hand" (Matthew 4:17). Repentance, in Jesus' teaching, is a turning away from sin and a turning toward God, embracing the new life offered in the Kingdom.

The Parable of the Lost Sheep (Luke 15:1-7) illustrates the joy in heaven over one sinner who repents. Jesus' ministry was characterized by a relentless pursuit of those who were lost, offering them the opportunity to repent and be restored to right relationship with God.

3.7. The Teachings on Discipleship and the Cost of Following Jesus

Jesus' teachings frequently addressed the nature of discipleship and the cost associated with following Him. He made it clear that discipleship requires total commitment and often involves sacrifice.

3.7.1. The Call to Discipleship

Jesus called individuals to follow Him, not just as students but as disciples who would dedicate their lives to His mission. This call to discipleship is seen in His invitation to the fishermen Peter, Andrew, James, and John, whom He called to leave their nets and become "fishers of men" (Matthew 4:18-22).

Discipleship, according to Jesus, involves more than just learning His teachings; it requires a complete reorientation of one's life. Jesus called His followers to prioritize the Kingdom of God above all else, even above family ties and personal ambitions (Luke 14:26-27).

3.7.2. The Cost of Discipleship

Jesus did not shy away from the reality that following Him would involve significant costs. In Luke 9:23, He stated, "If anyone would come after me, let him deny himself and take up his cross daily and follow me." The imagery of taking up one's cross points to the willingness to endure suffering, rejection, and even death for the sake of following Christ.

The Parable of the Pearl of Great Price (Matthew 13:45-46) emphasizes that the Kingdom of God is worth any sacrifice. The merchant in the parable sells all that he has to obtain the pearl, symbolizing the total commitment required to follow Jesus and enter the Kingdom.

3.7.3. The Rewards of Discipleship

While discipleship involves cost and sacrifice, Jesus also spoke of the rewards that come from following Him. He promised that those who leave everything for His sake will receive "a hundredfold" in this life and eternal life in the age to come (Mark 10:29-30). The rewards of discipleship are not just material but are found in the deep, abiding relationship with God and the joy of participating in His Kingdom.

Jesus also promised the presence and guidance of the Holy Spirit to His disciples, empowering them to continue His mission and to live out the teachings of the Kingdom.

This assurance of God's presence is a central aspect of the Christian life, offering strength and hope in the midst of the challenges of discipleship.

3.8. Conclusion

Jesus' core teachings and parables form the foundation of Christian faith and practice, offering profound insights into the nature of God, the Kingdom of God, and the way of life that He calls His followers to embrace. Through His teachings, Jesus revealed the heart of God's love, justice, mercy, and grace, challenging His listeners to live in a way that reflects the values of the Kingdom.

The parables of Jesus continue to resonate with believers, inviting them to explore the mysteries of the Kingdom and to apply these timeless truths to their own lives. The teachings on love, forgiveness, faith, prayer, judgment, grace, and discipleship remain central to the Christian journey, guiding believers in their relationship with God and their mission in the world.

As we continue to explore the person and work of Jesus Christ in the following chapters, these teachings will serve as a vital framework for understanding His mission, His identity, and the transformative impact of His life and message on the world. Jesus' teachings are not just historical lessons but living words that continue to shape and inspire the lives of millions today.

The Kingdom of God: Its Present and Future Aspects

3.1. Introduction

The Kingdom of God is a central theme in the teachings of Jesus Christ, serving as the focal point of His ministry and the message He proclaimed. The concept of the Kingdom of God is multifaceted, encompassing both present and future dimensions. It refers to God's sovereign reign and rule over all creation, which has been inaugurated through Jesus' life, death, and resurrection, and which will be fully realized in the future when God's will is perfectly established on earth as it is in heaven. This chapter explores the present and future aspects of the Kingdom of God, examining how these dimensions shape Christian understanding and practice.

3.2. The Present Aspect of the Kingdom of God

Jesus proclaimed that the Kingdom of God had arrived with His coming, indicating that the reign of God was already breaking into the world in a new and transformative way. This present aspect of the Kingdom is characterized by the active presence of God's rule in the lives of individuals and communities, bringing about redemption, healing, and renewal.

3.2.1. The Inauguration of the Kingdom

The beginning of Jesus' public ministry is marked by His proclamation of the Kingdom of God: "The time is fulfilled, and the kingdom of God is at hand; repent and believe in the gospel" (Mark 1:15). This declaration indicates that the Kingdom was not a distant future reality but something that was actively beginning in the here and now through Jesus' ministry.

The inauguration of the Kingdom of God is closely tied to Jesus' own person and work. Through His teachings, miracles, and exorcisms, Jesus demonstrated the power and presence of God's Kingdom. His healing of the sick, raising of the dead, and casting out of demons were signs that the Kingdom had arrived, as they showed God's authority over sin, sickness, death, and the forces of evil.

Jesus' proclamation of the Kingdom also called for a response. He urged people to repent and believe the good news, inviting them to enter into the Kingdom by aligning their lives with God's will. The present reality of the Kingdom is thus both a gift and a challenge, requiring individuals to turn away from sin and embrace the new life that God offers.

3.2.2. The Kingdom in the Lives of Believers

The present aspect of the Kingdom of God is most visibly manifest in the lives of those who follow Jesus. For believers, the Kingdom of God is a present reality that transforms their lives and relationships. Jesus taught that the Kingdom of God is within or among His followers (Luke 17:21), indicating that it is experienced in the community of faith where God's reign is acknowledged and lived out.

The Sermon on the Mount (Matthew 5-7) provides a vivid description of the ethics and values of the Kingdom. Jesus called His followers to live in a way that reflects the righteousness, mercy, and love of God, demonstrating the present reality of the Kingdom in their actions and attitudes. The Beatitudes, in particular, outline the characteristics of those who belong to the Kingdom, such as being poor in spirit, merciful, and peacemakers.

The present Kingdom is also characterized by the work of the Holy Spirit in the lives of believers. The Spirit empowers and guides Christians to live according to the principles of the Kingdom, producing the fruit of the Spirit such as love, joy, peace, patience, kindness, goodness, faithfulness, gentleness, and self-control (Galatians 5:22-23). Through the Spirit, believers experience the transformative power of the Kingdom in their daily lives, growing in holiness and becoming more like Christ.

3.2.3. The Kingdom as a Community of Justice and Love

The present Kingdom of God is not only a spiritual reality but also has social and communal implications. Jesus taught that the Kingdom is marked by justice, mercy, and love, and these values are to be reflected in the way His followers interact with others.

The parable of the Good Samaritan (Luke 10:25-37) illustrates the radical inclusivity and compassion of the Kingdom. In this parable, Jesus challenges social and ethnic boundaries, teaching that true neighborly love transcends prejudice and requires active compassion for those in need. The Kingdom of God, as envisioned by Jesus, is a community where the last are first, the marginalized are welcomed, and the oppressed find justice.

In the present age, the Church is called to be an embodiment of the Kingdom, living out its values in a world that often opposes them. This involves not only personal holiness but also social action—working to alleviate poverty, promote peace, and stand against injustice. The Kingdom of God is present wherever God's will is done on earth, and believers are called to be agents of that Kingdom, bringing the light of Christ into the darkness of the world.

3.3. The Future Aspect of the Kingdom of God

While the Kingdom of God is already present in the world, it is not yet fully realized. The New Testament teaches that the Kingdom will be fully established in the future when Christ returns, bringing about the final defeat of evil, the resurrection of the dead, and the renewal of all creation. This future aspect of the Kingdom provides hope and perspective for Christians, motivating them to live faithfully in the present while looking forward to the ultimate fulfillment of God's promises.

3.3.1. The Second Coming of Christ

The future aspect of the Kingdom is closely tied to the Second Coming of Christ. Throughout the New Testament, Jesus and the apostles spoke of a future time when Christ would return in glory to establish His Kingdom in its fullness. This event is often referred to as the Parousia, or the "coming" of Christ.

In the Olivet Discourse (Matthew 24-25), Jesus describes the signs of the end of the age and the coming of the Son of Man. He speaks of a time of great tribulation, followed by His return in power and glory to judge the nations and gather His elect. The future Kingdom will be a time of divine judgment, where the righteous will be vindicated, and the wicked will be punished.

The Second Coming is also described as a time of resurrection. Paul writes in 1 Corinthians 15:52 that at the last trumpet, "the dead will be raised imperishable, and we shall be changed." This resurrection is a key component of the future Kingdom, where believers will receive glorified bodies and share in the eternal life of the new creation.

3.3.2. The Final Judgment

The future aspect of the Kingdom of God includes the final judgment, where all people will be held accountable for their lives and actions. Jesus often spoke of this judgment, emphasizing that it would be a time of separation between the righteous and the wicked.

In the Parable of the Sheep and the Goats (Matthew 25:31-46), Jesus describes how the Son of Man will sit on His glorious throne and separate people as a shepherd separates the sheep from the goats. The righteous, who have shown compassion to the needy, will inherit the Kingdom prepared for them, while the wicked, who have neglected to care for others, will be cast into eternal punishment.

This final judgment underscores the seriousness of how one lives in relation to the Kingdom. It is a reminder that the choices made in the present have eternal consequences and that God's justice will ultimately prevail. However, it also emphasizes God's mercy, as those who have aligned themselves with the values of the Kingdom—especially in their treatment of others—will be welcomed into eternal life.

3.3.3. The Renewal of Creation

The future Kingdom of God is not just about the redemption of individuals but also about the renewal of the entire cosmos. The Bible speaks of a new heaven and a new earth, where God will dwell with His people, and all things will be made new (Revelation 21:1-5). This renewal is the ultimate fulfillment of God's redemptive plan, where the effects of sin and death are completely eradicated, and creation is restored to its original goodness.

Paul speaks of this cosmic renewal in Romans 8:19-22, where he describes how "the creation waits with eager longing for the revealing of the sons of God." He writes that the whole creation has been groaning as in the pains of childbirth, waiting to be set free from its bondage to decay and brought into the freedom and glory of the children of God. The future Kingdom will be a time of liberation for all of creation, where the curse of sin is lifted, and God's shalom (peace) is established.

This eschatological hope has profound implications for how Christians live in the present. It encourages a forward-looking faith that anticipates the fulfillment of God's promises and motivates believers to work toward the healing and restoration of the world. The future Kingdom is a vision of a world where justice, peace, and righteousness reign, and this vision calls Christians to embody these values in their lives today.

3.4. The Tension Between the "Already" and the "Not Yet"

One of the key theological insights into the Kingdom of God is the concept of the "already" and the "not yet." The Kingdom has already been inaugurated through the life, death, and resurrection of Jesus, but it has not yet been fully realized. This tension shapes the Christian experience, as believers live in the present reality of the Kingdom while awaiting its future fulfillment.

3.4.1. Living in the "Already"

The "already" aspect of the Kingdom means that God's reign is present and active in the world today. Through the Holy Spirit, believers experience the power and presence of the Kingdom in their lives. They are called to live out the values of the Kingdom, to seek justice, to love mercy, and to walk humbly with God (Micah 6:8).

This "already" reality is also seen in the Church, which is the visible manifestation of the Kingdom on earth. The Church is called to be a foretaste of the future Kingdom, a community where God's will is done, and His love is made manifest. Through its worship, sacraments, and mission, the Church participates in the ongoing work of the Kingdom, proclaiming the good news of Jesus and working for the transformation of society.

3.4.2. Anticipating the "Not Yet"

At the same time, the "not yet" aspect of the Kingdom reminds believers that the fullness of God's reign is still to come. The world is still marred by sin, suffering, and death, and the final victory of God's Kingdom has not yet been achieved. This eschatological tension calls Christians to live with a sense of hope and anticipation, looking forward to the day when Christ will return and make all things new.

This future hope is a source of comfort and strength in the midst of the trials and challenges of life. It assures believers that their present struggles are not the end of the story and that God's purposes will ultimately prevail. The "not yet" aspect of the Kingdom also encourages perseverance and faithfulness, as Christians are called to remain steadfast in their commitment to Christ and His Kingdom, even in the face of opposition.

3.4.3. The Role of Faith and Hope

Living in the tension between the "already" and the "not yet" requires both faith and hope. Faith involves trusting in the present reality of God's Kingdom, even when it is not fully visible or realized. It means believing that God is at work in the world, even when circumstances seem to suggest otherwise.

Hope, on the other hand, involves looking forward to the future fulfillment of God's promises. It is the confident expectation that the Kingdom will be fully realized and that

God's justice, peace, and love will ultimately triumph. This hope sustains believers as they navigate the challenges of life, giving them the strength to persevere and the courage to live out the values of the Kingdom in the present.

3.5. The Kingdom of God and the Mission of the Church

The tension between the present and future aspects of the Kingdom of God has direct implications for the mission of the Church. The Church is called to participate in the work of the Kingdom, both by proclaiming the good news of Jesus and by working to bring about the transformation of the world in accordance with God's will.

3.5.1. Proclaiming the Kingdom

The primary mission of the Church is to proclaim the Kingdom of God. This involves sharing the message of Jesus—the good news that the Kingdom has come near and that through Christ, people can enter into a relationship with God. The Church is called to make disciples of all nations, teaching them to observe everything that Jesus commanded (Matthew 28:19-20).

Proclaiming the Kingdom also involves calling people to repentance and faith, inviting them to turn away from sin and to embrace the new life that God offers in Christ. This proclamation is not just about words but is also demonstrated through the Church's actions, as it seeks to embody the love, justice, and mercy of the Kingdom in its life and witness.

3.5.2. Demonstrating the Kingdom

In addition to proclaiming the Kingdom, the Church is also called to demonstrate the Kingdom through its actions. This involves living out the values of the Kingdom in tangible ways, such as caring for the poor, advocating for justice, and promoting peace. The Church is called to be a sign and foretaste of the future Kingdom, showing the world what it looks like when God's will is done on earth as it is in heaven.

The Church's mission also includes working for the renewal of all creation. This involves caring for the environment, promoting sustainable practices, and advocating for policies that reflect God's concern for the earth and all its inhabitants. The future hope of the Kingdom inspires the Church to work for the restoration of creation, anticipating the day when God will make all things new.

3.5.3. Living in the Light of the Kingdom

Finally, the Church is called to live in the light of the Kingdom. This means that believers are to live with a sense of urgency and purpose, knowing that the time is short and that the Kingdom is at hand. It involves being vigilant, watching for the signs of Christ's return, and being ready to meet Him when He comes.

Living in the light of the Kingdom also means that the Church must be a community of hope, offering encouragement and support to one another as they await the fulfillment of God's promises. The Church is called to be a place where the values of the Kingdom are lived out in daily life, where love, forgiveness, and reconciliation are practiced, and where the presence of Christ is made known.

3.6. Conclusion

The Kingdom of God is both a present reality and a future hope, encompassing the fullness of God's redemptive work in the world. In the present, the Kingdom is manifest in the lives of believers, in the work of the Church, and in the transformative power of the Holy Spirit. It is a Kingdom of justice, mercy, and love, where God's will is done on earth as it is in heaven.

At the same time, the Kingdom is not yet fully realized. The future aspect of the Kingdom points to the return of Christ, the final judgment, and the renewal of all creation. This eschatological hope provides the Church with the motivation to live faithfully in the present, working to bring about the values of the Kingdom in a world that is still marred by sin and suffering.

Living in the tension between the "already" and the "not yet" requires faith, hope, and perseverance. It challenges believers to trust in the present reality of God's Kingdom while eagerly anticipating its future fulfillment. The mission of the Church is to proclaim and demonstrate the Kingdom, inviting others to enter into the life of God and to participate in the work of redemption.

As we continue to explore the teachings and mission of Jesus Christ, the Kingdom of God remains central to our understanding of His purpose and message. It is the lens through which we view His life, death, resurrection, and the ongoing work of the Church. The Kingdom of God is both a gift and a calling, a present reality and a future hope, inviting us to live in the light of God's reign and to work for the coming of His Kingdom in all its fullness.

Ethical Teachings: Love, Forgiveness, and Justice

3.1. Introduction

The ethical teachings of Jesus Christ form the core of Christian morality and provide a framework for how believers are to live in relation to God, others, and society. Among the most prominent of these teachings are the principles of love, forgiveness, and justice. These three concepts are deeply intertwined, shaping the way Christians are called to interact with the world and with each other. In this chapter, we will explore Jesus' ethical teachings on love, forgiveness, and justice, examining their significance, biblical foundations, and implications for Christian life.

3.2. The Teaching of Love

Love is at the heart of Jesus' ethical teachings and is the foundation upon which all other moral principles are built. Jesus emphasized that love for God and love for neighbor are the greatest commandments, and all the Law and the Prophets hang on these two commandments (Matthew 22:37-40).

3.2.1. Love for God

Jesus taught that the greatest commandment is to "love the Lord your God with all your heart and with all your soul and with all your mind" (Matthew 22:37). This commandment, rooted in the Shema of Deuteronomy 6:4-5, calls for a total and unwavering commitment to God. Love for God is not merely an emotional response but involves the whole being—heart, soul, and mind—dedicated to worship, obedience, and devotion.

Loving God with all one's heart means placing God at the center of one's affections and desires, making Him the priority in every aspect of life. It involves a deep and personal relationship with God, characterized by trust, reverence, and gratitude. Loving God with all one's soul refers to a complete surrender of one's life to God's will, aligning one's actions and decisions with His purposes. Loving God with all one's mind involves engaging one's intellect in the pursuit of understanding God's nature, His word, and His will.

This love for God is expressed through worship, prayer, and obedience to His commandments. Jesus emphasized that those who love Him will keep His commandments (John 14:15), showing that true love for God is demonstrated through a life of faithful discipleship.

3.2.2. Love for Neighbor

The second greatest commandment, according to Jesus, is to "love your neighbor as yourself" (Matthew 22:39). This commandment, based on Leviticus 19:18, expands the scope of love to include all people, not just fellow believers or those within one's immediate community.

Jesus' teaching on love for neighbor is radical in its inclusivity. In the Parable of the Good Samaritan (Luke 10:25-37), Jesus challenges His listeners to reconsider the boundaries of neighborly love. The parable tells the story of a Samaritan—an outsider and enemy in the eyes of the Jews—who shows compassion to a wounded man after others, including a priest and a Levite, pass by without helping. Jesus concludes the parable by instructing His listeners to "go and do likewise," teaching that true love for neighbor transcends ethnic, social, and religious boundaries.

Love for neighbor involves active compassion and service. It requires believers to seek the well-being of others, to care for the poor and marginalized, and to advocate for justice and peace. This love is not conditional on the worthiness or likability of the neighbor but is a reflection of the unconditional love that God shows to all people.

3.2.3. The New Commandment: Love One Another

In addition to the commandments to love God and neighbor, Jesus gave His disciples a "new commandment" to "love one another: just as I have loved you, you also are to love one another" (John 13:34). This commandment emphasizes the self-sacrificial love that Jesus demonstrated throughout His life and ministry, culminating in His willingness to lay down His life for the sake of others.

This love for one another is to be the defining characteristic of Jesus' followers: "By this all people will know that you are my disciples, if you have love for one another" (John 13:35). The love that Jesus commands is not merely a feeling but an active, intentional, and self-giving love that seeks the good of others, even at great personal cost.

The ethical teaching of love, therefore, permeates every aspect of Christian life. It is the guiding principle that shapes how believers relate to God, to each other, and to the world. It calls for a radical reorientation of one's life, away from self-centeredness and toward a life of sacrificial service and compassion.

3.3. The Teaching of Forgiveness

Forgiveness is another central theme in Jesus' ethical teachings, closely related to the principle of love. Jesus taught that forgiveness is essential for maintaining healthy relationships, both with God and with others. He emphasized the importance of receiving and extending forgiveness as a reflection of God's mercy.

3.3.1. Forgiveness and the Lord's Prayer

In the Lord's Prayer, Jesus taught His disciples to pray, "Forgive us our debts, as we also have forgiven our debtors" (Matthew 6:12). This petition highlights the reciprocal nature of forgiveness in the Kingdom of God. Jesus goes on to explain, "For if you forgive others their trespasses, your heavenly Father will also forgive you, but if you do not forgive others their trespasses, neither will your Father forgive your trespasses" (Matthew 6:14-15).

Forgiveness is presented as a non-negotiable requirement for those who seek to live in God's grace. The willingness to forgive others is a sign of having truly received and understood God's forgiveness. Jesus taught that an unforgiving heart is incompatible with the life of the Kingdom, where mercy and grace are central.

3.3.2. The Parable of the Unforgiving Servant

The Parable of the Unforgiving Servant (Matthew 18:21-35) provides a powerful illustration of the importance of forgiveness. In this parable, a servant who owes an enormous debt to his master is forgiven when he pleads for mercy. However, this same servant refuses to forgive a fellow servant who owes him a small amount. When the master hears of this, he is enraged and revokes his forgiveness, throwing the unforgiving servant into prison.

The parable teaches that those who have received God's mercy are obligated to show mercy to others. It underscores the principle that forgiveness must be generous and unconditional, reflecting the boundless grace that God offers to all. The parable also warns of the severe consequences of harboring an unforgiving heart, as it shows that refusing to forgive others can lead to the forfeiture of one's own forgiveness.

3.3.3. The Practice of Forgiveness

Forgiveness, according to Jesus, is not merely a one-time act but a continual practice. When Peter asked Jesus how many times he should forgive a brother who sins against him, suggesting seven times, Jesus replied, "I do not say to you seven times, but seventy-seven times" (Matthew 18:21-22). This response indicates that forgiveness should be limitless and ongoing, reflecting God's infinite capacity to forgive.

The practice of forgiveness is essential for healing and reconciliation in relationships. It involves letting go of resentment, bitterness, and the desire for revenge, and instead, extending grace and compassion to those who have wronged us. Forgiveness does not mean condoning or excusing wrongdoing, but it does involve releasing the offender from the debt they owe and seeking restoration and peace.

Jesus' teaching on forgiveness challenges believers to examine their own hearts and attitudes, encouraging them to cultivate a spirit of mercy and compassion. It also calls for a radical approach to conflict resolution, where forgiveness is prioritized over retribution, and where reconciliation is sought even in the most difficult circumstances.

3.4. The Teaching of Justice

Justice is another key element of Jesus' ethical teachings. Throughout His ministry, Jesus emphasized the importance of justice, particularly in how individuals and societies treat the poor, the marginalized, and the oppressed. His teachings on justice are rooted in the biblical understanding of God as a just and righteous judge, who cares deeply about the well-being of all people and who will hold the powerful accountable for their actions.

3.4.1. Justice and the Kingdom of God

The concept of justice is closely tied to the Kingdom of God. Jesus proclaimed that the Kingdom of God was at hand and that it was characterized by righteousness, justice, and peace. In His inaugural sermon in the synagogue in Nazareth, Jesus quoted the prophet Isaiah, saying, "The Spirit of the Lord is upon me, because he has anointed me to proclaim good news to the poor. He has sent me to proclaim liberty to the captives and recovering of sight to the blind, to set at liberty those who are oppressed, to proclaim the year of the Lord's favor" (Luke 4:18-19).

This proclamation reveals that the Kingdom of God is about more than just spiritual renewal; it is also about social justice and the restoration of right relationships. Jesus' ministry was marked by a concern for the marginalized and the oppressed, and He consistently challenged the social and religious structures that perpetuated injustice.

3.4.2. The Beatitudes and Justice

In the Beatitudes, Jesus highlighted the blessedness of those who hunger and thirst for righteousness, promising that they will be filled (Matthew 5:6). The term "righteousness" in this context can also be understood as "justice." Jesus is speaking of those who deeply desire to see God's justice established on earth, who long for a world where the poor are cared for, the oppressed are liberated, and the vulnerable are protected.

Jesus' teaching on justice is further emphasized in the Beatitude that blesses the merciful (Matthew 5:7) and the peacemakers (Matthew 5:9). Mercy and peace are closely related to justice, as they involve addressing the needs of those who suffer and working to bring about reconciliation and harmony in relationships and society.

3.4.3. The Parable of the Sheep and the Goats

The Parable of the Sheep and the Goats (Matthew 25:31-46) provides a vivid picture of the final judgment, where Jesus separates the righteous from the wicked based on how they have treated the "least of these"—the hungry, the thirsty, the stranger, the naked, the sick, and the imprisoned. In this parable, Jesus teaches that acts of justice and mercy toward the most vulnerable members of society are, in fact, acts of service to Him.

The parable emphasizes that justice is not an abstract concept but is lived out in concrete actions of care and compassion for those in need. It challenges believers to examine their own lives and to ask whether they are actively working to address the needs of the poor and the marginalized. The parable also underscores the seriousness of neglecting justice, as those who fail to care for the "least of these" are condemned for their indifference.

3.4.4. Justice in the Teachings of Jesus

Jesus' teachings on justice also include a strong critique of hypocrisy, particularly among religious leaders who neglect justice while focusing on outward religiosity. In Matthew 23:23, Jesus rebukes the Pharisees, saying, "Woe to you, scribes and Pharisees, hypocrites! For you tithe mint and dill and cumin, and have neglected the weightier matters of the law: justice and mercy and faithfulness. These you ought to have done, without neglecting the others."

This critique highlights the importance of justice as a central concern of God's law. Jesus teaches that true righteousness involves a commitment to justice, mercy, and faithfulness, not just in religious observance but in every aspect of life.

Jesus also emphasized the importance of justice in economic relationships. In the Parable of the Workers in the Vineyard (Matthew 20:1-16), Jesus teaches about the generosity of God's justice, where all are treated with fairness and compassion, regardless of their status or position. The parable challenges conventional notions of justice and fairness, pointing to the radical inclusivity and generosity of God's Kingdom.

3.5. The Interconnectedness of Love, Forgiveness, and Justice

Love, forgiveness, and justice are deeply interconnected in Jesus' ethical teachings. These principles are not separate or competing, but rather, they work together to create a holistic vision of life in the Kingdom of God.

3.5.1. Love as the Foundation of Forgiveness and Justice

Love is the foundation of both forgiveness and justice. It is out of love that God forgives, and it is out of love that God seeks justice for the oppressed. Jesus taught that love for God and neighbor is the greatest commandment because it encompasses all other ethical requirements. When believers love as God loves, they will naturally seek to forgive those who have wronged them and to work for justice in their relationships and communities.

3.5.2. Forgiveness and Justice in Harmony

Forgiveness and justice are not mutually exclusive but are meant to work in harmony. Forgiveness involves letting go of personal vengeance and resentment, while justice involves addressing the wrongs that have been committed and working to restore right relationships. In the Kingdom of God, forgiveness and justice go hand in hand, as God's justice is always tempered with mercy, and His forgiveness does not negate the need for accountability and restitution.

Jesus' teachings call believers to practice both forgiveness and justice, recognizing that true justice is restorative rather than retributive, and that forgiveness opens the door to reconciliation and healing.

3.5.3. The Role of the Church in Living Out These Ethics

The Church is called to be a community where love, forgiveness, and justice are lived out in tangible ways. The Church is to be a witness to the world of what it looks like when God's will is done on earth as it is in heaven. This involves creating a community where love is the guiding principle, where forgiveness is freely offered and received, and where justice is pursued for all, especially the vulnerable and marginalized.

The Church's mission is to embody these ethical teachings in its worship, fellowship, and service, demonstrating the values of the Kingdom of God in its life together and in its engagement with the wider world.

3.6. Conclusion

Jesus' ethical teachings on love, forgiveness, and justice provide a comprehensive framework for Christian living. These principles are not just moral guidelines but are expressions of the character of God and the values of His Kingdom. Love is the foundation upon which all other ethics are built, calling believers to a life of self-sacrificial service to God and others. Forgiveness is the practice of mercy that reflects God's grace and opens the way for healing and reconciliation. Justice is the pursuit of right relationships, where the dignity of every person is honored, and the needs of the vulnerable are met.

These teachings challenge believers to live in a way that reflects the heart of God, prioritizing love, mercy, and justice in all their interactions. They call the Church to be a community that embodies these values, both within its fellowship and in its mission to the world. As followers of Jesus, Christians are called to live out these ethical teachings in their daily lives, demonstrating the reality of God's

Kingdom in a world that is in desperate need of love, forgiveness, and justice.

CHAPTER 04

THE DEATH AND RESURRECTION OF JESUS: THE SIGNIFICANCE OF JESUS' CRUCIFIXION

4.1. Introduction

The crucifixion of Jesus Christ is one of the most significant events in Christian history and theology. It represents the climax of Jesus' earthly ministry and is the focal point of the Christian understanding of salvation. The significance of the crucifixion goes beyond a historical event; it embodies the depths of God's love, the fulfillment of divine justice, and the means by which humanity is reconciled to

God. This chapter explores the theological significance of Jesus' crucifixion, focusing on its role in the atonement, the fulfillment of prophecy, and its impact on the relationship between God and humanity.

4.2. The Crucifixion as Atonement for Sin

At the heart of the Christian understanding of Jesus' crucifixion is the belief that His death was an atoning sacrifice for the sins of humanity. The concept of atonement refers to the reconciliation of humanity with God through the removal or covering of sin. Jesus' crucifixion is seen as the ultimate sacrifice that satisfies divine justice, brings forgiveness, and restores the broken relationship between God and humanity.

4.2.1. The Problem of Sin

The Bible teaches that sin separates humanity from God. In the Garden of Eden, Adam and Eve's disobedience brought sin into the world, resulting in spiritual death and separation from God (Genesis 3). This separation affected all of humanity, as Paul writes in Romans 3:23, "For all have sinned and fall short of the glory of God." Sin creates a barrier between a holy God and sinful humanity, and this barrier can only be removed through atonement.

In the Old Testament, atonement was made through the sacrificial system, where animals were offered to God to cover the sins of the people (Leviticus 16). However, these sacrifices were temporary and ultimately insufficient to fully remove sin. The New Testament presents Jesus as the ultimate and final sacrifice, whose death on the cross atones for the sins of the whole world once and for all.

4.2.2. Jesus as the Lamb of God

Throughout the New Testament, Jesus is identified as the Lamb of God who takes away the sin of the world (John 1:29). This imagery draws on the sacrificial system of the Old Testament, particularly the Passover lamb, whose blood was shed to protect the Israelites from death during the Exodus (Exodus 12:1-14). Just as the Passover lamb's blood spared the Israelites from judgment, Jesus' blood, shed on the cross, spares humanity from the consequences of sin.

The sacrificial death of Jesus fulfills the prophetic imagery of the suffering servant in Isaiah 53, where the servant is described as being "pierced for our transgressions" and "crushed for our iniquities" (Isaiah 53:5). Jesus willingly took upon Himself the punishment that humanity deserved, offering His life as a ransom for many (Mark 10:45). His death was not merely a tragic execution but a divinely ordained act of redemption.

4.2.3. The Doctrine of Substitutionary Atonement

One of the central theological interpretations of Jesus' crucifixion is the doctrine of substitutionary atonement. This doctrine holds that Jesus died in the place of sinners, bearing the punishment that they deserved. Paul explains this concept in 2 Corinthians 5:21: "For our sake he made him to be sin who knew no sin, so that in him we might become the righteousness of God." Jesus, who was sinless, became a substitute for sinners, taking upon Himself the judgment for sin.

Substitutionary atonement highlights the justice and mercy of God. On one hand, God's justice demands that sin be punished. On the other hand, God's mercy provides a way for sinners to be forgiven without facing the full consequences of their sin. Jesus' death on the cross satisfies both the justice and the mercy of God, allowing for the reconciliation of humanity with their Creator.

4.3. The Fulfillment of Prophecy

The crucifixion of Jesus was not an unexpected event in the context of biblical prophecy. Throughout the Old

Testament, there are numerous prophecies that point to the suffering and death of the Messiah. Jesus' crucifixion is seen as the fulfillment of these prophecies, demonstrating that His death was part of God's redemptive plan from the beginning.

4.3.1. The Suffering Servant in Isaiah

One of the most significant Old Testament prophecies that foreshadows Jesus' crucifixion is found in Isaiah 53, the prophecy of the suffering servant. In this passage, the servant is described as being "despised and rejected by men," "a man of sorrows, and acquainted with grief" (Isaiah 53:3). The servant's suffering is not for his own sins but for the sins of others: "Surely he has borne our griefs and carried our sorrows" (Isaiah 53:4).

Isaiah 53:5-6 states, "He was pierced for our transgressions; he was crushed for our iniquities; upon him was the chastisement that brought us peace, and with his wounds we are healed. All we like sheep have gone astray; we have turned—every one—to his own way; and the Lord has laid on him the iniquity of us all." These verses describe the servant's substitutionary suffering, which results in the healing and restoration of those for whom he suffers.

The New Testament writers frequently reference this passage in connection with Jesus' crucifixion, seeing in it a clear prophecy of the Messiah's sacrificial death. Jesus' crucifixion fulfills the role of the suffering servant, who willingly takes on the punishment for the sins of humanity in order to bring about their redemption.

4.3.2. The Paschal Lamb

In addition to the suffering servant, the image of the Paschal (Passover) lamb is another prophetic symbol that finds its fulfillment in Jesus' crucifixion. The Passover lamb, whose blood was smeared on the doorposts of the Israelites' homes during the Exodus, protected them from the angel of death and secured their deliverance from slavery in Egypt (Exodus 12).

Jesus' crucifixion took place during the Passover festival, reinforcing the connection between His death and the Passover sacrifice. In 1 Corinthians 5:7, Paul explicitly refers to Jesus as "our Passover lamb," whose death brings about a new exodus from the bondage of sin and death. Just as the blood of the Passover lamb spared the Israelites, the blood of Jesus spares believers from the judgment of sin and brings them into the freedom of God's Kingdom.

4.3.3. Other Prophecies Fulfilled

Several other Old Testament prophecies are seen as being fulfilled in the events surrounding Jesus' crucifixion. For example, Psalm 22, a psalm of lament written by David, contains vivid descriptions of suffering that closely parallel the crucifixion. The psalmist cries out, "My God, my God, why have you forsaken me?" (Psalm 22:1), words that Jesus Himself quotes while hanging on the cross (Matthew 27:46). Psalm 22 also describes the piercing of hands and feet (Psalm 22:16), the dividing of garments (Psalm 22:18), and the mockery of onlookers, all of which are reflected in the crucifixion narrative.

Zechariah 12:10 prophesies, "They will look on me, the one they have pierced," which the Gospel of John sees fulfilled when Jesus is pierced by a soldier's spear after His death (John 19:34-37). These and other prophecies emphasize that the crucifixion was not a random or unforeseen event but part of God's predetermined plan to redeem humanity.

4.4. The Crucifixion and Reconciliation with God

The crucifixion of Jesus is the means by which humanity is reconciled to God. This reconciliation is central to the Christian understanding of salvation, as it addresses the problem of sin and restores the broken relationship between God and humanity.

4.4.1. Reconciliation through the Cross

Paul speaks of the reconciling power of the cross in several of his letters. In Colossians 1:19-20, he writes, "For in him all the fullness of God was pleased to dwell, and through him to reconcile to himself all things, whether on earth or in heaven, making peace by the blood of his cross." The cross is the instrument through which God brings peace, not only between Himself and humanity but between all of creation.

Reconciliation through the cross is made possible because Jesus bears the penalty for sin on humanity's behalf. Sin is what separates humanity from God, and only through the removal of sin can reconciliation take place. Jesus' death on the cross removes this barrier, allowing for a restored relationship with God.

In 2 Corinthians 5:18-19, Paul writes, "All this is from God, who through Christ reconciled us to himself and gave us the ministry of reconciliation; that is, in Christ God was reconciling the world to himself, not counting their trespasses against them." Jesus' death not only reconciles individuals to God but also initiates a broader mission of reconciliation, where believers are called to share this message of peace with the world.

4.4.2. Justification by Faith

The crucifixion is also the means by which believers are justified before God. Justification refers to the legal declaration that a person is righteous in God's sight, despite their sins. Paul explains in Romans 5:1, "Therefore, since we have been justified by faith, we have peace with God through our Lord Jesus Christ."

Justification is not earned by human effort but is received by faith in the finished work of Christ on the cross. Through His death, Jesus bears the penalty for sin, allowing believers to be declared righteous before God. As Paul writes in Romans 3:24-25, believers "are justified by his grace as a gift, through the redemption that is in Christ Jesus, whom God put forward as a propitiation by his blood, to be received by faith."

The crucifixion, therefore, is the foundation of Christian salvation. It is through Jesus' sacrificial death that believers are forgiven, justified, and reconciled to God. This act of grace is available to all who put their trust in Jesus and accept His atoning sacrifice on their behalf.

4.5. The Cosmic Significance of the Crucifixion

While the crucifixion has personal implications for the salvation of individuals, it also has cosmic significance. The New Testament presents Jesus' death as the decisive victory over the powers of sin, death, and evil. Through His crucifixion, Jesus defeats the forces that oppose God's rule and begins the process of cosmic renewal.

4.5.1. The Defeat of Evil Powers

In Colossians 2:14-15, Paul describes how Jesus "canceled the record of debt that stood against us with its legal demands. This he set aside, nailing it to the cross. He disarmed the rulers and authorities and put them to open shame, by triumphing over them in him." The "rulers and authorities" in this passage refer to the spiritual forces of evil that enslave humanity and oppose God's purposes. By dying on the cross, Jesus defeats these powers, liberating humanity from their control.

The crucifixion is often described as a "triumph" over evil, with Jesus' apparent defeat on the cross being, in reality, the moment of His greatest victory. Through His death, Jesus defeats Satan, the accuser, and breaks the power of death itself. Hebrews 2:14-15 states that through His death, Jesus "destroyed the one who has the power of death, that is, the devil, and delivered all those who through fear of death were subject to lifelong slavery."

4.5.2. The Restoration of Creation

The cosmic significance of the crucifixion extends beyond the defeat of evil to the restoration of creation. Paul writes in Romans 8:19-21 that "the creation waits with eager longing for the revealing of the sons of God. For the creation was subjected to futility, not willingly, but because of him who subjected it, in hope that the creation itself will be set free from its bondage to decay and obtain the freedom of the glory of the children of God."

Through the crucifixion, Jesus initiates the process of restoring all of creation to its original glory. The effects of sin, which have marred the world and brought about suffering and death, are being undone through the redemptive work of Christ. The crucifixion is, therefore, not only about individual salvation but also about the renewal of the entire cosmos.

This cosmic renewal will be fully realized at the second coming of Christ, but it has already begun through His death and resurrection. The crucifixion is the turning point in history, where the forces of evil are defeated, and the redemption of all things is set in motion.

4.6. The Crucifixion and the Love of God

One of the most profound aspects of Jesus' crucifixion is its demonstration of God's love for humanity. The cross is the ultimate expression of God's self-giving love, where He willingly sacrifices His Son for the sake of the world.

4.6.1. God's Love in Sending His Son

John 3:16 famously declares, "For God so loved the world, that he gave his only Son, that whoever believes in him should not perish but have eternal life." The motivation for the crucifixion is God's love for the world. Jesus' death is not the result of divine wrath alone, but it is the outpouring of God's love, where He provides the means of salvation for a fallen and broken humanity.

Paul echoes this sentiment in Romans 5:8, stating, "But God shows his love for us in that while we were still sinners, Christ died for us." God's love is not dependent on human goodness or merit. Rather, it is freely given, even to those who are in rebellion against Him. The crucifixion is the ultimate demonstration of God's grace, where He offers forgiveness and reconciliation to those who least deserve it.

4.6.2. The Love of Jesus in His Willing Sacrifice

Jesus' crucifixion is also an expression of His own love for humanity. Throughout His ministry, Jesus spoke of laying down His life for His followers. In John 10:17-18, Jesus says, "For this reason the Father loves me, because I lay down my life that I may take it up again. No one takes it from me, but I lay it down of my own accord."

Jesus' willingness to endure suffering and death on behalf of others is a powerful testament to His love. In John 15:13, He tells His disciples, "Greater love has no one than this, that someone lay down his life for his friends." The crucifixion is the ultimate act of self-sacrificial love, where Jesus willingly gives up His life so that others may live.

This love is transformative for those who receive it. The love demonstrated on the cross calls believers to respond with love for God and for others. As John writes in 1 John 4:19, "We love because he first loved us." The cross is not only a means of salvation but also the pattern for Christian living, where love, sacrifice, and service are the highest virtues.

4.7. Conclusion

The crucifixion of Jesus Christ holds profound theological and practical significance for the Christian faith. It is the means by which sin is atoned for, humanity is reconciled to God, and the powers of evil are defeated. Through His sacrificial death, Jesus fulfills Old Testament prophecies, demonstrates God's love, and inaugurates the process of cosmic renewal.

The crucifixion is not just an event in the past but a present reality that continues to shape the lives of believers. It calls Christians to live in the light of God's grace, to extend forgiveness to others, and to work for justice and reconciliation in the world. The cross is both a symbol of suffering and death and a sign of victory and hope, pointing to the ultimate triumph of God's love over sin and death.

As we continue to explore the significance of Jesus' resurrection in the next chapter, it is important to remember that the resurrection cannot be understood apart from the crucifixion. Together, the death and resurrection of Jesus form the foundation of Christian hope, offering the promise of eternal life and the renewal of all things.

Theological Implications of the Atonement

4.1. Introduction

The doctrine of the atonement is central to Christian theology, explaining how humanity is reconciled to God through the life, death, and resurrection of Jesus Christ. Atonement refers to the way in which Christ's sacrificial death repairs the broken relationship between humanity and God, which has been severed by sin. Understanding the theological implications of the atonement is crucial for grasping the significance of Christ's work on the cross and its impact on Christian faith and practice. This chapter explores the key theological dimensions of the atonement, including the nature of sin, the justice and mercy of God, Christ's role as a mediator, and the implications for Christian living.

4.2. The Nature of Sin and the Need for Atonement

At the heart of the atonement is the problem of sin, which is understood in Christian theology as humanity's rebellion against God and the corruption of human nature. Sin creates a fundamental separation between God and humanity, disrupting the relationship for which human beings were created. Because God is holy and just, He cannot ignore sin, and because human beings are sinful, they cannot bridge the gap that sin creates on their own. Therefore, atonement is necessary to restore the broken relationship between God and humanity.

4.2.1. Sin as Rebellion and Separation

The Bible presents sin not merely as individual acts of wrongdoing but as a pervasive condition that affects all of humanity. In Romans 3:23, Paul writes, "For all have sinned and fall short of the glory of God." Sin is both a state of being and a violation of God's moral law, resulting in separation from God and spiritual death. This separation is illustrated in the story of Adam and Eve in the Garden of Eden, where their disobedience leads to their expulsion from God's presence (Genesis 3).

Because sin separates humanity from God, atonement is necessary to reconcile the two. The Old Testament sacrificial system provided temporary atonement for sin, with animal sacrifices offered to God as a way of covering the people's transgressions. However, these sacrifices were insufficient to fully remove the guilt of sin, pointing forward to the need for a perfect and final atonement.

4.2.2. The Universal Need for Atonement

The universality of sin underscores the universal need for atonement. Sin affects every aspect of human existence—relationships, society, and the natural world—leading to suffering, injustice, and death. Human beings are unable to rectify this condition on their own, as their sinful nature prevents them from fully living according to God's will.

The New Testament teaches that Jesus Christ provides the only sufficient atonement for sin, offering Himself as a sacrifice that addresses the root problem of human sinfulness. In Hebrews 10:4, the author writes, "It is impossible for the blood of bulls and goats to take away sins." Christ's atonement is not only necessary but also sufficient, providing a once-for-all solution to the problem of sin.

4.3. The Justice and Mercy of God in the Atonement

The atonement is deeply connected to the attributes of God, particularly His justice and mercy. These two aspects of God's character are harmonized in the atonement, as God's justice requires that sin be punished, while His mercy offers forgiveness and reconciliation to sinners.

4.3.1. Divine Justice and the Necessity of Punishment

God's justice is one of His essential attributes, meaning that He must act in accordance with what is right and punish wrongdoing. Sin is an offense against God's holiness, and because of His just nature, He cannot simply overlook it. In Romans 6:23, Paul states that "the wages of sin is death," indicating that the rightful consequence of sin is both physical and spiritual death—separation from the life of God.

The justice of God, therefore, requires that the penalty for sin be paid. This presents a dilemma: if God is just, He must punish sin, but if He is merciful, He must find a way to forgive sinners. The doctrine of the atonement resolves this tension by providing a means through which justice is satisfied and mercy is extended.

4.3.2. Divine Mercy and the Offer of Forgiveness

God's mercy is equally central to His character, and the atonement reflects His desire to forgive and restore sinners to fellowship with Him. In His mercy, God does not leave humanity to suffer the consequences of sin but instead provides a way for them to be reconciled to Him.

This mercy is fully revealed in the person of Jesus Christ, who willingly takes upon Himself the punishment that humanity deserves. Paul expresses this in Romans 5:8, where he writes, "But God shows his love for us in that while we were still sinners, Christ died for us." The atonement is an act of divine love, where Jesus, the innocent Son of God, suffers in place of the guilty, bearing the full weight of God's justice so that sinners may experience His mercy.

4.3.3. The Harmony of Justice and Mercy

The cross of Christ is where God's justice and mercy meet. In the atonement, God does not compromise His justice but upholds it by placing the punishment for sin on Jesus. At the same time, He extends mercy to humanity, offering forgiveness and reconciliation to all who trust in Christ. This harmony is beautifully expressed in 1 John 1:9: "If we confess our sins, he is faithful and just to forgive us our sins and to cleanse us from all unrighteousness."

The theological significance of this harmony is profound. It shows that God is both holy and loving, both righteous and compassionate. Through the atonement, God demonstrates that He is not indifferent to sin, yet He is also deeply invested in the restoration of sinners.

4.4. Christ as the Mediator of the New Covenant

A key theological implication of the atonement is the role of Christ as the mediator between God and humanity. Through His life, death, and resurrection, Jesus establishes a new covenant between God and His people, fulfilling the promises of the Old Testament and inaugurating a new era of grace.

4.4.1. The Role of the Mediator

In biblical theology, a mediator is one who stands between two parties to reconcile them. In the Old Testament, Moses acted as a mediator between God and Israel, delivering the law and interceding on behalf of the people (Exodus 32:11-14). However, the law was unable to bring about true reconciliation because it could not fully deal with the problem of sin.

Jesus, as the perfect mediator, accomplishes what the law could not. In 1 Timothy 2:5, Paul writes, "For there is one God, and there is one mediator between God and men, the man Christ Jesus." Through His atoning death, Jesus bridges the gap between God and humanity, restoring the relationship that was broken by sin. His mediation is unique in that He not only represents humanity before God but also takes the penalty for sin upon Himself.

4.4.2. The New Covenant

The atonement establishes a new covenant between God and His people, fulfilling the promises of the Old Testament and offering a new way of relating to God. The prophet Jeremiah foretold this new covenant, where God would write His law on the hearts of His people and forgive their sins (Jeremiah 31:31-34). Jesus, during the Last Supper, identifies His sacrificial death as the inauguration of this new covenant, saying, "This is my blood of the covenant, which is poured out for many for the forgiveness of sins" (Matthew 26:28).

Under the new covenant, forgiveness and reconciliation with God are no longer dependent on the sacrificial system or adherence to the law. Instead, they are made possible through faith in Christ and His atoning work. The new covenant is characterized by grace, where believers are given the Holy Spirit to empower them to live in obedience to God's will.

4.4.3. The Priesthood of Christ

Christ's role as mediator is closely connected to His role as high priest. In the Old Testament, the high priest was responsible for offering sacrifices on behalf of the people and interceding for them before God. Jesus is described in the New Testament as the "great high priest" who offers not the blood of animals but His own blood as a sacrifice for sin (Hebrews 9:11-14).

Jesus' priesthood is superior to that of the Old Testament because it is eternal and perfect. As Hebrews 7:24-25 states, "But he holds his priesthood permanently, because he continues forever. Consequently, he is able to save to the uttermost those who draw near to God through him, since he always lives to make intercession for them." Jesus' priestly work continues even after His death, as He intercedes for believers and ensures their ongoing reconciliation with God.

4.5. The Atonement and Christian Life

The atonement has profound implications not only for theology but also for Christian living. It shapes the way believers understand their relationship with God, their relationship with others, and their participation in the mission of the Church.

4.5.1. Reconciliation with God

The primary implication of the atonement for Christian life is reconciliation with God. Through Christ's atoning work, believers are restored to fellowship with God and are no longer under the condemnation of sin. Paul captures this transformation in Romans 5:1, where he writes, "Therefore, since we have been justified by faith, we have peace with God through our Lord Jesus Christ."

This reconciliation is not merely a legal status but a relational reality. Believers are adopted into God's family and are invited to experience intimate communion with Him. The atonement opens the way for a restored relationship with God, where believers can approach Him with confidence and joy, knowing that their sins have been forgiven.

4.5.2. Forgiveness and Reconciliation with Others

The atonement also has ethical implications for how believers relate to others. Just as believers have received forgiveness through Christ's sacrificial death, they are called to extend forgiveness to others. In Colossians 3:13, Paul instructs believers to "forgive each other; as the Lord has forgiven you, so you also must forgive." The atonement serves as the model for Christian forgiveness, where the self-giving love of Christ empowers believers to forgive those who have wronged them.

Reconciliation is not limited to the vertical relationship between humanity and God but extends to horizontal relationships within the Christian community and the broader world. The atonement calls believers to work for peace and reconciliation in their relationships, reflecting the love and grace they have received from God.

4.5.3. Participation in the Mission of God

The atonement also invites believers to participate in the mission of God, sharing the message of reconciliation with others. In 2 Corinthians 5:18-20, Paul writes, "All this is from God, who through Christ reconciled us to himself and gave us the ministry of reconciliation. Therefore, we are ambassadors for Christ, God making his appeal through us."

Believers are called to be ambassadors of the Gospel, sharing the good news of Christ's atoning work with the world and inviting others to experience the reconciliation that God offers. This mission is not only about proclaiming the message of the cross but also about living out its implications in daily life—demonstrating love, mercy, and justice in a world marked by division and strife.

4.5.4. Sanctification and the Power of the Cross

Finally, the atonement is central to the process of sanctification—the ongoing transformation of believers into the likeness of Christ. Through the cross, believers are freed not only from the penalty of sin but also from its power. Paul writes in Romans 6:6, "We know that our old self was crucified with him in order that the body of sin might be brought to nothing, so that we would no longer be enslaved to sin."

The atonement empowers believers to live holy lives, not by their own strength but through the grace of God. The Holy Spirit, given to believers as a result of Christ's work, enables them to resist sin and grow in righteousness. The cross, therefore, is not only the means of justification but also the source of sanctification, as believers continually die to sin and live in the new life that Christ has secured for them.

4.6. Conclusion

The atonement is the heart of the Christian Gospel, revealing the depths of God's love, justice, and mercy. Through the sacrificial death of Jesus Christ, humanity is reconciled to God, sin is forgiven, and the way to eternal life is opened. The theological implications of the atonement are vast, touching on the nature of sin, the attributes of God, the work of Christ as mediator and high priest, and the practical outworking of salvation in the lives of believers.

The atonement shapes Christian life in profound ways, calling believers to live in gratitude for the forgiveness they have received, to extend forgiveness to others, and to participate in the mission of reconciliation. It also empowers believers to live holy lives, freed from the power of sin and transformed by the grace of God.

As we continue to reflect on the significance of Christ's death and resurrection, the atonement remains central to our understanding of God's redemptive work and our role in His ongoing mission of reconciliation and renewal.

The Resurrection: Its Role in Christian Faith and Doctrine

4.1. Introduction

The resurrection of Jesus Christ is the cornerstone of Christian faith and doctrine. It is the event that defines Christianity and distinguishes it from other religious beliefs. The resurrection is not just an isolated event in history but is deeply interconnected with the entire narrative of God's redemptive work. It validates Jesus' identity as the Son of God, demonstrates the power of God over death, and serves as the foundation for the hope of eternal life for all believers. This chapter explores the theological and doctrinal significance of the resurrection, its role in Christian faith, and its implications for both individual believers and the Church as a whole.

4.2. The Resurrection as the Validation of Jesus' Identity

The resurrection of Jesus is the ultimate validation of His identity as the Son of God and the Messiah. Throughout His ministry, Jesus made radical claims about His divine nature, His authority to forgive sins, and His mission to bring the Kingdom of God. The resurrection serves as the divine affirmation of these claims and is the proof that Jesus is who He said He was.

4.2.1. Jesus' Predictions of His Resurrection

Jesus repeatedly foretold His own death and resurrection. In Matthew 16:21, for example, He began to explain to His disciples that He "must go to Jerusalem and suffer many things…and on the third day be raised to life." These predictions were integral to Jesus' understanding of His mission. By predicting His resurrection, Jesus linked His future rising from the dead with His Messianic role and the fulfillment of Old Testament prophecies.

If Jesus had not been raised from the dead, His claims to divinity and His role as the Messiah would have been discredited. The resurrection, therefore, is the vindication of Jesus' identity, confirming that He is not only the prophesied Messiah but also the eternal Son of God.

4.2.2. The Declaration of Jesus as Lord and Christ

The New Testament repeatedly emphasizes the resurrection as the key event that declares Jesus' lordship. In Romans 1:4, Paul states that Jesus was "declared to be the Son of God in power according to the Spirit of holiness by his resurrection from the dead." The resurrection is the moment when Jesus' divine authority is fully revealed, marking Him as Lord over all creation.

In Peter's sermon on the day of Pentecost, he proclaims that "God has raised this Jesus to life, and we are all witnesses of it. Exalted to the right hand of God...God has made this Jesus, whom you crucified, both Lord and Messiah" (Acts 2:32-36). Peter's message is clear: the resurrection is the divine endorsement of Jesus as both the promised Messiah and the sovereign Lord.

4.3. The Resurrection and the Defeat of Death and Sin

The resurrection is the ultimate demonstration of God's power over death and sin. In Christian theology, death is the consequence of sin, and sin separates humanity from God. By rising from the dead, Jesus breaks the power of sin and death, offering the hope of eternal life to all who believe in Him.

4.3.1. Victory Over Death

One of the most profound implications of the resurrection is the defeat of death. Death, which entered the world through Adam's sin (Romans 5:12), is portrayed in Scripture as the final enemy of humanity. Yet, through Jesus' resurrection, death is no longer victorious.

Paul triumphantly declares in 1 Corinthians 15:54-55, "Death is swallowed up in victory. O death, where is your victory? O death, where is your sting?" Jesus' resurrection proves that death does not have the final word. This victory is not just a triumph for Jesus but a promise to all believers that they, too, will share in His resurrection and overcome death.

4.3.2. The Defeat of Sin

The resurrection is also integral to the defeat of sin. Sin brings about death, both physically and spiritually, and separates humanity from God. Through Jesus' sacrificial death on the cross, the penalty for sin was paid, but the resurrection is what seals the victory over sin and its consequences.

In Romans 6:9-10, Paul writes, "We know that Christ, being raised from the dead, will never die again; death no longer has dominion over him. For the death he died he died to sin, once for all, but the life he lives he lives to God." The resurrection signifies that sin's hold on humanity has been broken, and believers are now free to live new lives in Christ, empowered by His resurrection life.

4.4. The Resurrection and Justification

The resurrection plays a crucial role in the Christian doctrine of justification. Justification refers to being declared righteous before God, and it is through the resurrection that believers are justified and made right with God.

4.4.1. Justification Through the Resurrection

In Romans 4:25, Paul writes that Jesus "was delivered up for our trespasses and raised for our justification." While Jesus' death atones for sin, His resurrection is essential for the believer's justification. By rising from the dead, Jesus conquers death and makes it possible for believers to be declared righteous in God's sight.

The resurrection proves that the sacrifice of Jesus was accepted by God. If Jesus had remained in the grave, it would have indicated that His death had no power to overcome sin. However, because He was raised, believers can have confidence that His sacrifice was sufficient and that they are now justified before God.

4.4.2. Union with Christ in His Resurrection

Justification is not only about being declared righteous but also about being united with Christ in His resurrection. Paul emphasizes this union in Romans 6:5, stating, "For if we have been united with him in a death like his, we shall certainly be united with him in a resurrection like his." Believers share in the resurrection life of Christ, experiencing the transformative power of His victory over sin and death.

This union with Christ's resurrection is both a present reality and a future hope. In the present, believers experience the new life that comes from being raised with Christ, marked by freedom from sin and the indwelling of the Holy Spirit. In the future, believers look forward to the full realization of this union in the resurrection of their own bodies at the return of Christ.

4.5. The Resurrection and the Hope of Eternal Life

The resurrection of Jesus is the foundation of Christian hope, particularly the hope of eternal life. The resurrection assures believers that death is not the end and that they, too, will experience resurrection and eternal life with God.

4.5.1. The Promise of Resurrection for Believers

One of the most significant promises in the New Testament is that believers will share in Jesus' resurrection. In 1 Corinthians 15:20-22, Paul writes, "But in fact Christ has been raised from the dead, the firstfruits of those who have fallen asleep. For as by a man came death, by a man has come also the resurrection of the dead. For as in Adam all die, so also in Christ shall all be made alive."

Jesus' resurrection is described as the "firstfruits," meaning that it is the first of many resurrections to come. Just as Jesus was raised, so too will all who are in Christ be raised from the dead at His return. This promise gives believers the hope of eternal life, free from the pain, suffering, and death that characterize the present world.

4.5.2. The Nature of Resurrection Life

The resurrection also points to the nature of the life that believers will experience in the age to come. In 1 Corinthians 15:42-44, Paul describes the resurrection body as imperishable, glorious, and powerful. He contrasts the present physical body, which is subject to decay and weakness, with the resurrection body, which is immortal and perfect.

The resurrection life is not merely a continuation of the present existence but a transformation into a new, glorified state. Believers will share in the fullness of life in the presence of God, free from sin, death, and suffering. This hope of resurrection life gives meaning to the present life, as believers live in anticipation of the eternal glory that awaits them.

4.6. The Resurrection and the Mission of the Church

The resurrection of Jesus is not only central to individual faith but also to the mission of the Church. The early Church's proclamation of the resurrection was the foundation of its preaching and teaching, and it remains the central message of the Christian Gospel.

4.6.1. The Apostolic Witness to the Resurrection

The resurrection was the defining message of the apostles and the early Church. In the book of Acts, the apostles repeatedly emphasize the resurrection in their preaching. Peter's sermon at Pentecost centers on the fact that God "raised Jesus from the dead" (Acts 2:32), and Paul declares in Acts 17:31 that God has given assurance of judgment and salvation by "raising him from the dead."

The apostles were witnesses to the resurrection, and their testimony formed the basis for the spread of the Christian faith. The resurrection confirmed the truth of Jesus' message and mission, and it gave the apostles the boldness to proclaim the Gospel, even in the face of persecution and death.

4.6.2. The Power of the Resurrection in the Church's Mission

The resurrection continues to empower the Church's mission today. Paul writes in Philippians 3:10-11 of his desire "to know Christ and the power of his resurrection." The power of the resurrection is not only a future hope but a present reality that strengthens believers for their mission in the world.

Through the resurrection, the Church is empowered to live out the values of the Kingdom of God, bringing hope, healing, and justice to a broken world. The resurrection also fuels the Church's hope in the ultimate renewal of all things, motivating believers to work for God's purposes in the present while looking forward to the future consummation of His Kingdom.

4.7. The Resurrection and Christian Worship

The resurrection has also profoundly shaped Christian worship and the practice of the faith. It is the reason why Christians gather for worship on Sunday, the day of Jesus' resurrection, and it is the focus of the celebration of Easter, the most significant event in the Christian liturgical calendar.

4.7.1. Sunday Worship and the Resurrection

The early Church began to gather for worship on the first day of the week, Sunday, in commemoration of the resurrection. This practice continues in Christian communities today, where Sunday is viewed as the "Lord's Day" (Revelation 1:10) and a weekly reminder of the victory of Christ over death.

In worship, Christians celebrate the resurrection as the foundation of their faith, proclaiming the risen Christ through hymns, prayers, and the reading of Scripture. The Eucharist, or Lord's Supper, is also a central act of worship that commemorates Jesus' death and resurrection, as believers remember His sacrifice and anticipate His return.

4.7.2. Easter: The Celebration of the Resurrection

The annual celebration of Easter is the high point of the Christian liturgical year, marking the resurrection of Jesus as the central event in salvation history. Easter is a time of rejoicing in the victory of Christ over death and the hope of eternal life that His resurrection brings.

Easter is also a time of renewal and transformation, as believers reflect on the significance of the resurrection for their own lives. Just as Christ was raised from the dead, so too are Christians called to live in the power of the resurrection, experiencing new life and participating in God's ongoing work of redemption in the world.

4.8. Conclusion

The resurrection of Jesus Christ is the foundation of Christian faith and doctrine, shaping the way believers understand God, salvation, and their own lives. It is the validation of Jesus' identity as the Son of God, the defeat of sin and death, and the source of hope for eternal life. The resurrection is not only a past event but a present reality that empowers the Church's mission and worship.

For Christians, the resurrection is both a historical fact and a theological truth that transforms every aspect of life. It gives meaning to suffering, offers hope in the face of death, and promises the ultimate restoration of all things in the new creation. The resurrection is the reason for Christian faith, and it will remain the heart of the Church's proclamation until the day when Christ returns to make all things new.

CHAPTER 05

JESUS AS THE MESSIAH: JESUS' ROLE IN FUFLLING OLD TESTAMENT PROPHECIES

5.1. Introduction

The concept of the Messiah, or the "Anointed One," is deeply rooted in Jewish tradition and the Hebrew Scriptures. The Messiah was expected to be a divinely appointed figure who would bring salvation to Israel, restore the Davidic kingdom, and establish God's reign of justice and peace. For Christians, Jesus of Nazareth is identified as the long-awaited Messiah, fulfilling the prophecies of the Old Testament in His life, death, and resurrection. This chapter explores the role of Jesus in fulfilling Old Testament Messianic prophecies and how these prophecies reveal the nature and mission of Jesus as the Messiah.

5.2. The Concept of the Messiah in the Old Testament

Before examining how Jesus fulfills Old Testament prophecies, it is important to understand the concept of the Messiah as it developed in the Hebrew Scriptures. The term "Messiah" (Hebrew: Mashiach) means "Anointed One" and refers to someone who is chosen and consecrated by God for a specific mission. In the Old Testament, kings, priests, and prophets were anointed, but the Messiah came to signify a future figure who would deliver Israel and bring about God's Kingdom.

5.2.1. The Davidic Covenant and the Promise of a King

One of the foundational passages for Messianic expectations is found in 2 Samuel 7:12-16, where God makes a covenant with King David. God promises David that his descendants will always rule over Israel and that his kingdom will be established forever: "Your house and your kingdom shall be made sure forever before me. Your throne shall be established forever" (2 Samuel 7:16). This promise led to the hope for a future descendant of David who would rule as the ideal king, bringing peace, justice, and righteousness to Israel and the world.

The Davidic Messiah was expected to be a righteous and just ruler who would restore the fortunes of Israel. Prophecies in the books of Isaiah, Jeremiah, and Ezekiel envision a king who will reign in the line of David and lead Israel to triumph over its enemies (Isaiah 9:6-7, Jeremiah 23:5-6, Ezekiel 34:23-24).

5.2.2. The Suffering Servant and the Role of Redemption

In addition to the expectation of a Davidic king, the Old Testament contains prophecies about a "Suffering Servant" who would bring redemption to Israel through suffering and sacrifice. Isaiah 52:13-53:12 is one of the most striking Messianic passages, describing a servant who is "pierced for our transgressions" and "crushed for our iniquities" (Isaiah 53:5). This figure is not only a king but also a servant who suffers on behalf of the people, bearing their sins and bringing them peace and healing.

This dual expectation—of a conquering king and a suffering servant—shapes the Messianic hope of Israel. For Christians, Jesus embodies both of these roles, fulfilling the prophecies of the Old Testament in ways that reveal the full scope of God's redemptive plan.

5.3. Jesus as the Fulfillment of the Davidic Covenant

One of the key aspects of Jesus' role as the Messiah is His fulfillment of the Davidic covenant, where God promised that a descendant of David would reign over an eternal kingdom. Throughout the New Testament, Jesus is identified as the rightful heir to the throne of David, fulfilling the promises made to Israel's greatest king.

5.3.1. The Genealogy of Jesus

The Gospels of Matthew and Luke both emphasize Jesus' Davidic lineage. In Matthew 1:1-17, the genealogy of Jesus is traced through Joseph, His legal father, back to David, showing that Jesus is the rightful heir to the Davidic throne. Similarly, Luke 3:23-38 traces Jesus' lineage through Mary, also connecting Him to David. This genealogical emphasis demonstrates that Jesus is the fulfillment of the promise that a descendant of David would reign forever.

The angel Gabriel, when announcing Jesus' birth to Mary, explicitly ties Jesus to the Davidic covenant: "He will be great and will be called the Son of the Most High. And the Lord God will give to him the throne of his father David, and he will reign over the house of Jacob forever, and of his kingdom there will be no end" (Luke 1:32-33). This declaration affirms that Jesus is the promised Davidic king who will establish God's eternal kingdom.

5.3.2. The Kingship of Jesus

Throughout His ministry, Jesus demonstrates His authority as the Messiah and King. He proclaims the arrival of the Kingdom of God (Mark 1:15) and teaches that He is the King who will rule over this kingdom. Jesus' entry into Jerusalem on Palm Sunday, riding on a donkey, fulfills the prophecy of Zechariah 9:9: "Rejoice greatly, O daughter of Zion! Shout aloud, O daughter of Jerusalem! Behold, your king is coming to you; righteous and having salvation is he, humble and mounted on a donkey."

By entering Jerusalem in this manner, Jesus presents Himself as the humble yet righteous King, in fulfillment of the Messianic prophecy. The crowds recognize this and shout, "Hosanna to the Son of David!" (Matthew 21:9), acknowledging Jesus as the Davidic Messiah.

However, Jesus' kingship is not one of political power or military conquest, as many expected. Instead, His kingdom is spiritual and eternal. Jesus declares to Pilate, "My kingdom is not of this world" (John 18:36), indicating that His reign transcends earthly kingdoms and is focused on establishing God's reign in the hearts of His followers.

5.4. Jesus as the Suffering Servant

In addition to fulfilling the Davidic covenant, Jesus also fulfills the prophecies concerning the Suffering Servant in Isaiah. The New Testament writers frequently connect Jesus' suffering, death, and resurrection to the servant's mission described in Isaiah 53.

5.4.1. Jesus' Suffering and Death as Fulfillment

Isaiah 53 presents a vivid picture of a servant who suffers on behalf of others, bearing their sins and bringing them healing and peace. Christians see this passage as a clear prophecy of Jesus' crucifixion. Isaiah 53:5 states, "He was pierced for our transgressions; he was crushed for our iniquities." This is fulfilled in Jesus' death on the cross, where He takes upon Himself the punishment for sin.

The New Testament frequently refers to this prophecy in relation to Jesus' suffering. In Matthew 8:17, after Jesus heals the sick, the Gospel writer quotes Isaiah 53:4: "He took our illnesses and bore our diseases," showing that Jesus' healing ministry is part of His fulfillment of the Suffering Servant's role.

Peter also explicitly connects Jesus' suffering to Isaiah's prophecy, writing in 1 Peter 2:24, "He himself bore our sins in his body on the tree, that we might die to sin and live to righteousness. By his wounds you have been healed." This echoes Isaiah's words in 53:5, confirming that Jesus' suffering and death are the fulfillment of the servant's mission to bring redemption through sacrifice.

5.4.2. The Atonement and Jesus' Sacrificial Role

One of the key theological implications of Jesus as the Suffering Servant is the doctrine of atonement. Isaiah 53 describes the servant as making an offering for sin: "He was oppressed, and he was afflicted, yet he opened not his mouth… like a lamb that is led to the slaughter" (Isaiah 53:7). Jesus' death is understood as the ultimate sacrifice, fulfilling the Old Testament sacrificial system and providing atonement for the sins of humanity.

Jesus Himself identifies His death as a sacrifice for sin, saying in Matthew 20:28, "The Son of Man came not to be served but to serve, and to give his life as a ransom for many." This sacrificial death is the means by which humanity is reconciled to God, fulfilling the Messianic role of bringing salvation and healing to the world.

5.5. Jesus and the Prophecies of a New Covenant

Another important aspect of Jesus' Messianic role is His fulfillment of the prophecies concerning a new covenant between God and His people. The Old Testament prophets, particularly Jeremiah and Ezekiel, foretold a time when God would establish a new covenant that would bring about spiritual renewal and forgiveness of sins.

5.5.1. The Promise of a New Covenant

In Jeremiah 31:31-34, God promises to make a new covenant with the house of Israel and the house of Judah, saying, "I will put my law within them, and I will write it on their hearts. And I will be their God, and they shall be my people." This new covenant would involve an internal transformation, where God's law would be written on the hearts of His people, leading to a deep, personal relationship with Him.

Ezekiel also speaks of this new covenant, where God will give His people a new heart and a new spirit: "I will remove the heart of stone from your flesh and give you a heart of flesh. And I will put my Spirit within you, and cause you to walk in my statutes and be careful to obey my rules" (Ezekiel 36:26-27).

These prophecies point to a future time when God's people would be spiritually renewed, forgiven of their sins, and empowered by the Holy Spirit to live in obedience to Him.

5.5.2. Jesus' Establishment of the New Covenant

At the Last Supper, Jesus explicitly identifies His death as the means by which the new covenant is established. He takes the cup and says, "This cup that is poured out for you is the new covenant in my blood" (Luke 22:20). Through His sacrificial death, Jesus inaugurates the new covenant, fulfilling the promises of Jeremiah and Ezekiel.

The new covenant brings about the forgiveness of sins and the gift of the Holy Spirit, which empowers believers to live in accordance with God's will. As the Messiah, Jesus fulfills the role of mediator of this new covenant, making it possible for humanity to be reconciled to God and to experience the fullness of His grace and presence.

5.6. Jesus as the Messiah of All Nations

While the Old Testament prophecies often focus on the Messiah's role in redeeming Israel, there are also numerous prophecies that point to the Messiah's mission to bring salvation to the entire world. Jesus fulfills these prophecies by extending His mission beyond Israel to include all nations.

5.6.1. The Universal Mission of the Messiah

Isaiah 49:6 contains a powerful statement about the Messiah's mission: "It is too light a thing that you should be my servant to raise up the tribes of Jacob and to bring back the preserved of Israel; I will make you as a light for the nations, that my salvation may reach to the end of the earth." This prophecy reveals that the Messiah's mission is not limited to Israel but extends to all peoples.

Similarly, in Psalm 72:8-11, the future king is described as ruling over all nations, and "all kings shall fall down before him; all nations serve him." These passages reveal the global scope of the Messiah's reign, where His salvation and rule will encompass the entire world.

5.6.2. Jesus' Commission to the Nations

Jesus fulfills this aspect of the Messianic mission by commissioning His disciples to take the message of salvation to all nations. After His resurrection, Jesus tells His disciples, "Go therefore and make disciples of all nations, baptizing them in the name of the Father and of the Son and of the Holy Spirit" (Matthew 28:19). This Great Commission marks the beginning of the Church's mission to bring the Gospel to the ends of the earth, fulfilling the Old Testament prophecies of the Messiah's global reign.

The Book of Acts records the expansion of the early Church beyond Israel, as the apostles preach the message of Jesus' resurrection to Jews and Gentiles alike. Paul, in particular, emphasizes that Jesus is the Messiah not only of Israel but of the entire world, proclaiming that "there is neither Jew nor Greek... for you are all one in Christ Jesus" (Galatians 3:28).

5.7. Conclusion

Jesus' role as the Messiah is deeply rooted in the fulfillment of Old Testament prophecies. He is the promised descendant of David, the righteous King who establishes God's eternal kingdom. He is the Suffering Servant, who bears the sins of the world and brings redemption through His sacrificial death. He is the mediator of the new covenant, bringing about forgiveness, spiritual renewal, and the indwelling of the Holy Spirit. Finally, He is the light to the nations, extending God's salvation to all people, fulfilling the prophecies that foretold the global scope of the Messiah's reign.

For Christians, the fulfillment of these prophecies in the person of Jesus confirms that He is the true Messiah, the One through whom God's redemptive plan for the world is accomplished. As we continue to explore the life, death, and resurrection of Jesus, the prophetic witness of the Old Testament serves as a powerful testimony to the divine mission of the Messiah and the unfolding of God's plan for humanity's salvation.

Different Messianic Expectations and How Jesus Met or Redefined Them

5.1. Introduction

In the centuries leading up to Jesus' life and ministry, Jewish expectations of the Messiah were diverse and multifaceted. These messianic hopes were shaped by various religious, political, and social factors, all rooted in the Hebrew Scriptures. Some expected a political leader to overthrow oppressive regimes, while others anticipated a spiritual or priestly figure who would restore Israel's religious purity. Jesus of Nazareth met many of these expectations, but He also redefined and transformed them in ways that confounded both His followers and His opponents. This chapter will explore the key messianic expectations of the time and examine how Jesus fulfilled or reshaped them, leading to a new understanding of what it means for Him to be the Messiah.

5.2. The Expectation of a Political and Military Messiah

One of the most prominent messianic hopes in the first century was for a political and military leader who would deliver Israel from Roman occupation. The Jewish people, under Roman rule, longed for a descendant of King David who would rise up and restore Israel's independence and sovereignty, just as David had once delivered Israel from its enemies and established a powerful kingdom.

5.2.1. The Political Messiah in Jewish Thought

The idea of a political Messiah was rooted in the Davidic covenant and the promises of the Hebrew Scriptures. Prophecies like 2 Samuel 7:12-16, which speak of an everlasting kingdom for David's line, and Isaiah 9:6-7, which describes a government established in peace and justice, fueled expectations that the Messiah would be a warrior-king who would defeat Israel's enemies and rule with power and authority.

During the time of Jesus, several Jewish groups and movements, such as the Zealots, actively pursued the overthrow of Roman rule and sought a Messiah who would lead them in battle. They envisioned a Messiah who would use force to liberate Israel and establish a new political order.

5.2.2. Jesus' Rejection of a Political Messiahship

While Jesus was indeed a descendant of David and entered Jerusalem as a king (Matthew 21:1-11), He did not conform to the expectation of a political and military leader. Instead of rallying an army or engaging in violent rebellion, Jesus preached a message of peace, love, and forgiveness. When asked about paying taxes to Caesar, Jesus responded, "Render to Caesar the things that are Caesar's, and to God the things that are God's" (Mark 12:17), showing that His kingdom was not in direct opposition to Roman political authority.

Jesus made it clear that His kingdom was not of this world (John 18:36). His mission was not to establish a political kingdom but a spiritual one—the Kingdom of God, which transcended national borders and was not based on military might. By redefining the concept of kingship and the Messiah's role, Jesus transformed messianic expectations from a political agenda to a spiritual mission aimed at the hearts and souls of individuals.

5.2.3. The Disappointment and Confusion of the People

Many were disappointed or confused by Jesus' refusal to take on a political role. Even His own disciples struggled to understand this redefinition of Messiahship. After Jesus' death and resurrection, the disciples asked Him, "Lord, will you at this time restore the kingdom to Israel?" (Acts 1:6). Their question reveals the persistence of political expectations, but Jesus redirects them toward their mission of spreading the Gospel, signifying that the kingdom He was establishing was not a political entity but a spiritual movement.

5.3. The Expectation of a Priestly or Religious Messiah

Alongside the hope for a political Messiah, there was also an expectation for a priestly or religious leader who would restore Israel's purity and lead the people back to covenant faithfulness. This expectation was influenced by the priestly tradition and the role of figures like Moses and Aaron, who mediated between God and the people.

5.3.1. The Priestly Role in Jewish Messianism

Some Jewish traditions, particularly those associated with the Essenes and other ascetic communities, emphasized the Messiah's role in renewing the religious life of Israel. These groups, who retreated from mainstream Jewish society to live in purity, anticipated a Messiah who would cleanse the temple, purify the priesthood, and restore true worship.

This expectation was based on passages like Malachi 3:1-3, which spoke of a messenger who would purify the Levites and bring about a renewal of sacrificial worship. The Messiah was seen as one who would restore the religious order, ensuring that Israel's covenant relationship with God was renewed and preserved.

5.3.2. Jesus as the Ultimate High Priest

Jesus met this expectation but in a way that far exceeded traditional understandings of the priestly role. Rather than simply reforming the temple worship or restoring the priesthood, Jesus redefined the very concept of sacrifice and priesthood. The author of Hebrews identifies Jesus as the ultimate high priest who offers not the blood of animals but

His own life as a sacrifice for sin (Hebrews 9:11-14). Jesus' sacrifice is perfect and final, fulfilling the role of the priest and rendering the old sacrificial system obsolete.

Jesus also challenged the religious authorities of His day, calling out the corruption within the temple and the hypocrisy of the religious leaders. In cleansing the temple (Matthew 21:12-13), Jesus demonstrated that He was concerned with true worship and purity, but His focus was on spiritual purity rather than ritual observance.

5.3.3. The Fulfillment of the New Covenant

Jesus also fulfilled the messianic expectation for a new covenant, which was anticipated by prophets like Jeremiah and Ezekiel. At the Last Supper, Jesus declared that His blood was the blood of the new covenant (Luke 22:20), signaling the establishment of a new relationship between God and His people, not based on the law or temple rituals, but on faith in His redemptive work.

In this way, Jesus met the expectation for a priestly Messiah by becoming the ultimate mediator between God and humanity, offering Himself as the perfect sacrifice and establishing a new covenant of grace and forgiveness.

5.4. The Expectation of a Prophetic Messiah

Another important messianic expectation was that the Messiah would be a prophet like Moses, who would speak God's word to the people and lead them in faithfulness. Deuteronomy 18:15-19 contains a promise that God would raise up a prophet like Moses, and many in Jesus' time looked for this prophetic figure to arise and lead Israel.

5.4.1. The Role of the Prophet in Jewish Tradition

In Jewish tradition, prophets were seen as God's messengers, sent to call the people back to faithfulness and obedience. Prophets like Elijah, Isaiah, and Jeremiah not only foretold future events but also interpreted God's will and rebuked the people for their sins. The idea of a prophetic Messiah was that this figure would act as the ultimate spokesman for God, leading the people in righteousness and delivering God's message of salvation.

5.4.2. Jesus as the Fulfillment of the Prophetic Role

Jesus fulfilled the expectation of a prophetic Messiah by being the ultimate prophet who not only spoke God's word but embodied it. In Luke 4:18-21, Jesus reads from the book of Isaiah in the synagogue and applies the prophecy to Himself: "The Spirit of the Lord is upon me, because he has anointed me to proclaim good news to the poor... Today this Scripture has been fulfilled in your hearing."

Throughout His ministry, Jesus acted as a prophet, teaching the people, performing miracles, and proclaiming the coming of God's Kingdom. He also challenged the religious and social systems of the day, calling the people to repentance and warning them of coming judgment. Like the prophets of old, Jesus confronted injustice, hypocrisy, and false piety, but He also revealed God's plan for salvation in ways that no previous prophet had done.

5.4.3. The Ultimate Revelation of God

While Jesus fulfilled the prophetic role, He also redefined it by being more than just a messenger from God—He was the Word made flesh (John 1:14). In Jesus, God's revelation is complete. As the writer of Hebrews states, "In these last days he has spoken to us by his Son, whom he appointed the heir of all things" (Hebrews 1:2). Jesus is not just a prophet among prophets; He is the divine Son, who reveals the fullness of God's character and will.

5.5. Jesus' Redefinition of Messianic Expectations

Throughout His ministry, Jesus consistently met and exceeded Jewish messianic expectations, but He also redefined what it meant to be the Messiah in profound ways. His rejection of political power, His radical reinterpretation of religious authority, and His self-sacrificial role as both priest and prophet led to a new understanding of the Messiah that extended beyond the boundaries of Jewish thought.

5.5.1. The Suffering Messiah

Perhaps the most significant way in which Jesus redefined messianic expectations was through His suffering and death. While many expected the Messiah to be a victorious leader, Jesus embraced the role of the suffering servant described in Isaiah 53. He redefined victory not as military conquest but as self-sacrifice and love. By willingly going to the cross, Jesus showed that true Messianic power lies in humility, service, and obedience to God's will, even to the point of death.

Jesus' suffering and death were not failures but the ultimate fulfillment of God's redemptive plan. Through His crucifixion, He accomplished the forgiveness of sins and the reconciliation of humanity with God. His resurrection then confirmed His identity as the true Messiah, victorious not over political enemies but over sin and death.

5.5.2. The Messiah of All People

While Jewish expectations of the Messiah were often focused on the restoration of Israel, Jesus expanded the scope of Messiahship to include all people. He redefined the Kingdom of God as a spiritual reality that transcended ethnic and national boundaries. Jesus welcomed Gentiles, tax collectors, sinners, and the marginalized into His kingdom, demonstrating that the Messiah's mission was to bring salvation to all humanity, not just to Israel.

In Matthew 28:19-20, Jesus commissions His disciples to "go and make disciples of all nations," signaling the universal scope of His Messianic mission. The early Church, particularly through the ministry of Paul, continued this expansion, proclaiming Jesus as the Messiah for both Jews and Gentiles alike.

5.6. Conclusion

Jesus met the diverse messianic expectations of His time but did so in ways that were unexpected and transformative. He fulfilled the political, priestly, and prophetic roles expected of the Messiah, but He redefined them according to God's plan of redemption. Rather than being a political conqueror, Jesus established a spiritual kingdom marked by peace, justice, and love. Rather than restoring temple worship, He became the ultimate High

Priest, offering Himself as a sacrifice for sin. Rather than being a mere prophet, He was the full and final revelation of God's Word.

In reinterpreting and fulfilling messianic expectations, Jesus revealed that God's plans for the Messiah were far greater than what many had imagined. His life, death, and resurrection transformed not only Jewish expectations but also the entire course of human history, as He became the Savior and King of all who believe. Through Jesus, the true nature of the Messiah is revealed—a servant king, a suffering savior, and the divine Son who brings God's Kingdom to earth.

The Concept of Jesus as the Suffering Servant

5.1. Introduction

The idea of the "Suffering Servant" is one of the most profound and defining elements of Christian theology. Rooted in the Old Testament, particularly in the writings of the prophet Isaiah, the concept of the Suffering Servant speaks of a figure who would bring redemption to God's people not through political might or conquest, but through suffering, humility, and self-sacrifice. For Christians, this prophecy finds its ultimate fulfillment in Jesus Christ. This chapter explores the biblical foundations of the Suffering Servant, how Jesus embodies this role, and the theological implications of His suffering and death for salvation.

5.2. The Old Testament Foundation: Isaiah's Servant Songs

The concept of the Suffering Servant originates from four passages in the book of Isaiah, often referred to as the "Servant Songs." These passages describe a mysterious servant of God who is chosen for a divine mission of justice, redemption, and restoration. However, the servant's path to fulfilling this mission is marked by suffering, rejection, and even death.

5.2.1. The Servant's Mission

In Isaiah 42:1-4, the first of the Servant Songs, the servant is introduced as God's chosen one who will bring justice to the nations: "Here is my servant, whom I uphold, my chosen one in whom I delight; I will put my Spirit on him, and he will bring justice to the nations." The servant is described as humble and gentle, one who will not shout or break a bruised reed. This picture of the servant already contrasts with the common expectation of a powerful, conquering leader.

The second Servant Song (Isaiah 49:1-6) further expands on the servant's mission, emphasizing that the servant will be a light to the nations and bring salvation not only to Israel but to the ends of the earth. This global vision of the servant's work begins to align with the Messianic hope of the restoration of all humanity.

5.2.2. The Suffering and Rejection of the Servant

The third and fourth Servant Songs (Isaiah 50:4-9 and 52:13-53:12) take a dramatic turn, revealing that the servant will endure intense suffering and rejection. Isaiah 50:6 describes the servant's mistreatment: "I offered my back to those who beat me, my cheeks to those who pulled out my beard; I did not hide my face from mocking and spitting."

However, it is in Isaiah 52:13-53:12, the most famous of the Servant Songs, that the full extent of the servant's suffering is revealed. Here, the servant is "despised and rejected by men," "a man of sorrows, and acquainted with grief" (Isaiah 53:3). The servant's suffering is not for his own sins, but for the sins of others: "He was pierced for our transgressions; he was crushed for our iniquities" (Isaiah

53:5). The servant's death is described as a substitutionary sacrifice, one that brings healing and peace to those for whom he suffers.

This portrait of the servant as one who suffers in the place of others, bearing their iniquities and offering his life as a sacrifice, sets the stage for understanding Jesus' role as the Suffering Servant in Christian theology.

5.3. Jesus as the Fulfillment of the Suffering Servant

The New Testament repeatedly identifies Jesus as the fulfillment of Isaiah's Suffering Servant. Jesus' life, ministry, death, and resurrection are seen as the ultimate realization of the Servant Songs, particularly the prophecy in Isaiah 53. By embracing suffering and willingly offering Himself as a sacrifice for sin, Jesus redefines what it means to be the Messiah, embodying the servant's role in a way that transcends traditional Messianic expectations.

5.3.1. Jesus' Life and Ministry as a Servant

From the beginning of His ministry, Jesus positioned Himself as a servant. In Mark 10:45, Jesus says, "For even the Son of Man came not to be served but to serve, and to give his life as a ransom for many." This statement encapsulates the heart of Jesus' mission: He came not as a political ruler or military leader, but as a servant who would offer His life for the salvation of others.

Throughout His ministry, Jesus demonstrated this servant-hearted approach in both word and deed. He healed the sick, fed the hungry, and showed compassion to the marginalized and oppressed. He consistently identified with the poor and lowly, embodying the humility described in Isaiah's Servant Songs. Even His actions at the Last Supper, where He washed His disciples' feet, symbolized His role as a servant, willing to take the lowest position for the sake of others (John 13:1-17).

5.3.2. The Passion and Crucifixion of Jesus

It is in Jesus' suffering and death that the connection to the Suffering Servant becomes most explicit. The events of Jesus' passion—His arrest, trial, crucifixion, and death— parallel the descriptions of the servant's suffering in Isaiah 53. Jesus is mocked, beaten, and led to His death in much the same way that Isaiah's servant is depicted as being "oppressed and afflicted" (Isaiah 53:7).

The New Testament writers frequently cite Isaiah 53 in connection with Jesus' death. For example, in Matthew 8:17, the Gospel writer quotes Isaiah 53:4 ("He took our illnesses and bore our diseases") to explain Jesus' healing ministry, showing that His suffering was not only physical but also redemptive. Similarly, in Acts 8:32-35, Philip explains to the Ethiopian eunuch that Isaiah 53 points directly to Jesus, identifying Him as the Suffering Servant who gave His life for the salvation of humanity.

The theological heart of this connection lies in the doctrine of substitutionary atonement. As Isaiah 53:5 declares, "He was pierced for our transgressions; he was crushed for our iniquities; upon him was the chastisement that brought us peace, and with his wounds we are healed." Jesus, as the Suffering Servant, bears the penalty for sin, offering Himself as a sacrifice so that others might be forgiven and reconciled to God.

5.3.3. The Resurrection and Vindication of the Servant

Isaiah's prophecy does not end with the servant's suffering and death. In Isaiah 53:11, the servant is vindicated: "After he has suffered, he will see the light of life and be satisfied." This prophecy points to the resurrection of the servant, who, despite His death, will be vindicated by God and exalted.

Jesus' resurrection is the ultimate fulfillment of this vindication. By raising Jesus from the dead, God demonstrates that Jesus' suffering was not in vain but was part of His divine plan for salvation. The resurrection confirms that Jesus is the Messiah, the Suffering Servant who has been exalted by God and now reigns as Lord. In Philippians 2:8-9, Paul writes that Jesus "humbled himself by becoming obedient to the point of death, even death on a cross. Therefore God has highly exalted him and bestowed on him the name that is above every name."

5.4. The Theological Implications of Jesus as the Suffering Servant

The identification of Jesus as the Suffering Servant has profound theological implications, particularly in the areas of atonement, discipleship, and the nature of God's Kingdom. Jesus' willingness to suffer and die for the sake of others reveals the depth of God's love for humanity and sets the pattern for how Christians are to live as His followers.

5.4.1. The Atonement and Substitutionary Sacrifice

One of the central theological implications of Jesus' role as the Suffering Servant is the doctrine of atonement. In Isaiah 53, the servant's suffering is described as a substitutionary act: the servant suffers not for his own sins but for the sins of others. This concept finds its ultimate fulfillment in Jesus' death on the cross, where He bears the punishment for the sins of the world.

The New Testament teaches that Jesus' death is the means by which humanity is reconciled to God. In 1 Peter 2:24, Peter writes, "He himself bore our sins in his body on the tree, that we might die to sin and live to righteousness. By his wounds you have been healed." Jesus' death as the Suffering Servant is the ultimate act of love and sacrifice, providing a way for sinners to be forgiven and restored to a right relationship with God.

5.4.2. Discipleship and the Call to Suffer

Jesus' role as the Suffering Servant also has implications for Christian discipleship. Just as Jesus embraced suffering for the sake of others, so too are His followers called to take up their cross and follow Him (Luke 9:23). Discipleship, according to Jesus, involves self-sacrifice, service, and a willingness to endure suffering for the sake of the Gospel.

In Philippians 2:5-8, Paul urges Christians to adopt the same mindset as Christ, who "made himself nothing, taking the form of a servant." Jesus' humility, obedience, and willingness to suffer serve as a model for how believers are to live. The path of discipleship is not one of worldly power or glory but one of service, sacrifice, and suffering in the name of Christ.

5.4.3. The Nature of God's Kingdom

Finally, Jesus' identification as the Suffering Servant redefines

the nature of God's Kingdom. In contrast to the expectations of a political Messiah who would overthrow Israel's enemies, Jesus reveals that God's Kingdom is not established through force or violence but through love, humility, and sacrifice. The cross, rather than a throne, becomes the symbol of Jesus' kingship.

God's Kingdom, as revealed through the Suffering Servant, is a kingdom where the last are first, where the meek inherit the earth, and where power is perfected in weakness. Jesus' suffering and death demonstrate that God's Kingdom operates on entirely different principles than the kingdoms of this world. It is a kingdom of justice, mercy, and peace, established through the self-giving love of the Suffering Servant.

5.5. Conclusion

The concept of Jesus as the Suffering Servant is central to Christian theology and the understanding of Jesus' mission. By fulfilling the prophecies of Isaiah, Jesus redefines the nature of the Messiah, showing that true salvation comes not through political power or military might, but through suffering, sacrifice, and self-giving love. As the Suffering Servant, Jesus bears the sins of the world, offering Himself as a sacrifice for the redemption of humanity.

The theological implications of Jesus' role as the Suffering Servant are profound. His death on the cross provides the means of atonement and reconciliation with God, while His example of humility and service sets the pattern for Christian discipleship. Finally, Jesus' suffering reveals the nature of God's Kingdom—a kingdom where love triumphs over hate, humility over pride, and life over death.

As we continue to explore the person and work of Jesus Christ, the image of the Suffering Servant serves as a powerful reminder of the depths of God's love and the cost of our salvation. Through His suffering, Jesus not only redeems humanity but also reveals the true nature of the Messiah as one who comes not to be served but to serve, and to give His life as a ransom for many.

CHAPTER 06

THE ROLE OF THE HOLY SPIRIT

6.1. Introduction

The Holy Spirit plays a vital role in both the ministry of Jesus Christ and the lives of His followers. As the third person of the Trinity, the Holy Spirit is the active presence of God in the world, working to bring about God's will and purpose. In the ministry of Jesus, the Holy Spirit empowered Him for His mission, guided Him, and confirmed His identity as the Son of God. After Jesus' resurrection and ascension, the Holy Spirit became the promised gift to all believers, empowering them to live out their faith and participate in the mission of God. This chapter explores the role of the Holy Spirit in Jesus' ministry and how the Spirit continues to work in the lives of believers.

6.2. The Holy Spirit in the Ministry of Jesus

From the beginning of Jesus' earthly life, the Holy Spirit was central to His ministry. The Spirit was active in His conception, baptism, and throughout His public ministry, empowering Jesus to proclaim the Kingdom of God and perform mighty works.

6.2.1. The Holy Spirit and Jesus' Birth

The role of the Holy Spirit in Jesus' life begins with His miraculous conception. The angel Gabriel announced to Mary that she would conceive and bear a son by the power of the Holy Spirit. Luke 1:35 records Gabriel's words: "The Holy Spirit will come upon you, and the power of the Most High will overshadow you; therefore, the child to be born will be called holy—the Son of God."

This miraculous event, in which Jesus was conceived by the Holy Spirit, affirmed His divine origin and His unique identity as both fully God and fully human. The Holy Spirit's involvement in Jesus' birth establishes the divine nature of His mission from the very beginning.

6.2.2. The Holy Spirit at Jesus' Baptism

The baptism of Jesus marks a pivotal moment in His ministry, and it is a moment in which the Holy Spirit plays a significant role. As Jesus emerged from the waters of the Jordan River, the Holy Spirit descended upon Him "like a dove" (Matthew 3:16). At the same time, a voice from heaven declared, "This is my beloved Son, with whom I am well pleased" (Matthew 3:17).

The descent of the Holy Spirit upon Jesus at His baptism signifies the Spirit's anointing and empowerment for His public ministry. This event publicly affirmed Jesus' identity as the Son of God and the Messiah, while also marking the beginning of His mission to proclaim the Kingdom of God.

6.2.3. The Holy Spirit's Empowerment in Jesus' Ministry

Throughout His ministry, Jesus operated in the power of the Holy Spirit. Luke 4:1 records that Jesus, "full of the Holy Spirit," was led by the Spirit into the wilderness for a period of testing and preparation before beginning His public ministry. After His time in the wilderness, Jesus returned to Galilee "in the power of the Spirit" (Luke 4:14) and began preaching, teaching, and performing miracles.

In Luke 4:18-19, Jesus Himself explicitly connects His ministry to the empowerment of the Holy Spirit when He reads from the scroll of Isaiah in the synagogue: "The Spirit of the Lord is upon me, because he has anointed me to proclaim good news to the poor. He has sent me to proclaim liberty to the captives and recovering of sight to the blind, to set at liberty those who are oppressed, to proclaim the year of the Lord's favor." Here, Jesus reveals that the Holy Spirit has anointed Him for the specific purpose of proclaiming and enacting the Kingdom of God.

Jesus' miracles—healing the sick, casting out demons, raising the dead, and performing other mighty works—were all carried out by the power of the Holy Spirit. The Spirit empowered Jesus to demonstrate God's authority and bring about the restoration of individuals and communities, pointing to the ultimate redemption that would be accomplished through His death and resurrection.

6.2.4. The Holy Spirit and Jesus' Resurrection

The Holy Spirit also played a crucial role in Jesus' resurrection. Paul writes in Romans 8:11, "If the Spirit of him who raised Jesus from the dead dwells in you, he who raised Christ Jesus from the dead will also give life to your mortal bodies through his Spirit who dwells in you." This verse indicates that the Holy Spirit was actively involved in raising Jesus from the dead, demonstrating the Spirit's power over life and death.

The resurrection, empowered by the Holy Spirit, is the climactic event of Jesus' earthly ministry, affirming His victory over sin, death, and the forces of evil. It is also the foundation for the hope of believers, who are promised the same resurrection power through the Spirit.

6.3. The Role of the Holy Spirit in the Lives of Believers

After Jesus' ascension, the Holy Spirit became the promised gift to all who follow Christ. In the lives of believers, the Holy Spirit works to guide, empower, and transform them into the likeness of Christ, equipping them to participate in God's mission in the world.

6.3.1. The Promise of the Holy Spirit

Before His crucifixion, Jesus promised His disciples that the Holy Spirit would come to them after His departure. In John 14:16-17, Jesus says, "And I will ask the Father, and he will give you another Helper, to be with you forever, even the Spirit of truth, whom the world cannot receive, because it neither sees him nor knows him. You know him, for he dwells with you and will be in you."

This promise is fulfilled after Jesus' resurrection, at Pentecost, when the Holy Spirit is poured out on the disciples in the form of tongues of fire, and they are filled with the Spirit's power (Acts 2:1-4). The coming of the Holy Spirit marks the birth of the Church and the beginning of its mission to spread the Gospel to all nations. The Spirit's presence empowers believers for the task of bearing witness to Christ and participating in His mission.

6.3.2. The Holy Spirit as Counselor, Comforter, and Guide

One of the key roles of the Holy Spirit in the lives of believers is to serve as a Counselor or Comforter. The Greek word used for the Holy Spirit in the New Testament is parakletos, meaning one who comes alongside to help. Jesus promises His disciples that the Holy Spirit will guide them into all truth (John 16:13), reminding them of everything He has taught (John 14:26) and giving them the wisdom and courage they need to live as His followers.

The Holy Spirit also provides comfort and encouragement in times of difficulty. In Romans 8:26-27, Paul explains that the Holy Spirit intercedes for believers when they are weak, helping them in their prayers and sustaining them in their faith.

6.3.3. The Empowerment of the Holy Spirit

Just as the Holy Spirit empowered Jesus for His ministry, the Spirit also empowers believers to carry out God's work. At Pentecost, the disciples were filled with the Holy Spirit and began proclaiming the Gospel in various languages, demonstrating the Spirit's power to equip believers for their mission (Acts 2:4). Peter, filled with the Spirit, boldly preached to the crowds, and thousands were converted (Acts 2:14-41).

The Spirit continues to empower believers today by equipping them with spiritual gifts for the edification of the Church and the advancement of God's Kingdom. In 1 Corinthians 12, Paul lists various gifts of the Spirit, including wisdom, knowledge, healing, prophecy, and discernment, which are given "for the common good" (1 Corinthians 12:7).

The Holy Spirit also empowers believers with boldness and courage to proclaim the Gospel, even in the face of opposition and persecution.

6.3.4. The Holy Spirit and Sanctification

Another critical role of the Holy Spirit is in the process of sanctification, whereby believers are transformed into the likeness of Christ. The Spirit works within believers to convict them of sin (John 16:8), renew their minds (Romans 12:2), and produce the fruit of righteousness in their lives.

In Galatians 5:22-23, Paul describes the "fruit of the Spirit" as love, joy, peace, patience, kindness, goodness, faithfulness, gentleness, and self-control. These virtues are the result of the Spirit's transformative work in the hearts of believers, shaping them to reflect the character of Christ and enabling them to live according to God's will.

6.3.5. The Assurance and Hope of the Holy Spirit

The Holy Spirit also plays a crucial role in providing assurance and hope to believers. Paul teaches in Romans 8:16 that "the Spirit himself bears witness with our spirit that we are children of God." The Holy Spirit confirms the believer's identity as a child of God and an heir of eternal life, giving them confidence in their relationship with God.

In addition, the Holy Spirit is described as a "guarantee" or "down payment" of the inheritance that believers will receive in the future. In Ephesians 1:13-14, Paul writes, "In him you also, when you heard the word of truth, the gospel of your salvation, and believed in him, were sealed with the promised Holy Spirit, who is the guarantee of our inheritance until we acquire possession of it." The Spirit's presence in the lives of believers is a foretaste of the future glory that awaits them in the new creation.

6.4. The Holy Spirit and the Mission of the Church

The Holy Spirit is not only active in the individual lives of believers but is also the driving force behind the mission of the Church. From the day of Pentecost, the Holy Spirit has been empowering the Church to bear witness to Christ and to carry out God's redemptive mission in the world.

6.4.1. The Spirit's Empowerment for Mission

The book of Acts makes it clear that the Holy Spirit is the source of the Church's power and effectiveness in its mission. Jesus instructs His disciples to wait in Jerusalem until they are "clothed with power from on high" (Luke 24:49), referring to the coming of the Holy Spirit at Pentecost. When the Spirit comes, the disciples are empowered to preach the

Gospel boldly, perform miracles, and establish communities of believers throughout the Roman Empire.

The same Spirit who empowered the early Church continues to empower the Church today. The Spirit gives believers the courage and boldness to share the Gospel, the wisdom to lead and serve others, and the gifts to build up the body of Christ. Without the Holy Spirit, the Church's mission would be impossible, but with the Spirit's power, the Church can carry out God's work in the world.

6.4.2. The Spirit's Role in Unity and Diversity

The Holy Spirit also plays a crucial role in creating unity within the Church, despite its diversity. In 1 Corinthians 12, Paul emphasizes that while there are many different gifts, all believers are united by the same Spirit: "For in one Spirit we were all baptized into one body—Jews or Greeks, slaves or free—and all were made to drink of one Spirit" (1 Corinthians 12:13).

The Spirit creates a sense of unity among believers, transcending cultural, ethnic, and social barriers. At the same time, the Spirit distributes different gifts to each believer, ensuring that the Church is a diverse and multifaceted community where every member has a role to play.

6.4.3. The Spirit and the Church's Growth

Throughout history, the Holy Spirit has been responsible for the growth and expansion of the Church. In Acts 2, after Peter's sermon at Pentecost, about 3,000 people were added to the Church in a single day. This explosive growth was a result of the Holy Spirit's power working through the apostles.

Today, the Holy Spirit continues to lead the Church into new areas of mission and ministry, bringing people to faith and transforming lives. The growth of the Church, both in numbers and in spiritual maturity, is a testament to the ongoing work of the Holy Spirit in guiding, empowering, and sustaining God's people.

6.5. Conclusion

The Holy Spirit plays a central role in both the ministry of Jesus and the lives of believers. From the moment of Jesus' conception to His resurrection, the Holy Spirit was at work, empowering Him for His mission and confirming His identity as the Son of God. After Jesus' ascension, the Holy Spirit became the promised gift to believers, empowering them for mission, guiding them in truth, and transforming them into the likeness of Christ.

In the lives of believers, the Holy Spirit serves as a counselor, comforter, and guide, empowering them to live out their faith and bear witness to the Gospel. The Spirit also plays a crucial role in the mission of the Church, uniting believers, equipping them with spiritual gifts, and leading the Church into God's redemptive work in the world.

Ultimately, the Holy Spirit is the active presence of God in the world, working to bring about His Kingdom and to draw people into a deeper relationship with Him. Through the power of the Holy Spirit, believers are able to participate in God's mission, grow in their faith, and live as witnesses to the transforming power of Christ.

The Theological Understanding of Pentecost and Its Implications

6.1. Introduction

Pentecost marks one of the most significant events in Christian history, representing the outpouring of the Holy Spirit on the disciples and the birth of the Church. Recorded in Acts 2, Pentecost is a momentous occasion when the Holy Spirit descends upon the followers of Jesus, empowering them to proclaim the Gospel to all nations. Theologically, Pentecost fulfills the promises of the Old Testament and

Jesus' prophecies about the coming of the Holy Spirit. This chapter will explore the theological significance of Pentecost, its implications for the mission of the Church, and its ongoing relevance in the lives of believers.

6.2. The Significance of Pentecost in the Biblical Narrative

Pentecost is rooted in both the Old and New Testaments and serves as the fulfillment of God's promises to His people. The events of Pentecost are not isolated but are part of the larger story of God's plan for salvation and the establishment of His Kingdom.

6.2.1. Pentecost in the Old Testament

Pentecost, or the Feast of Weeks (Shavuot), was originally a Jewish festival that occurred 50 days after Passover and celebrated the harvest and the giving of the Law to Moses at Mount Sinai. It was a time of thanksgiving for God's provision and the covenant He established with Israel through the giving of the Law (Leviticus 23:15-21). For Jews, Pentecost commemorated both physical and spiritual sustenance.

This historical backdrop provides a rich theological foundation for understanding the Christian Pentecost. Just as the Old Testament Pentecost celebrated the harvest, the New Testament Pentecost marks the beginning of a spiritual harvest, as the Holy Spirit empowers the disciples to preach the Gospel and bring people into the Kingdom of God. Additionally, while the giving of the Law at Sinai established the old covenant, the outpouring of the Holy Spirit at Pentecost inaugurates the new covenant, in which God's law is written on the hearts of believers (Jeremiah 31:33).

6.2.2. The Fulfillment of Jesus' Promise

Pentecost also fulfills Jesus' promise to His disciples that the Holy Spirit would come and empower them for their mission. Before His ascension, Jesus instructed the disciples to wait in Jerusalem until they received the Holy Spirit: "You will receive power when the Holy Spirit has come upon you, and you will be my witnesses in Jerusalem and in all Judea and Samaria, and to the end of the earth" (Acts 1:8).

The events of Pentecost in Acts 2 fulfill this promise. As the disciples were gathered in Jerusalem, "suddenly there came from heaven a sound like a mighty rushing wind, and it filled the entire house where they were sitting. And divided tongues as of fire appeared to them and rested on each one of them. And they were all filled with the Holy Spirit" (Acts 2:2-4). The arrival of the Holy Spirit not only fulfilled Jesus' promise but also signaled the beginning of a new era in salvation history—the age of the Church, empowered by the Spirit to carry out God's mission.

6.3. Theological Implications of Pentecost

Theologically, Pentecost has profound implications for the Church and the life of every believer. It marks the beginning of the Church's mission in the world, the fulfillment of Old Testament prophecies, and the establishment of a new way of relating to God through the Holy Spirit.

6.3.1. The Inauguration of the Church

Pentecost is often referred to as the "birthday of the Church" because it is the moment when the followers of Jesus were empowered to go out and proclaim the Gospel. Before Pentecost, the disciples were uncertain and afraid, hiding in an upper room after Jesus' crucifixion and resurrection. However, after receiving the Holy Spirit, they boldly began preaching in different languages, proclaiming the wonders of God to people from various nations gathered in Jerusalem for the festival (Acts 2:4-12).

Peter's sermon at Pentecost, empowered by the Holy Spirit, resulted in the conversion of about 3,000 people (Acts

2:41). This marked the beginning of the Church as a community of believers, united by the Spirit and sent out to bear witness to the risen Christ. Theologically, this demonstrates the essential role of the Holy Spirit in the Church's life and mission. Without the Spirit's empowerment, the Church would not have the boldness, unity, or power to carry out its mission.

6.3.2. The Fulfillment of Prophecy

Pentecost also fulfills Old Testament prophecies about the outpouring of the Holy Spirit. In his sermon at Pentecost, Peter quotes the prophet Joel: "And in the last days it shall be, God declares, that I will pour out my Spirit on all flesh, and your sons and your daughters shall prophesy, and your young men shall see visions, and your old men shall dream dreams" (Acts 2:17-18; cf. Joel 2:28-32).

This outpouring of the Spirit is significant because it represents the fulfillment of God's promise to establish a new covenant with His people. In the Old Testament, the Spirit's presence was often limited to specific individuals—prophets, kings, and judges—whom God called for special tasks. However, Joel's prophecy speaks of a time when the Spirit would be poured out on all people, regardless of age, gender, or social status. Pentecost marks the beginning of this new era, in which the Spirit is given to all who believe in Christ, empowering them for ministry and witness.

6.3.3. The Empowerment for Mission

Pentecost underscores the essential role of the Holy Spirit in empowering believers for mission. Before Pentecost, the disciples were not equipped to fulfill the Great Commission that Jesus had given them. But after receiving the Holy Spirit, they were transformed into bold witnesses who proclaimed the Gospel with power and authority.

The Holy Spirit empowers believers for mission by giving them the gifts and abilities they need to fulfill God's calling. As Paul explains in 1 Corinthians 12, the Spirit distributes various spiritual gifts to believers for the common good and the edification of the Church. These gifts include wisdom, knowledge, faith, healing, prophecy, and discernment, among others. The Spirit also gives believers the courage and boldness to share their faith, even in the face of opposition and persecution.

Pentecost reminds believers that the mission of the Church is not something they can accomplish in their own strength. It is only through the power of the Holy Spirit that the Church can effectively proclaim the Gospel, disciple nations, and live out the values of God's Kingdom.

6.3.4. The Unity of Believers

Another key theological implication of Pentecost is the unity of believers through the Holy Spirit. When the disciples began speaking in different languages at Pentecost, people from various nations and cultures heard the Gospel in their own tongues (Acts 2:6-12). This miracle of speaking in tongues symbolizes the reversal of the confusion and division caused by the Tower of Babel (Genesis 11:1-9), where God confused human language and scattered people across the earth.

At Pentecost, the Holy Spirit brings unity out of diversity. The Spirit unites people from different backgrounds and cultures into one body—the Church. Paul emphasizes this unity in Ephesians 4:4-6: "There is one body and one Spirit...one Lord, one faith, one baptism, one God and Father of all, who is over all and through all and in all." Pentecost reveals that the Church is meant to be a diverse yet unified community, reflecting the unity of the Trinity and the reconciling power of the Gospel.

6.3.5. The Presence of the Holy Spirit in Believers' Lives

Pentecost also signifies the indwelling of the Holy Spirit in the lives of believers. Before Pentecost, the Holy Spirit came upon individuals for specific tasks, but now, through the new covenant, the Spirit permanently dwells in all who belong to Christ. This indwelling presence of the Holy Spirit is a defining mark of the Christian life.

In Romans 8:9-11, Paul teaches that "anyone who does not have the Spirit of Christ does not belong to him." The Holy Spirit is the source of spiritual life, regeneration, and sanctification. Through the Spirit, believers are transformed into the likeness of Christ, empowered to resist sin, and equipped to live holy lives. The Spirit's presence in believers' lives is also a guarantee of their future inheritance in God's Kingdom (Ephesians 1:13-14).

6.4. The Continuing Relevance of Pentecost for the Church Today

Pentecost was not just a one-time event in history but has ongoing significance for the Church today. The same Holy Spirit who empowered the first disciples continues to work in and through believers, guiding, equipping, and sustaining the Church's mission.

6.4.1. The Spirit's Ongoing Work in the Church

The outpouring of the Holy Spirit at Pentecost marked the beginning of the Spirit's work in the Church, but it was not the end. Throughout the book of Acts and the New Testament, the Holy Spirit continues to guide, empower, and direct the early Christians. The Spirit provides guidance to the apostles, leads them to new mission fields, and empowers them to perform signs and wonders that confirm the message of the Gospel.

Today, the Holy Spirit remains active in the life of the Church. The Spirit continues to equip believers with spiritual gifts, guide them in discerning God's will, and empower them to carry out God's mission in the world. Pentecost serves as a reminder that the Church is dependent on the Spirit for its effectiveness and vitality.

6.4.2. The Spirit and Global Mission

Pentecost also highlights the global scope of the Church's mission. The fact that people from many nations were present in Jerusalem at Pentecost and heard the Gospel in their own languages emphasizes that the message of salvation is for all people, regardless of their ethnic or cultural background. Jesus' commission to His disciples to be His witnesses "to the ends of the earth" (Acts 1:8) is fulfilled through the empowering work of the Holy Spirit.

In the same way, the Church today is called to continue the global mission of proclaiming the Gospel to all nations. The Holy Spirit equips believers to cross cultural, linguistic, and geographical barriers, bringing the message of Christ's redemption to the entire world.

6.4.3. The Spirit's Role in Renewal and Revival

Pentecost is also a reminder of the potential for spiritual renewal and revival through the Holy Spirit. Just as the outpouring of the Spirit at Pentecost transformed the early Church, the Spirit can bring renewal and revival to the Church today. Throughout history, there have been moments of spiritual awakening, often marked by a fresh outpouring of the Holy Spirit, that have led to widespread repentance, conversion, and a renewed commitment to God's mission.

The Church is called to seek the Spirit's presence and power continually, praying for revival and renewal both within the Church and in the broader society. Pentecost serves as a model for what is possible when the Church is filled with the Spirit and empowered to proclaim the Gospel with boldness.

6.5. Conclusion

The theological understanding of Pentecost reveals its profound significance for the life of the Church and the individual believer. At Pentecost, the Holy Spirit descended upon the disciples, empowering them to carry out the mission of Jesus and inaugurating the age of the Church. Pentecost fulfills Old Testament prophecies, initiates the global mission of the Church, and marks the beginning of a new covenant in which the Holy Spirit dwells in all believers.

The implications of Pentecost are far-reaching. The Holy Spirit unites believers, empowers them for mission, equips them with spiritual gifts, and transforms them into the likeness of Christ. Pentecost is not just a historical event but an ongoing reality for the Church, as the Holy Spirit continues to guide, empower, and renew believers in every generation. The Church is called to live in the power of the Holy Spirit, participating in God's mission to proclaim the Gospel to the ends of the earth.

The Ongoing Work of the Holy Spirit in the Church

6.1. Introduction

The Holy Spirit plays a central role in the life of the Church, continuing the work that began at Pentecost and empowering believers to live out their faith. While the Holy Spirit was foundational in the birth of the Church, His work did not end with the events of Acts 2. The Holy Spirit's ongoing presence is essential for the growth, mission, and sanctification of the Church. This chapter explores how the Holy Spirit continues to guide, empower, and sustain the Church today, influencing every aspect of Christian life and community.

6.2. The Holy Spirit as the Source of Power for the Church's Mission

One of the most significant roles of the Holy Spirit is empowering the Church to fulfill its mission in the world. Jesus commissioned His disciples to be His witnesses "in Jerusalem and in all Judea and Samaria, and to the end of the earth" (Acts 1:8), and this global mission would be impossible without the Holy Spirit's enabling power.

6.2.1. Empowerment for Proclamation

The Holy Spirit gives believers the courage, boldness, and ability to proclaim the Gospel. Just as the disciples, filled with the Holy Spirit at Pentecost, boldly preached the message of salvation, so too does the Spirit empower modern believers to share their faith. Peter, who had previously denied Jesus, became a bold and effective preacher after receiving the Holy Spirit, leading thousands to faith (Acts 2:14-41).

Today, the Holy Spirit continues to embolden Christians to share the message of Christ, even in hostile environments. Through the Spirit, believers are given the words to speak and the wisdom to present the Gospel in ways that resonate with their audience (Matthew 10:19-20). The Spirit also convicts hearts and opens the way for people to respond to the Gospel message (John 16:8).

6.2.2. Guidance in Mission

The Holy Spirit not only empowers the proclamation of the Gospel but also provides guidance in the Church's mission. Throughout the book of Acts, the Spirit directed the apostles to specific places and people. For example, the Spirit led Philip to the Ethiopian eunuch (Acts 8:26-40), guided Paul and his companions on their missionary journeys (Acts 16:6-10), and even instructed the Church in Antioch to send out Paul and Barnabas for missionary work (Acts 13:2).

In the same way, the Holy Spirit continues to guide the Church today, leading believers to new opportunities for ministry and mission. Whether through direct prompting or through prayerful discernment, the Spirit opens doors for the Gospel to be shared and provides direction for the Church's activities in the world.

6.3. The Holy Spirit in the Sanctification of Believers

Another key role of the Holy Spirit is in the process of sanctification—the ongoing transformation of believers into the likeness of Christ. Sanctification is the work of the Spirit in making Christians holy, empowering them to resist sin, grow in righteousness, and live according to God's will.

6.3.1. Conviction of Sin

The Holy Spirit works within believers to convict them of sin, guiding them toward repentance and deeper obedience to God. In John 16:8, Jesus describes the Spirit's role in convicting the world "concerning sin and righteousness and judgment." This conviction is not just a feeling of guilt but a transformative awareness of God's holiness and the need for personal growth and spiritual renewal.

The Spirit prompts believers to examine their lives, repent of sinful behaviors, and strive for holiness. This process of conviction and repentance is a lifelong journey, as the Spirit continually refines believers and conforms them to the image of Christ.

6.3.2. Producing the Fruit of the Spirit

The evidence of the Spirit's work in a believer's life is seen in the transformation of character, often referred to as the "fruit of the Spirit." In Galatians 5:22-23, Paul lists the fruit of the Spirit as "love, joy, peace, patience, kindness, goodness, faithfulness, gentleness, and self-control." These qualities are the result of the Spirit's sanctifying work, as He empowers believers to live according to God's will.

As Christians walk in step with the Holy Spirit, their lives increasingly reflect these virtues, displaying the character of Christ to the world. This transformation is not a product of human effort alone but is the result of the Spirit's ongoing work within each believer, enabling them to live lives that are pleasing to God.

6.3.3. The Role of the Spirit in Prayer

The Holy Spirit also plays a crucial role in the prayer life of believers. Paul writes in Romans 8:26-27 that "the Spirit helps us in our weakness. For we do not know what to pray for as we ought, but the Spirit himself intercedes for us with groanings too deep for words." The Spirit intercedes on behalf of believers, aligning their prayers with God's will and strengthening them in times of spiritual need.

In prayer, the Holy Spirit provides believers with both the desire and the ability to communicate with God. The Spirit deepens their relationship with God, helping them to grow in their understanding of His will and His purposes for their lives.

6.4. The Holy Spirit and the Unity of the Church

The Holy Spirit is also central to creating and maintaining unity within the Church. Despite differences in background, culture, and spiritual gifts, the Holy Spirit unites all believers into one body, the Body of Christ.

6.4.1. Unity in Diversity

One of the Spirit's most remarkable works is creating unity within the Church while preserving diversity. In 1 Corinthians 12, Paul explains that while there are "varieties of gifts" and "varieties of service," there is the same Spirit who works through them all. The Spirit distributes spiritual gifts to each believer as He wills, but these gifts are meant to work together for the common good and the building up of the Church (1 Corinthians 12:4-7).

The Spirit's unity is not based on uniformity but on the recognition that all believers are part of the same body and are empowered by the same Spirit. This unity allows the Church to function as a cohesive whole, with each member contributing to the mission of God according to their spiritual gifts and calling.

6.4.2. The Bond of Peace

The Holy Spirit also creates the "bond of peace" that unites believers in love and fellowship. In Ephesians 4:3, Paul urges the Church to "maintain the unity of the Spirit in the bond of peace." The Spirit fosters peace and reconciliation among believers, helping them to overcome divisions, forgive one another, and live in harmony.

Through the Holy Spirit, the Church becomes a community that reflects the love, forgiveness, and peace of Christ. This unity in the Spirit is not only essential for the health of the Church but also serves as a powerful witness to the world of the transforming power of the Gospel.

6.5. The Gifts of the Spirit for the Edification of the Church

The Holy Spirit equips the Church for its mission by distributing spiritual gifts to believers. These gifts, given for the building up of the body of Christ, enable the Church to fulfill its calling in the world.

6.5.1. The Distribution of Spiritual Gifts

In 1 Corinthians 12, Romans 12, and Ephesians 4, Paul describes various spiritual gifts that the Holy Spirit gives to believers, including gifts of wisdom, knowledge, faith, healing, prophecy, teaching, and leadership. These gifts are diverse, reflecting the many different ways that the Spirit empowers believers for service in the Church.

The Holy Spirit distributes these gifts according to His will, and each believer is given a unique role to play in the life of the Church. No one gift is more important than another, as all are necessary for the functioning of the body of Christ. Paul emphasizes that these gifts are given "for the common good" (1 Corinthians 12:7) and that they should be exercised in love (1 Corinthians 13).

6.5.2. The Purpose of Spiritual Gifts

The primary purpose of spiritual gifts is to edify, or build up, the Church. These gifts are not given for personal glory or self-promotion but for the benefit of the entire

Christian community. As believers use their gifts in service to one another, the Church grows in maturity and unity, becoming a more effective witness to the world.

In Ephesians 4:11-13, Paul explains that the gifts of the Spirit are given "to equip the saints for the work of ministry, for building up the body of Christ, until we all attain to the unity of the faith and of the knowledge of the Son of God." The gifts of the Spirit, when used properly, enable the Church to grow in faith, knowledge, and love, equipping believers to live out their calling as followers of Christ.

6.6. The Role of the Holy Spirit in Renewal and Revival

Throughout history, the Holy Spirit has played a crucial role in renewing the Church and bringing about spiritual revival. Times of renewal and revival are marked by a fresh outpouring of the Holy Spirit, resulting in widespread repentance, conversion, and a renewed commitment to the mission of God.

6.6.1. Spiritual Renewal

Spiritual renewal occurs when the Holy Spirit breathes new life into the Church, awakening believers to a deeper sense of God's presence and purpose. This renewal often leads to greater devotion to prayer, worship, and the study of Scripture, as well as a renewed sense of mission and outreach to the world.

The Holy Spirit initiates renewal by convicting believers of areas in their lives where they need to grow and change. This process of renewal is not limited to individual believers but can spread throughout entire communities, resulting in a revitalized Church that is more attuned to God's will and more effective in its witness to the world.

6.6.2. Revival and Evangelism

Revival is a powerful work of the Holy Spirit that often leads to mass conversions and a widespread turning to God. Throughout history, revivals have occurred when the Holy Spirit moves in extraordinary ways, bringing conviction of sin, repentance, and transformation to individuals and communities.

Revivals often lead to a renewed focus on evangelism, as believers, empowered by the Holy Spirit, boldly proclaim the Gospel and share the message of salvation with others. The outpouring of the Holy Spirit at Pentecost is the model for revival, as it resulted in the rapid expansion of the Church and the conversion of thousands of people.

6.7. Conclusion

The ongoing work of the Holy Spirit is essential for the life and mission of the Church. From the empowerment of believers for mission to the process of sanctification and the distribution of spiritual gifts, the Holy Spirit is the driving force behind the Church's growth and effectiveness in the world. The Holy Spirit unites believers, equips them for service, and continually renews and revives the Church, enabling it to fulfill God's purpose in every generation.

Pentecost may have been the beginning of the Church's mission, but the work of the Holy Spirit continues to this day, guiding, empowering, and sustaining the Church as it proclaims the Gospel and lives out the values of God's Kingdom. The Church is called to rely on the Holy Spirit, seeking His guidance and empowerment as it participates in God's redemptive work in the world.

CHAPTER 07

THE CHRISTOLOGICAL CONTROVERSIES

7.1. Introduction

The early centuries of Christian history were marked by significant debates and controversies regarding the nature of Jesus Christ. Central to these discussions was the question of how to understand Jesus as both fully divine and fully human, a mystery that lies at the heart of Christian belief. As the Church sought to articulate its understanding of Christ, various theological positions emerged, some of which were later condemned as heresies. Among the most significant of these debates were the controversies over Arianism, Nestorianism, and Monophysitism, which sparked intense theological and political conflict within the Church. This chapter explores the nature of these Christological controversies, the key figures involved, and the eventual resolution of these debates through the ecumenical councils.

7.2. The Arian Controversy

The Arian controversy was one of the earliest and most significant Christological debates in the history of the Church. It centered on the question of whether Jesus Christ, the Son of God, was truly divine or a created being, subordinate to God the Father. This debate ultimately led to the Council of Nicaea in 325 AD and the formulation of the Nicene Creed.

7.2.1. Arius and the Origins of the Controversy

The controversy began with the teachings of Arius, a priest from Alexandria, Egypt, in the early 4th century. Arius taught that Jesus, the Son of God, was not co-eternal with the Father but was a created being. According to Arius, there was a time when the Son did not exist, and He was brought into existence by the Father. Arius reasoned that since Jesus was begotten by the Father, He could not be of the same substance (homoousios) as the Father and must therefore be subordinate to Him.

Arius' teaching gained considerable support but was also met with strong opposition, particularly from his bishop, Alexander of Alexandria, and later from Athanasius, who became one of the most vocal opponents of Arianism. The central concern for Arius' opponents was that his teachings undermined the full divinity of Christ, which was essential for the doctrine of salvation. If Christ were not truly God, they argued, He could not fully reconcile humanity to God.

7.2.2. The Council of Nicaea and the Nicene Creed

In response to the growing controversy, Emperor Constantine convened the First Council of Nicaea in 325 AD to address the issue and restore unity within the Church. At the council, over 300 bishops gathered to debate the nature of Christ and to resolve the Arian controversy.

The key theological issue at Nicaea was the relationship between the Father and the Son. The council ultimately rejected Arius' teaching and affirmed that Jesus Christ is "begotten, not made, being of one substance (homoousios) with the Father." This formulation emphasized that the Son is co-eternal with the Father and fully divine, sharing the same essence as God the Father.

The Nicene Creed, which was produced at the council, became the foundational statement of orthodox Christian belief, affirming the full divinity of Christ. However, the controversy did not end with Nicaea. Arianism continued to persist, leading to further debates and councils in the years that followed.

7.2.3. The Legacy of Arianism

Although Arianism was formally condemned at Nicaea, it continued to influence parts of the Church, particularly in the Eastern Roman Empire and among various Germanic tribes. The Arian controversy highlighted the importance of Christ's divinity in Christian theology and set the stage for future debates about how to understand the relationship between Christ's divinity and humanity. Ultimately, the resolution of the Arian controversy helped to clarify the Church's doctrine of the Trinity and the nature of Christ's divine personhood.

7.3. The Nestorian Controversy

Following the Arian controversy, another major Christological debate emerged in the 5th century, this time concerning the relationship between the divine and human natures of Christ. This controversy centered on the teachings of Nestorius, the Patriarch of Constantinople, and led to the Council of Ephesus in 431 AD.

7.3.1. Nestorius and the Question of Christ's Two Natures

Nestorius' Christology emphasized the distinction between Christ's divine and human natures. He was concerned that the unity of these two natures might lead to confusion or a mixing of the divine and human, a position he believed would undermine the full humanity of Jesus. In particular, Nestorius objected to the title Theotokos ("God-bearer") for Mary, the mother of Jesus, arguing that Mary should be called Christotokos ("Christ-bearer") instead. He believed that Mary gave birth to the human nature of Christ, not to His divine nature.

Nestorius' position implied that there were two distinct persons in Christ—one divine and one human—united in a loose moral or relational union rather than in a single person. His opponents argued that this view effectively divided Christ into two separate beings, which would undermine the unity of His person and the efficacy of His redemptive work.

7.3.2. The Council of Ephesus and the Condemnation of Nestorianism

The controversy over Nestorius' teachings led to the convening of the Council of Ephesus in 431 AD. At this council, the Church decisively rejected Nestorius' Christology and affirmed that Christ is one person (hypostasis) with two distinct natures—divine and human—that are united without confusion or division. The council also upheld the use of the title Theotokos for Mary, affirming that she gave birth to the one person of Christ, who is both fully God and fully man.

The Council of Ephesus emphasized the importance of the unity of Christ's person for the doctrine of salvation. The Church affirmed that Jesus Christ is one person, and His divine and human natures are united in such a way that His redemptive work is fully effective. Nestorianism was condemned as heretical, and Nestorius was deposed as Patriarch of Constantinople.

7.3.3. The Ongoing Debate over Christ's Natures

The Nestorian controversy highlighted the challenge of articulating the relationship between Christ's divine and human natures in a way that preserved both His full humanity and His full divinity. While the Council of Ephesus resolved the immediate controversy, debates about the nature of Christ continued, leading to further developments in Christological doctrine at subsequent councils.

7.4. The Monophysite Controversy

The third major Christological controversy in the early Church was the Monophysite controversy, which focused on the relationship between Christ's divine and human natures after the Incarnation. This debate culminated in the Council of Chalcedon in 451 AD, which produced one of the most definitive statements on the nature of Christ in Christian history.

7.4.1. The Rise of Monophysitism

Monophysitism (from the Greek monos, meaning "one," and physis, meaning "nature") arose in response to the Nestorian controversy and emphasized the unity of Christ's person. However, Monophysites took this emphasis to the extreme, arguing that after the Incarnation, Christ had only one nature, which was primarily divine. This position was associated with the teachings of Eutyches, a monk from Constantinople, who argued that Christ's human nature was absorbed or subsumed into His divine nature, leaving Him with only one, unified nature.

Monophysitism sought to protect the unity of Christ's person, but it did so at the expense of His full humanity. By downplaying or denying Christ's human nature, Monophysitism raised concerns that Christ was not truly human and therefore could not fully identify with humanity or accomplish a complete redemption.

7.4.2. The Council of Chalcedon and the Definition of Faith

In response to the Monophysite controversy, the Church convened the Council of Chalcedon in 451 AD. At this council, the Church rejected Monophysitism and affirmed that Jesus Christ is one person with two distinct and complete natures—divine and human—that are united in one person "without confusion, without change, without division, and without separation."

The Chalcedonian Definition, produced at the council, became the standard of orthodox Christology. It emphasized that Christ's divine and human natures remain fully intact and are not mixed or absorbed into one another. The council upheld the full divinity and full humanity of Christ, affirming that He is "truly God and truly man," possessing both a divine nature and a human nature in perfect unity.

7.4.3. The Aftermath of Chalcedon

While the Council of Chalcedon established a clear and orthodox understanding of Christ's two natures, the controversy did not end with the council's conclusions. Many Christians, particularly in Egypt and Syria, rejected the Chalcedonian Definition, arguing that it compromised the unity of Christ's person. These non-Chalcedonian Christians, who held to a version of Monophysitism, eventually formed what became known as the Oriental Orthodox Churches.

The Monophysite controversy, like the Arian and Nestorian controversies before it, demonstrated the difficulty of articulating the mystery of Christ's nature in a way that preserved both His divinity and His humanity. Nevertheless, the Chalcedonian Definition remains one of the most important theological achievements in the history of the Church, providing a lasting framework for understanding the person of Christ.

7.5. Conclusion

The Christological controversies of the early Church were foundational in shaping Christian theology and doctrine. Through debates over Arianism, Nestorianism, and Monophysitism, the Church grappled with the mystery of

Christ's nature, seeking to articulate how He could be both fully divine and fully human. These controversies were not just theological exercises; they were central to the Church's understanding of salvation, as the nature of Christ directly impacted the efficacy of His redemptive work.

The resolutions of these controversies, particularly at the Councils of Nicaea, Ephesus, and Chalcedon, provided the Church with a clear and orthodox understanding of Christ's nature. The Nicene Creed and the Chalcedonian Definition remain essential statements of Christian faith, affirming that Jesus Christ is one person with two distinct natures, divine and human, united in perfect harmony. These theological developments continue to shape the faith and practice of Christians today, as they point to the profound mystery of the Incarnation and the saving work of Christ.

The Councils of Nicaea, Chalcedon, and Their Outcomes

7.1. Introduction

The early centuries of Christian history were marked by theological debates that profoundly shaped the doctrines of the Church, particularly concerning the nature of Jesus Christ and the Trinity. Among the most significant of these debates were the discussions about Christ's divinity and humanity, which led to the convening of the great ecumenical councils of Nicaea (325 AD) and Chalcedon (451 AD). These councils, driven by efforts to combat heresies and clarify orthodox beliefs, played a critical role in defining key doctrines of the Christian faith. This chapter explores the background, proceedings, and outcomes of these councils, focusing on their significance for the development of Christology and the doctrine of the Trinity.

7.2. The Council of Nicaea (325 AD)

The Council of Nicaea, convened in 325 AD by the Roman Emperor Constantine, was the first ecumenical council in the history of the Church. It was called primarily to address the Arian controversy, which centered on the nature of Jesus Christ and His relationship to God the Father.

7.2.1. The Arian Controversy

The primary issue that led to the convening of the Council of Nicaea was the teachings of Arius, a priest from Alexandria. Arius argued that Jesus, the Son of God, was not co-eternal with the Father but was a created being, subordinate to the Father. He famously declared, "There was a time when the Son was not," implying that Christ was not of the same essence as God the Father.

Arius' views created a theological crisis within the Church. If Christ were not fully divine, then the Christian understanding of salvation and the Trinity would be jeopardized. Arius' opponents, particularly his bishop, Alexander of Alexandria, and later Athanasius, argued that Jesus must be fully divine for His redemptive work to be effective.

7.2.2. The Proceedings of Nicaea

Constantine called for the council in an effort to restore unity within the Church and to settle the Arian controversy. Over 300 bishops from across the Roman Empire gathered in the city of Nicaea (modern-day İznik, Turkey) to debate the issue.

At the heart of the debate was the Greek term homoousios, meaning "of the same substance" or "essence." Arius and his followers argued that the Son was of a similar but not the same essence as the Father (homoiousios), whereas the majority of bishops, led by Athanasius, insisted that the Son was homoousios with the Father, meaning that the Father and the Son shared the same divine essence.

7.2.3. The Outcome: The Nicene Creed

The council ultimately rejected Arius' teachings and affirmed that Jesus Christ is "begotten, not made, being of one substance (homoousios) with the Father." This statement was formalized in the Nicene Creed, which declared the full divinity of the Son and articulated the relationship between the Father and the Son within the Godhead. The original form of the Nicene Creed reads:

> "We believe in one God, the Father Almighty, Maker of heaven and earth, and of all things visible and invisible.

> And in one Lord Jesus Christ, the only-begotten Son of God, begotten of the Father before all worlds; Light of Light, very God of very God; begotten, not made, being of one substance with the Father, by whom all things were made."

The Nicene Creed became the definitive statement of orthodox Christian belief regarding the nature of Christ and the Trinity. However, the Arian controversy did not end with the council. Arianism continued to persist in parts of the Church, leading to further theological debates in the following decades.

7.3. The Council of Chalcedon (451 AD)

The Council of Chalcedon, convened in 451 AD, was the fourth ecumenical council of the Church and addressed the ongoing debates over the relationship between Christ's divine and human natures. This council was particularly concerned with the rise of Monophysitism, which taught that Christ had only one nature following the Incarnation.

7.3.1. The Context of the Chalcedonian Controversy

In the years following the Council of Nicaea, the Church faced new theological challenges concerning how to understand the union of Christ's divine and human natures. The teachings of Nestorius, the Patriarch of Constantinople, had sparked controversy in the early 5th century by emphasizing a strong distinction between Christ's two natures. This led to the Council of Ephesus in 431 AD, which condemned Nestorianism and affirmed that Christ is one person with two natures, fully divine and fully human.

However, the debate did not end with Ephesus. In response to Nestorianism, some theologians, particularly Eutyches, argued that after the Incarnation, Christ's human nature was absorbed into His divine nature, leaving Him with only one nature. This view, known as Monophysitism (from the Greek monos meaning "one" and physis meaning "nature"), became a source of significant controversy within the Church.

7.3.2. The Proceedings of Chalcedon

The Council of Chalcedon was convened by the Roman Emperor Marcian to resolve the Monophysite controversy and to clarify the Church's understanding of Christ's two natures. Over 500 bishops attended the council, making it one of the largest gatherings in the history of the early Church.

At Chalcedon, the bishops sought to balance the need to affirm both Christ's full divinity and His full humanity. They were concerned that Monophysitism, by emphasizing the divine nature, effectively denied the reality of Christ's human experience. On the other hand, they wanted to avoid the opposite extreme of Nestorianism, which seemed to divide Christ into two separate persons.

7.3.3. The Outcome: The Chalcedonian Definition

The Council of Chalcedon produced the Chalcedonian Definition, which became one of the most important Christological statements in the history of the Church. The definition affirmed that Jesus Christ is one person (hypostasis) in two natures—divine and human—that are united "without confusion, without change, without division, and without separation." It reads in part:

> "We, then, following the holy Fathers, all with one consent, teach men to confess one and the same Son, our Lord Jesus Christ, the same perfect in Godhead and also perfect in manhood; truly God and truly man, of a reasonable soul and body; consubstantial with the Father according to the Godhead, and consubstantial with us according to the Manhood; in all things like unto us, without sin; begotten before all ages of the Father according to the Godhead, and in these latter days, for us and for our salvation, born of the Virgin Mary, the Mother of God, according to the Manhood."

This definition preserved the unity of Christ's person while affirming the distinctness of His two natures. It rejected both Nestorianism and Monophysitism, establishing the orthodox doctrine that Christ is fully God and fully human, with both natures coexisting in one person.

7.3.4. The Legacy of Chalcedon

The Chalcedonian Definition became the cornerstone of Christological orthodoxy in the Christian tradition. It provided a clear and balanced articulation of the Church's belief in the Incarnation, affirming both the divinity and humanity of Christ. However, the definition was not accepted by all Christians. Many in the Eastern Church, particularly in Egypt and Syria, rejected the Chalcedonian formula, leading to the formation of the Oriental Orthodox Churches, which continue to uphold a version of Monophysitism.

Despite these divisions, the Chalcedonian Definition remains a key theological document for most branches of Christianity, including Roman Catholic, Eastern Orthodox, and Protestant traditions. It continues to serve as a foundational expression of the mystery of the Incarnation and the Church's understanding of Jesus Christ as both God and man.

7.4. The Lasting Impact of the Councils

The Councils of Nicaea and Chalcedon were pivotal in shaping Christian orthodoxy and addressing the theological challenges that arose in the early centuries of the Church. Their outcomes had profound and lasting effects on Christian doctrine, particularly in the areas of Christology and the doctrine of the Trinity.

7.4.1. The Establishment of Orthodox Christology

The councils clarified key aspects of Christology, affirming that Jesus Christ is both fully divine and fully human. Nicaea resolved the question of Christ's divinity, rejecting Arianism and affirming that Christ is of the same substance (homoousios) as the Father. Chalcedon, in turn, provided a definitive statement on the relationship between Christ's divine and human natures, rejecting both Nestorianism and Monophysitism.

These theological affirmations have shaped Christian understanding of the person and work of Christ for centuries. They ensure that the mystery of the Incarnation is understood in a way that preserves the full reality of both Christ's divinity and humanity, which is central to the doctrine of salvation.

7.4.2. The Development of the Doctrine of the Trinity

While the primary focus of the councils was Christology, their decisions also had significant implications for the development of the doctrine of the Trinity. The Council of Nicaea, in particular, was foundational in clarifying the relationship between the Father and the Son within the Godhead, affirming that the Son is co-eternal and consubstantial with the Father.

The debates surrounding these councils helped the Church to develop a more precise understanding of the Trinity, which was further articulated in the later councils of Constantinople (381 AD) and later theological developments.

7.4.3. The Role of Ecumenical Councils in Church Authority

The Councils of Nicaea and Chalcedon also established the precedent for ecumenical councils as authoritative gatherings that could define and clarify doctrine. These councils set a pattern for how the Church would address theological disputes in the future, emphasizing the importance of collective discernment and consensus in matters of faith.

7.5. Conclusion

The Councils of Nicaea and Chalcedon were watershed moments in the history of the Church, shaping the core doctrines of Christianity regarding the nature of Christ and the Trinity. Nicaea clarified that Jesus Christ is fully divine, sharing the same essence as the Father, while Chalcedon affirmed that He is also fully human, with two natures united in one person. These councils not only resolved key theological debates but also provided the Church with lasting doctrinal statements that continue to define Christian orthodoxy.

The outcomes of these councils have had a profound and enduring impact on Christian theology, worship, and practice. The Nicene Creed and the Chalcedonian Definition remain central to Christian confession and are recited in churches around the world to this day. Through these councils, the Church was able to articulate the mystery of the Incarnation and the Trinity in a way that safeguarded the essential truths of the Christian faith.

How the Christological Controversies Shaped Christian Doctrine

7.1. Introduction

The Christological controversies of the early Church were not merely theological disputes; they were decisive moments that shaped the fundamental doctrines of Christianity. The intense debates over the nature of Christ—whether He was divine, human, or a combination of both—directly influenced the Church's understanding of salvation, the Trinity, and the relationship between God and humanity. The resolution of these controversies through the ecumenical councils of Nicaea (325 AD) and Chalcedon (451 AD), among others, provided the foundation for what would become orthodox Christian doctrine. This chapter explores how these controversies shaped key aspects of Christian belief and the lasting theological, liturgical, and spiritual impact they had on the Church.

7.2. Clarifying the Divinity of Christ: The Legacy of the Arian Controversy

One of the earliest and most significant Christological controversies was Arianism, which questioned the full divinity of Jesus Christ. The resolution of this debate at the Council of Nicaea profoundly shaped the Christian understanding of the relationship between Jesus and God the Father.

7.2.1. Affirmation of Christ's Full Divinity

At the heart of the Arian controversy was the question of whether Christ was truly God or a created being. Arius, a priest from Alexandria, argued that Christ was subordinate to the Father and was not co-eternal or co-equal with Him. According to Arius, Christ was a superior creature but not fully divine. This view raised concerns about the nature of salvation, as only God could truly redeem humanity from sin.

The Council of Nicaea in 325 AD rejected Arius' teachings and affirmed that Christ is homoousios (of the same substance) with the Father, meaning that He shares the same divine essence as God. The Nicene Creed, formulated at this council, became the standard for orthodox Christian belief. By affirming the full divinity of Christ, the Church established that Jesus is truly God, equal with the Father in all respects. This affirmation had profound implications for Christian theology, particularly in relation to the doctrine of the Trinity and the nature of salvation.

7.2.2. Shaping the Doctrine of the Trinity

The resolution of the Arian controversy was also crucial for the development of the doctrine of the Trinity. In affirming that the Son is of the same substance as the Father, the Church laid the groundwork for a clearer understanding of the relationship between the persons of the Trinity. Nicaea emphasized the unity of essence between the Father and the Son while also recognizing their distinct persons.

This emphasis on unity and distinction within the Godhead later became the foundation for the full articulation of Trinitarian doctrine. The Council of Constantinople in 381 AD built upon Nicaea by affirming the divinity of the Holy Spirit, completing the Trinitarian framework that has since defined Christian orthodoxy: one God in three persons—Father, Son, and Holy Spirit.

7.2.3. The Eternal Relevance of the Nicene Creed

The Nicene Creed, which emerged from the Arian controversy, has become one of the most important confessional statements in Christian history. Recited in Christian liturgies across the world, the creed continues to serve as a unifying statement of faith for believers, encapsulating the Church's core beliefs about the nature of God, Christ, and the Holy Spirit. It remains a central part of Christian identity and worship, reminding believers of the foundational truths of the faith.

7.3. Defining the Union of Christ's Natures: The Impact of the Nestorian and Monophysite Controversies

The debates over Christ's divinity did not end with Nicaea. In the centuries that followed, the Church faced new challenges in defining how Christ's divinity and humanity were united in one person. The controversies surrounding Nestorianism and Monophysitism led to further doctrinal developments, culminating in the Council of Chalcedon in 451 AD.

7.3.1. The Nestorian Controversy and the Hypostatic Union

Nestorius, the Patriarch of Constantinople, argued that Christ's divine and human natures were separate, effectively resulting in two persons—the divine Logos and the human Jesus—united in a moral or relational way. Nestorius objected to the title Theotokos ("God-bearer") for Mary, preferring Christotokos ("Christ-bearer"), emphasizing that Mary gave birth only to Christ's human nature.

The Council of Ephesus (431 AD) condemned Nestorianism and affirmed that Christ is one person (hypostasis) with two distinct natures—divine and human—united in a single person. This concept, known as the hypostatic union, became a central tenet of Christian Christology. By affirming the unity of Christ's person, the Church preserved the integrity of both His divinity and humanity. This union was essential for understanding how Christ could act as a mediator between God and humanity, fully representing both in His redemptive work.

7.3.2. The Monophysite Controversy and the Chalcedonian Definition

In response to the Nestorian controversy, another extreme position emerged: Monophysitism. This view, championed by Eutyches, argued that after the Incarnation, Christ had only one nature, which was primarily divine.

Monophysitism downplayed or denied Christ's full humanity, raising concerns that Christ could not fully identify with humanity in His redemptive work.

The Council of Chalcedon in 451 AD rejected Monophysitism and issued the Chalcedonian Definition, which affirmed that Christ is "truly God and truly man" with two distinct natures—divine and human—united in one person "without confusion, without change, without division, and without separation." This formulation preserved the fullness of both Christ's divinity and humanity and provided a balanced and comprehensive understanding of the mystery of the Incarnation.

7.3.3. Theological and Soteriological Implications of the Hypostatic Union

The Chalcedonian Definition had profound theological and soteriological (salvation-related) implications. By affirming that Christ is fully divine and fully human, the Church upheld the belief that Christ's divinity was necessary for His role as the Savior of humanity. Only a fully divine Christ could conquer sin and death and reconcile humanity to God. At the same time, Christ's full humanity ensured that He could truly represent humanity and act as its substitute, offering Himself as a perfect sacrifice for sin.

The doctrine of the hypostatic union remains a cornerstone of Christian theology, influencing the way the Church understands the person and work of Christ, the nature of salvation, and the believer's relationship with God.

7.4. Preserving Orthodoxy and Unity: The Role of the Ecumenical Councils

The Christological controversies not only shaped Christian doctrine but also highlighted the importance of preserving orthodoxy and unity within the Church. The ecumenical councils, particularly Nicaea and Chalcedon, played a critical role in defining orthodox beliefs and maintaining the unity of the Church in the face of heresy.

7.4.1. The Development of Conciliar Authority

The councils set a precedent for how the Church would address theological disputes in the future. By gathering bishops from across the Christian world to deliberate and reach consensus, the councils established a model of conciliar authority. This process of collective discernment and decision-making ensured that the Church could respond to heresies with a unified voice and maintain doctrinal continuity.

The authority of these councils was recognized across the Christian world, and their decisions were seen as binding for the whole Church. The outcomes of the councils, particularly the Nicene Creed and the Chalcedonian Definition, became the foundation for orthodox Christian theology, shaping the faith of generations of believers.

7.4.2. The Councils and the Preservation of Christian Unity

The ecumenical councils also played a crucial role in preserving the unity of the Church. While the controversies often led to divisions, the councils sought to articulate a unified, orthodox faith that could be embraced by all Christians. The decisions made at Nicaea and Chalcedon, although not universally accepted at the time, provided a doctrinal foundation that helped to maintain the theological integrity and unity of the Church.

Although some schisms emerged from these controversies—such as the split between the Chalcedonian and non-Chalcedonian (Oriental Orthodox) Churches—the councils' role in defining orthodoxy and preserving unity remains a defining feature of their legacy.

7.5. The Lasting Influence on Christian Theology and Spirituality

The Christological controversies and the councils that resolved them had a profound and lasting impact on Christian theology, worship, and spirituality.

7.5.1. The Incarnation and Christian Worship

The affirmation of Christ's full divinity and humanity has shaped the way Christians approach worship and the sacraments. In Christian liturgy, Christ is worshipped as both fully divine and fully human, the incarnate Son of God who redeemed the world through His life, death, and resurrection. The Eucharist, in particular, reflects the mystery of the Incarnation, as believers partake in the body and blood of Christ, affirming His real presence in the sacrament.

The Christological debates also deepened the Church's understanding of the mystery of God's self-revelation in Christ. By clarifying the nature of Christ, the councils helped Christians to approach the Incarnation not only as a theological concept but as a profound spiritual reality that shapes the believer's relationship with God.

7.5.2. Theological Foundations for Future Doctrines

The theological formulations that emerged from the Christological controversies provided a foundation for future doctrinal developments in areas such as soteriology (the study of salvation), ecclesiology (the study of the Church), and Christian anthropology (the study of human nature). The doctrine of the hypostatic union, for example, has been essential for understanding how Christ's redemptive work affects humanity, while the Nicene Creed has served as a framework for discussions on the Trinity and the nature of God.

The councils also shaped the way theologians have approached theological discourse, emphasizing the importance of balancing mystery and clarity, and the need to preserve the fullness of Christian truth without oversimplifying complex theological realities.

7.6. Conclusion

The Christological controversies of the early Church were pivotal moments in the development of Christian doctrine. Through intense debate and the careful deliberation of ecumenical councils, the Church clarified its understanding of the person and nature of Jesus Christ, affirming that He is both fully divine and fully human. These controversies, particularly the Arian, Nestorian, and Monophysite debates, shaped the way the Church understands salvation, the Incarnation, and the Trinity, laying the foundation for Christian theology.

The outcomes of the Councils of Nicaea and Chalcedon provided a lasting framework for orthodox belief, defining the doctrines that continue to shape Christian faith and practice today. These theological developments not only preserved the integrity of Christian doctrine but also deepened the Church's understanding of the mystery of God's revelation in Christ, enriching the spiritual life of believers and strengthening the unity of the Church across generations.

How the Christological Controversies Shaped Christian Doctrine

7.1. Introduction

The Christological controversies that emerged in the early centuries of the Church profoundly influenced the development of Christian doctrine. These debates revolved around understanding the nature of Jesus Christ—how He could be both fully divine and fully human, and how His two natures interacted within one person. From the Arian controversy to Nestorianism and Monophysitism, these theological disputes forced the Church to clarify essential aspects of its faith. The outcomes of these controversies, solidified in the ecumenical councils such as Nicaea (325 AD) and Chalcedon (451 AD), laid the foundation for orthodox Christian belief and had lasting implications on the theology of the Incarnation, the Trinity, and salvation. This chapter explores how these early Christological controversies shaped key Christian doctrines and their enduring legacy within the Church.

7.2. The Arian Controversy and the Affirmation of Christ's Divinity

The Arian controversy, one of the earliest and most significant theological conflicts, centered on the question of whether Jesus Christ was truly divine or merely a created being. This debate, which arose in the early 4th century, led to the Council of Nicaea and resulted in a definitive statement on Christ's divinity that has shaped Christian doctrine ever since.

7.2.1. The Nature of the Controversy

Arius, a priest from Alexandria, taught that Jesus, while exalted and divine in some sense, was a created being and thus not co-eternal or co-equal with God the Father.

Arius famously declared, "There was a time when the Son was not," implying that Christ was subordinate to the Father and did not share the same divine essence. Arius' views threatened the core Christian belief in salvation, as a created being could not fully redeem humanity.

Arius' teaching sparked a theological crisis that divided the Church. His opponents, including Athanasius, argued that Jesus must be fully divine and consubstantial (homoousios, of the same substance) with the Father, for only God could provide salvation for humanity.

7.2.2. The Council of Nicaea and the Nicene Creed

In 325 AD, Emperor Constantine convened the Council of Nicaea to resolve the Arian controversy and restore unity within the Church. The council condemned Arianism and affirmed that Jesus Christ is "begotten, not made, being of one substance with the Father." This formulation, articulated in the Nicene Creed, affirmed that Jesus is fully divine, co-eternal with the Father, and shares the same divine essence. The council's ruling preserved the Church's belief in the full divinity of Christ, safeguarding the integrity of the doctrine of salvation.

The Nicene Creed, produced at this council, became one of the most important theological statements in Christian history. It established that Christ is not a created being but is of the same essence as God the Father, affirming the Church's belief in the Trinity. This doctrinal affirmation was crucial for developing a coherent understanding of God's nature and the relationship between the Father, Son, and Holy Spirit.

7.2.3. The Legacy of Nicaea and the Doctrine of the Trinity

The Arian controversy and the Council of Nicaea were pivotal in shaping the doctrine of the Trinity. By affirming that the Father and the Son are of the same substance, Nicaea established the principle that the persons of the Trinity share the same divine essence. This clarification laid the foundation for the full development of Trinitarian theology, which was further articulated at the Council of Constantinople in 381 AD, where the divinity of the Holy Spirit was affirmed.

The Nicene Creed remains central to Christian orthodoxy and is recited in churches worldwide. Its affirmation of Christ's full divinity continues to be a cornerstone of Christian theology, preserving the Church's understanding of Jesus as both fully God and fully capable of saving humanity from sin.

7.3. Nestorianism and the Hypostatic Union

Following the resolution of the Arian controversy, the Church faced new challenges in articulating the relationship between Christ's divine and human natures. The Nestorian controversy, which emerged in the 5th century, focused on the question of how these two natures interacted within the person of Jesus Christ. This debate ultimately led to the Council of Ephesus (431 AD) and the doctrine of the hypostatic union.

7.3.1. Nestorius and the Two Natures of Christ

Nestorius, the Patriarch of Constantinople, taught that Christ's divine and human natures were distinct and separate, to the point that He effectively became two persons: the divine Logos and the human Jesus. Nestorius objected to the use of the title Theotokos ("God-bearer") for Mary, arguing that Mary gave birth only to Christ's human nature, not His divine nature. Nestorius preferred the title Christotokos ("Christ-bearer"), emphasizing that Jesus' human and divine natures were only loosely united.

This teaching raised concerns that Nestorianism divided Christ into two separate beings, undermining the unity of His person and the integrity of His redemptive work. Nestorius' opponents, led by Cyril of Alexandria, argued that Christ is one person (hypostasis) with two natures, fully divine and fully human, united in a single person.

7.3.2. The Council of Ephesus and the Hypostatic Union

The Council of Ephesus, convened in 431 AD, condemned Nestorianism and affirmed the doctrine of the hypostatic union, which teaches that Christ's divine and human natures are united in one person without confusion or separation. The council declared that Mary could rightly be called Theotokos, as the one she bore was both fully God and fully man. This affirmation was crucial for maintaining the belief that Christ's divinity and humanity were inseparable and fully integrated in His person.

The doctrine of the hypostatic union became a foundational element of Christology, emphasizing that Christ is not two persons but one, and that His divine and human natures coexist in perfect unity. This understanding was essential for the doctrine of salvation, as it affirmed that

Christ, in His humanity, could truly represent humanity, and in His divinity, could effectively reconcile humanity to God.

7.4. Monophysitism and the Chalcedonian Definition

In response to the Nestorian controversy, another extreme view emerged, known as Monophysitism, which asserted that Christ had only one nature after the Incarnation. This view threatened to undermine Christ's full humanity, leading to further theological conflict and the eventual resolution at the Council of Chalcedon in 451 AD.

7.4.1. The Rise of Monophysitism

Monophysitism, championed by Eutyches, a monk from Constantinople, taught that after the Incarnation, Christ's human nature was absorbed into His divine nature, leaving Him with only one nature. This view was an overreaction to Nestorianism and sought to protect the unity of Christ's person. However, by emphasizing Christ's divine nature to the exclusion of His humanity, Monophysitism raised concerns that Christ could not fully identify with humanity and thus could not fully redeem it.

7.4.2. The Council of Chalcedon and the Two Natures of Christ

The Council of Chalcedon, convened in 451 AD, rejected Monophysitism and issued the Chalcedonian Definition, which affirmed that Jesus Christ is one person with two distinct natures—divine and human—united "without confusion, without change, without division, and without separation." This definition preserved the integrity of both Christ's divinity and humanity, ensuring that both natures remained fully intact and complete.

The Chalcedonian Definition provided a balanced and nuanced understanding of the mystery of the Incarnation. It affirmed that Christ is both fully God and fully human, and that His two natures coexist in perfect harmony within one person. This formulation has become the standard of orthodox Christology and remains a central tenet of Christian belief to this day.

7.5. Theological and Soteriological Implications of the Christological Controversies

The resolution of the Christological controversies had far-reaching implications for Christian theology, particularly in the areas of soteriology (the doctrine of salvation), the Incarnation, and the believer's relationship with God.

7.5.1. The Doctrine of Salvation

The Christological controversies were ultimately about the nature of salvation. The Church recognized that only a fully divine and fully human Christ could redeem humanity. If Christ were not fully divine, as Arius taught, He could not conquer sin and death. If Christ were not fully human, as the Monophysites suggested, He could not represent humanity or offer Himself as a perfect sacrifice for sin.

By affirming that Christ is both fully God and fully man, the councils ensured that Christ's redemptive work was both effective and complete. His divinity enabled Him to defeat the powers of sin and death, while His humanity allowed Him to stand in humanity's place, offering Himself as a substitute and mediator.

7.5.2. The Incarnation and the Trinity

The Christological controversies also shaped the Church's understanding of the Incarnation and the Trinity. The doctrine of the Incarnation, as defined at Chalcedon, clarified how God became man in the person of Jesus Christ, emphasizing that the two natures of Christ are united in one person. This understanding has been essential for Christian worship, devotion, and theology, influencing everything from the Eucharist to the practice of prayer.

The Arian controversy, in particular, was crucial for the development of Trinitarian doctrine. By affirming the full divinity of the Son at Nicaea, the Church laid the groundwork for a clearer understanding of the relationships between the persons of the Trinity—Father, Son, and Holy Spirit. This understanding has shaped Christian theology and liturgy for centuries.

7.6. Conclusion

The Christological controversies of the early Church were foundational in shaping Christian doctrine. Through the intense debates surrounding Arianism, Nestorianism, and Monophysitism, the Church clarified its beliefs about the nature of Jesus Christ, affirming that He is both fully divine and fully human. These controversies and their resolutions, particularly at the Councils of Nicaea, Ephesus, and Chalcedon, provided the theological framework for understanding the mystery of the Incarnation, the doctrine of the Trinity, and the nature of salvation.

The outcomes of these controversies have had a lasting impact on Christian theology and continue to shape the faith of believers today. The doctrines of the hypostatic union and the Nicene Creed remain central to Christian orthodoxy, providing a foundation for understanding who

Jesus Christ is and how His person and work bring about the redemption of humanity. Through these theological developments, the Church preserved the essential truths of the Christian faith, ensuring that the mystery of Christ's person would continue to be proclaimed and celebrated for generations to come.

CHAPTER 08

JESUS AND SALVATION: THE CONCEPT OF SALAVATION THROUGH JESUS CHRIST

8.1. Introduction

Salvation lies at the heart of the Christian faith and is the central message of the Gospel. The belief that Jesus Christ is the Savior of the world, who offers redemption from sin and eternal life to all who believe in Him, is the cornerstone of Christian theology. Salvation through Jesus encompasses His life, death, and resurrection, all of which contribute to His role as the redeemer of humanity. This chapter explores the concept of salvation through Jesus Christ, the theological foundations of His saving work, and the implications of His sacrifice for humanity's relationship with God.

8.2. The Need for Salvation

In Christian theology, salvation is understood as God's response to the human condition of sin and separation from Him. The Bible presents sin as the fundamental problem of humanity, which distorts the relationship between God and creation. Salvation, therefore, is the means by which God restores that relationship and reconciles humanity to Himself.

8.2.1. The Fall and Original Sin

The story of salvation begins with the fall of humanity in Genesis. Adam and Eve's disobedience in the Garden of Eden introduced sin into the world, resulting in a broken relationship between humanity and God. This original sin, according to Christian teaching, affected all of creation, leading to suffering, death, and the need for redemption.

The Apostle Paul emphasizes the universality of sin in Romans 3:23, stating, "For all have sinned and fall short of the glory of God." Sin not only separates humanity from God but also results in spiritual death (Romans 6:23). The need for salvation, therefore, arises from humanity's inability to reconcile itself to God through its own efforts.

8.2.2. The Promise of Redemption

From the moment of the fall, the Bible presents God's plan for salvation. In Genesis 3:15, often called the "protoevangelium" or "first gospel," God promises that the offspring of the woman would crush the head of the serpent, symbolizing the defeat of sin and evil. This promise foreshadows the coming of a Savior who would bring redemption to humanity.

Throughout the Old Testament, God continues to promise redemption through covenants with His people. The covenant with Abraham, the giving of the Law to Moses, and the promise of a Davidic king all point toward a future act of salvation that would restore the broken relationship between God and humanity. The prophets, particularly Isaiah, speak of a suffering servant who would bear the sins of the people and bring about their salvation (Isaiah 53:5-6).

8.3. Jesus as the Savior

In Christian belief, Jesus Christ is the fulfillment of God's promises of redemption. His life, death, and resurrection are seen as the definitive acts of salvation through which God reconciles humanity to Himself. The concept of salvation through Jesus rests on the belief that He is both fully God and fully human, and that He accomplished what no human could—offering Himself as a perfect sacrifice for sin.

8.3.1. The Incarnation: God Becoming Human

The incarnation, the belief that God became human in the person of Jesus Christ, is the foundation of Christian salvation. In Jesus, God enters into the human experience, taking on flesh and identifying with humanity. As both fully divine and fully human, Jesus is uniquely qualified to mediate between God and humanity.

The incarnation is crucial to the concept of salvation because it means that God Himself enters into the brokenness of the world to bring about redemption. As the Apostle John writes, "The Word became flesh and made his dwelling among us" (John 1:14). Jesus, as God incarnate, perfectly reveals the nature of God and demonstrates His love for humanity by coming to save it.

8.3.2. Jesus' Life and Ministry

The Gospels portray Jesus' life and ministry as central to His saving work. Through His teaching, miracles, and actions, Jesus proclaims the coming of the Kingdom of God—a kingdom characterized by justice, mercy, and reconciliation. His ministry demonstrates God's desire to save, heal, and restore the world.

Jesus' miracles, such as healing the sick, raising the dead, and casting out demons, are signs of the in-breaking of God's kingdom and a foretaste of the salvation He brings. His teachings on love, forgiveness, and justice reveal the ethical implications of salvation and call His followers to live as citizens of God's kingdom.

8.3.3. The Atonement: Jesus' Death on the Cross

At the center of Christian belief in salvation is the atonement—Jesus' sacrificial death on the cross. The word "atonement" refers to the act of reconciling or making amends for sin, and Jesus' death is seen as the means by which humanity is reconciled to God.

The New Testament presents several theological understandings of the atonement, each highlighting different aspects of Jesus' saving work:

- Substitutionary Atonement: Jesus takes humanity's place by bearing the penalty for sin. As Isaiah 53:5 states, "He was pierced for our transgressions; he was crushed for our iniquities." Jesus' death is understood as a substitutionary sacrifice, in which He takes upon Himself the punishment that humanity deserves, allowing believers to be forgiven and reconciled to God.

- Christus Victor: This view emphasizes Jesus' victory over the powers of sin, death, and evil. Through His death and resurrection, Jesus defeats the forces of darkness that have enslaved humanity, liberating them and establishing God's reign of justice and peace.

- Moral Influence: Jesus' death is seen as the ultimate demonstration of God's love, inspiring believers to turn away from sin and live lives of love and holiness. As Jesus said in John 15:13, "Greater love has no one than this, that someone lay down his life for his friends."

Each of these views of the atonement contributes to a fuller understanding of the significance of Jesus' death. At the core of all these perspectives is the belief that Jesus' death on the cross is the decisive act through which God deals with sin and makes salvation possible.

8.3.4. The Resurrection: Triumph Over Death

The resurrection of Jesus is the climax of the Christian understanding of salvation. By rising from the dead, Jesus demonstrates His victory over sin and death, confirming His identity as the Son of God and the truth of His saving work. The resurrection is not merely an isolated event but the beginning of a new creation in which death no longer has the final word.

Paul emphasizes the importance of the resurrection in 1 Corinthians 15:17, saying, "If Christ has not been raised, your faith is futile; you are still in your sins." The resurrection is proof that God's plan for salvation has been accomplished and that eternal life is available to all who trust in Christ. It also provides believers with the hope of their own resurrection and the promise of eternal life in the presence of God.

8.4. Salvation Through Faith in Jesus

Salvation, according to the New Testament, is a gift of God's grace, received through faith in Jesus Christ. It is not something that can be earned through human effort or good works but is a result of God's initiative in Christ.

8.4.1. Justification by Faith

One of the central teachings of the Apostle Paul is that believers are justified—that is, made right with God— through faith in Jesus Christ. In Romans 3:24-25, Paul writes,

"All are justified freely by his grace through the redemption that came by Christ Jesus. God presented Christ as a sacrifice of atonement, through the shedding of his blood—to be received by faith."

Justification is a legal term that refers to being declared righteous in the sight of God. Through faith in Christ, believers are forgiven of their sins and credited with Christ's righteousness. This doctrine of justification by faith alone (sola fide) became one of the foundational tenets of the Protestant Reformation, emphasizing that salvation is a gift of God's grace, not something that can be earned through human merit.

8.4.2. Sanctification and the Transforming Work of the Holy Spirit

Salvation is not only about being forgiven and justified; it also involves the ongoing process of sanctification, in which believers are transformed into the likeness of Christ. Sanctification is the work of the Holy Spirit, who empowers believers to live holy lives and to grow in love, obedience, and faithfulness.

Paul speaks of this transformative process in 2 Corinthians 3:18, saying, "And we all, who with unveiled faces contemplate the Lord's glory, are being transformed into his image with ever-increasing glory, which comes from the Lord, who is the Spirit." Salvation, therefore, is not merely about being saved from sin but also about being renewed and conformed to the image of Christ.

8.5. The Scope of Salvation: Personal and Cosmic Dimensions

The concept of salvation in Jesus Christ encompasses both personal and cosmic dimensions. It involves the redemption of individual believers as well as the restoration of the entire created order.

8.5.1. Personal Salvation

On a personal level, salvation is about the forgiveness of sins, reconciliation with God, and the promise of eternal life. Through faith in Jesus, individuals are saved from the consequences of sin and are brought into a new relationship with God. This personal salvation includes the assurance of God's love, the indwelling of the Holy Spirit, and the hope of resurrection.

8.5.2. Cosmic Salvation

In addition to personal salvation, the New Testament teaches that Jesus' saving work has cosmic implications. Through His death and resurrection, Jesus inaugurates the renewal of all creation. Paul speaks of this cosmic dimension in

Colossians 1:19-20, saying, "For God was pleased to have all his fullness dwell in him, and through him to reconcile to himself all things, whether things on earth or things in heaven, by making peace through his blood, shed on the cross."

The final hope of salvation is not just the salvation of individuals but the restoration of the entire created order. In Revelation 21:1, John describes the new creation: "Then I saw a new heaven and a new earth, for the first heaven and the first earth had passed away." The promise of salvation through Jesus extends to the whole cosmos, where God will dwell with His people in perfect harmony, and all things will be made new.

8.6. Conclusion

The concept of salvation through Jesus Christ is central to Christian theology and shapes the entirety of Christian belief and practice. Through His incarnation, life, death, and resurrection, Jesus accomplishes the salvation of humanity, reconciling us to God and offering us eternal life. His sacrifice on the cross addresses the problem of sin and makes possible the forgiveness and transformation of all who trust in Him.

Salvation is both a gift of God's grace and an invitation to participate in the ongoing work of sanctification through the power of the Holy Spirit. It encompasses both personal redemption and the ultimate restoration of all creation. Through faith in Jesus Christ, believers experience the fullness of God's saving love, both now and in the age to come.

Theories of Atonement: Substitutionary Atonement, Christus Victor, and Moral Influence

8.1. Introduction

Atonement refers to the reconciliation between God and humanity, accomplished through the life, death, and resurrection of Jesus Christ. Throughout Christian history, theologians have sought to understand how Jesus' death on the cross brings salvation to humanity, leading to the development of various theories of atonement. While all these theories agree on the significance of Christ's sacrificial death, they emphasize different aspects of how that sacrifice works. Three of the most influential theories are Substitutionary Atonement, Christus Victor, and the Moral Influence theory. This chapter explores these key theories of atonement, their theological foundations, and their implications for Christian belief and practice.

8.2. Substitutionary Atonement

Substitutionary atonement, often referred to as penal substitution, is one of the most prominent atonement theories in Christian theology. It emphasizes Jesus' role as a substitute for humanity, bearing the penalty of sin on behalf of others. This theory is deeply rooted in both Scripture and the legal framework of justice, and it underscores the seriousness of sin and the necessity of divine justice.

8.2.1. The Concept of Substitution

Substitutionary atonement holds that humanity, because of sin, stands guilty before a holy and righteous God. In this view, sin incurs a penalty—spiritual death and eternal separation from God—that must be satisfied to restore the broken relationship between humanity and God. As Paul writes in Romans 6:23, "For the wages of sin is death, but the gift of God is eternal life in Christ Jesus our Lord." According to this theory, human beings cannot pay the debt of sin themselves because they are imperfect and guilty. Therefore, Jesus, who is sinless and perfect, willingly takes the place of humanity, suffering the punishment they deserve.

The concept of substitution is best illustrated in Isaiah 53:5, where the Suffering Servant "was pierced for our transgressions, he was crushed for our iniquities; the punishment that brought us peace was on him, and by his wounds we are healed." This passage is often seen as a prophetic description of Jesus' sacrificial death, in which He takes upon Himself the penalty that was rightfully due to humanity.

8.2.2. Penal Substitution and Divine Justice

Penal substitution, a specific form of substitutionary atonement, emphasizes the legal framework of justice. In this view, sin is an offense against God's law, and divine justice demands that the penalty for sin be paid. Jesus, by dying on the cross, satisfies God's justice, bearing the wrath of God that was meant for sinners. This understanding is grounded in passages like Romans 3:25-26, which speaks of God presenting Christ as a "sacrifice of atonement" to demonstrate

His justice, while also providing a way for humanity to be justified through faith.

In penal substitution, Christ's death is not only an expression of God's love but also a legal requirement to uphold divine justice. By standing in humanity's place and enduring the punishment for sin, Jesus reconciles humanity to God, making forgiveness and eternal life possible.

8.2.3. Criticisms and Alternatives

While substitutionary atonement is a central theme in much of Christian theology, it has been criticized for its focus on divine wrath and punishment. Some argue that this view can make God seem vengeful, rather than merciful, and that it may overly emphasize legalistic aspects of atonement at the expense of relational ones. Others express concern that penal substitution portrays God as needing to be appeased, rather than as a loving Father who freely forgives.

Despite these criticisms, substitutionary atonement remains a foundational theory for many Christian traditions, especially within Reformed and evangelical theology. It highlights the gravity of sin, the necessity of justice, and the profound sacrifice of Jesus as the one who takes humanity's place in bearing the consequences of sin.

8.3. Christus Victor

The Christus Victor (Latin for "Christ the Victor") model of atonement emphasizes Jesus' victory over the powers of sin, death, and Satan. Rather than focusing on substitution or punishment, this theory sees Christ's death and resurrection as the decisive triumph of God over the forces of evil that have enslaved humanity. Christus Victor has its roots in the early Church and remains influential in various Christian traditions today.

8.3.1. The Cosmic Struggle Against Evil

In the Christus Victor model, the human condition is understood not primarily as legal guilt, but as enslavement to the powers of sin, death, and Satan. These forces hold humanity captive, preventing them from living in relationship with God. The biblical narrative depicts this cosmic struggle in various places, such as in Genesis 3, where the serpent (representing Satan) deceives Adam and Eve, leading to their fall into sin. As a result, humanity becomes subject to the power of death and the dominion of Satan.

In Christus Victor, Jesus' death on the cross is not primarily about satisfying God's justice but about defeating these oppressive powers. Through His crucifixion and resurrection, Jesus breaks the hold that sin and death have over humanity, liberating them from their bondage and restoring them to life in God's kingdom.

Colossians 2:15 is often cited in support of this view: "Having disarmed the powers and authorities, he made a public spectacle of them, triumphing over them by the cross." This passage portrays Christ's death as a cosmic victory, in which He exposes and defeats the spiritual powers that oppose God's reign.

8.3.2. The Cross as Victory Over Death and Satan

The Christus Victor model emphasizes that Jesus' resurrection is the ultimate proof of His victory. Death, which had entered the world through sin, is now defeated through Christ's resurrection, and with it, the power of Satan is broken. The resurrection is seen not only as a reversal of death but also as the inauguration of God's new creation, in which all things will be made new.

This victory over death and Satan is central to the Christian hope of eternal life. As Paul writes in 1 Corinthians 15:54-57, "Death has been swallowed up in victory. Where, O death, is your victory? Where, O death, is your sting?... But thanks be to God! He gives us the victory through our Lord Jesus Christ."

8.3.3. Christus Victor and the Human Experience

Christus Victor resonates with the human experience of oppression and suffering, as it presents Jesus as the one who liberates humanity from the forces of darkness that hold them in bondage. This model of atonement highlights the relational and redemptive aspects of salvation, focusing on how Christ's victory brings freedom, healing, and restoration to individuals and communities.

The Christus Victor model has been influential in various Christian traditions, including Eastern Orthodoxy, where the theme of Christ's victory over death is central to liturgy and theology. It offers a perspective that sees salvation not just as legal justification but as liberation from evil powers that distort human life and relationships.

8.4. Moral Influence Theory

The Moral Influence theory of atonement focuses on the ethical and transformative impact of Jesus' life and death. This theory, associated with the medieval theologian Peter Abelard, views the cross as the ultimate demonstration of God's love, designed to inspire humanity to turn away from sin and live a life of love and righteousness. Rather than emphasizing legal or cosmic dimensions, the moral influence theory highlights the way Jesus' death changes the hearts and minds of individuals.

8.4.1. The Cross as a Demonstration of God's Love

At the heart of the moral influence theory is the belief that Jesus' death on the cross is a powerful demonstration of God's love for humanity. In laying down His life for others, Jesus reveals the depth of God's compassion and mercy, showing that God is willing to go to any length to save humanity. This revelation of divine love is meant to inspire a response of repentance, faith, and transformation.

The Apostle John captures this idea in 1 John 4:9-10: "This is how God showed his love among us: He sent his one and only Son into the world that we might live through him. This is love: not that we loved God, but that he loved us and sent his Son as an atoning sacrifice for our sins." Jesus' death is seen as the ultimate act of self-giving love, intended to move humanity to love God in return and to live in accordance with His will.

8.4.2. Transformation Through Love

The moral influence theory emphasizes that the atonement is not primarily about satisfying divine justice or defeating cosmic powers but about transforming the human heart. Jesus' example of love and self-sacrifice provides a moral and ethical example for believers to follow. As they reflect on the love demonstrated at the cross, they are moved to live lives of love, compassion, and forgiveness.

This emphasis on transformation through love aligns with Jesus' teachings, particularly His call to love others as He has loved (John 13:34). In this view, the cross is not just an event in history but a source of ongoing inspiration for how Christians are to live.

8.4.3. Criticisms and Contributions

While the moral influence theory highlights the power of God's love and the ethical impact of Jesus' life, it has been criticized for not adequately addressing the problem of sin and the need for divine justice. Critics argue that this theory overlooks the seriousness of sin and the need for Christ's death to deal with the penalty of sin in a more objective way.

Nevertheless, the moral influence theory offers a valuable perspective on atonement by emphasizing the relational and ethical dimensions of salvation. It reminds believers that the cross is not only about forgiveness but also about transformation, calling them to respond to God's love by living lives of holiness and love.

8.5. Conclusion

Theories of atonement, including Substitutionary Atonement, Christus Victor, and Moral Influence, offer different perspectives on how Jesus' death brings about salvation. Each theory emphasizes a different aspect of Christ's work on the cross—whether it is the satisfaction of divine justice, the victory over sin and death, or the demonstration of God's love that transforms human hearts.

While these theories may differ in emphasis, they all affirm the central truth of the Christian faith: that through Jesus' life, death, and resurrection, God has reconciled the world to Himself. Together, these theories provide a rich and multifaceted understanding of the atonement, highlighting the depth of Christ's sacrifice and the various ways in which His work brings salvation to humanity. Through these different lenses, Christians are invited to explore the mystery of the cross and to experience the transforming power of God's love and grace.

Implications of Salvation for Humanity

8.1. Introduction

The doctrine of salvation is central to Christian theology and shapes every aspect of the believer's relationship with God, the Church, and the world. Salvation through Jesus Christ offers forgiveness of sins, reconciliation with God, and the promise of eternal life. But its implications extend beyond the individual to encompass all of humanity and the entirety of creation. This chapter explores the various dimensions of salvation—personal, communal, ethical, and eschatological—and how salvation through Jesus Christ impacts the lives of individuals and humanity as a whole.

8.2. Personal Implications of Salvation

Salvation has profound implications for individuals, both in their present lives and their eternal destinies. When a person accepts Jesus Christ as their Savior, they experience forgiveness, regeneration, and the gift of eternal life. These transformations affect not only the believer's relationship with God but also their inner life and outward behavior.

8.2.1. Forgiveness of Sins

The first and most immediate implication of salvation is the forgiveness of sins. The Bible teaches that all people have sinned and fallen short of God's glory (Romans 3:23), and that the wages of sin is death (Romans 6:23). However, through Jesus' sacrificial death on the cross, the penalty for sin is paid, and forgiveness is offered to all who believe in Him.

Forgiveness means that the guilt of sin is removed, and the believer is no longer under condemnation. As Paul writes in Romans 8:1, "There is now no condemnation for those who are in Christ Jesus." This release from guilt and condemnation restores the believer's relationship with God and offers them a fresh start.

8.2.2. Justification and Reconciliation

Salvation also involves justification, which is the act by which God declares a sinner righteous through faith in Jesus Christ. Justification is a legal term that signifies a change in status, where the believer moves from a position of guilt to a position of righteousness before God. This is possible not because of the believer's own merits, but because of Christ's atoning work on the cross. Paul explains this in 2 Corinthians 5:21: "God made him who had no sin to be sin for us, so that in him we might become the righteousness of God."

Justification leads to reconciliation with God, which is the restoration of the broken relationship between humanity and the Creator. In Christ, believers are no longer estranged from God but are brought into a loving and intimate relationship with Him. As Paul writes in Romans 5:10-11, "For if, while we were God's enemies, we were reconciled to him through the death of his Son, how much more, having been reconciled, shall we be saved through his life!"

8.2.3. Regeneration and New Life

Another personal implication of salvation is regeneration, or the spiritual rebirth of the believer. Jesus described this process to Nicodemus in John 3:3 when He said, "Very truly I tell you, no one can see the kingdom of God unless they are born again." Regeneration is the work of the Holy Spirit, who brings new life to those who put their faith in Christ. It involves the transformation of the heart and mind, enabling believers to live in obedience to God.

This new life in Christ also brings a new identity. Believers are no longer defined by their past sins or failures but are now "new creations" in Christ (2 Corinthians 5:17). They are adopted into God's family, becoming His children and heirs of His promises (Romans 8:15-17). This transformation changes how believers view themselves, their purpose, and their destiny.

8.2.4. Assurance of Eternal Life

One of the greatest personal implications of salvation is the promise of eternal life. Jesus offers this assurance in John 10:28: "I give them eternal life, and they shall never perish; no one will snatch them out of my hand." Through faith in Christ, believers are given the hope of living forever in the presence of God.

Eternal life is not just a future reality but begins in the present. It is a life marked by fellowship with God, the indwelling of the Holy Spirit, and participation in the life of the Church. While believers look forward to the full realization of eternal life in the new creation, they already experience the blessings of salvation in their relationship with God and their transformation by His grace.

8.3. Communal Implications of Salvation

Salvation is not just an individual experience; it has profound implications for the community of believers—the Church. Through salvation, individuals are united with Christ and with one another, forming a spiritual family that transcends social, cultural, and ethnic barriers.

8.3.1. The Church as the Body of Christ

One of the key communal implications of salvation is the formation of the Church, which is described in the New Testament as the "Body of Christ" (1 Corinthians 12:27). Through faith in Christ, believers are united with Him and with one another in a spiritual body. This unity is expressed through shared worship, mutual care, and the practice of the sacraments, such as baptism and the Lord's Supper.

The Church is not just a gathering of individuals but a community that reflects the love and unity of the Triune God. In Ephesians 4:4-6, Paul emphasizes the unity of the Church: "There is one body and one Spirit, just as you were called to one hope when you were called; one Lord, one faith, one baptism; one God and Father of all, who is over all and through all and in all." Salvation brings believers into this unified community, where they are called to serve one another and advance the mission of God in the world.

8.3.2. The Universal Church and Global Mission

Salvation has a global dimension, as it unites believers across the world in the mission of God. Jesus' Great Commission in Matthew 28:19-20 calls His followers to "go and make disciples of all nations." Salvation is not limited to any particular people or nation but is offered to all humanity. The Church, as the Body of Christ, is called to proclaim the Gospel to every corner of the earth and to invite all people into the saving relationship with Jesus.

This global mission underscores the communal aspect of salvation. Believers are not isolated individuals but part of a worldwide family of faith, united in their worship of God and their witness to the world. The Church's mission of evangelism, service, and justice is a reflection of the salvation that believers have experienced in Christ and a response to His command to share that salvation with others.

8.4. Ethical Implications of Salvation

Salvation also has significant ethical implications. Those who have been saved by grace are called to live lives that reflect the character of Christ, marked by love, holiness, and justice. Salvation is not just about being forgiven but about being transformed into the likeness of Christ, which involves a commitment to ethical living.

8.4.1. The Call to Holiness

Salvation involves a call to holiness, which is the process of becoming more like Christ in character and behavior. This process, known as sanctification, is a lifelong journey of spiritual growth, guided by the Holy Spirit. Paul speaks of this transformation in Romans 12:1-2, urging believers to "offer your bodies as a living sacrifice, holy and pleasing to God" and to "be transformed by the renewing of your mind."

Holiness involves both personal and relational aspects. Personally, believers are called to live lives of integrity, purity, and obedience to God's commands. Relationally, they are called to love others as Christ loved them, demonstrating compassion, forgiveness, and humility in their relationships.

8.4.2. Justice, Compassion, and Social Responsibility

Salvation also has implications for how believers engage with the world around them. The Gospel calls believers to be agents of justice and compassion, reflecting God's heart for the poor, the oppressed, and the marginalized. In Matthew 25:31-46, Jesus teaches that those who have experienced salvation will demonstrate their faith through acts of mercy, such as feeding the hungry, clothing the naked, and caring for the sick.

The ethical implications of salvation extend to issues of social justice, as believers are called to advocate for the oppressed, work for peace, and seek the common good. This is not an optional part of the Christian life but a natural outworking of the salvation that believers have received in Christ. As James 2:17 reminds us, "Faith by itself, if it is not accompanied by action, is dead."

8.4.3. Stewardship and Creation Care

In addition to justice and compassion, salvation has ethical implications for how believers relate to the created world. The Bible teaches that creation itself was affected by the fall and is awaiting redemption (Romans 8:19-22). As recipients of salvation, believers are called to care for the environment and to steward God's creation responsibly. This involves living in harmony with the natural world and working to protect it for future generations.

8.5. Eschatological Implications of Salvation

Salvation has not only present but also future implications, pointing toward the fulfillment of God's redemptive plan at the end of history. The Christian hope of salvation is ultimately eschatological, meaning it looks forward to the final consummation of God's kingdom and the restoration of all things.

8.5.1. The Resurrection and Eternal Life

One of the most significant eschatological implications of salvation is the promise of resurrection and eternal life. Just as Christ was raised from the dead, believers are promised that they too will be raised to new life in the age to come. In 1 Corinthians 15:52-54,

Paul speaks of the resurrection as the final victory over death: "For the trumpet will sound, the dead will be raised imperishable, and we will be changed… then the saying that is written will come true: 'Death has been swallowed up in victory.'"

Eternal life in the presence of God is the ultimate fulfillment of the promise of salvation. Believers look forward to a future where sin, death, and suffering are no more, and where they will dwell with God in perfect harmony and peace.

8.5.2. The New Creation

The eschatological hope of salvation extends beyond the individual to encompass the entire created order. The Bible teaches that God's plan of salvation includes the renewal of all creation. In Revelation 21:1-5, John describes the vision of a new heaven and a new earth, where God will dwell with His people, and "there will be no more death or mourning or crying or pain."

This vision of the new creation is the culmination of God's redemptive work. Salvation, therefore, is not only about the redemption of individuals but about the restoration of the entire cosmos. The promise of the new creation offers hope for a future in which all things will be made new and God's perfect will is fully realized.

8.6. Conclusion

The implications of salvation for humanity are vast and transformative. Salvation through Jesus Christ offers individuals forgiveness, justification, regeneration, and the assurance of eternal life. It brings believers into the community of the Church, uniting them with other believers and calling them to participate in God's mission in the world. Salvation also has profound ethical implications, calling believers to live lives of holiness, justice, and stewardship, and it offers the hope of resurrection and the renewal of all creation.

Through salvation, humanity is not only saved from sin but is also invited into a new way of life, characterized by love, service, and hope. The work of salvation, both personal and cosmic, reveals the depth of God's love for humanity and the greatness of His redemptive plan, which will ultimately culminate in the new creation and the full realization of His kingdom.

CHAPTER 09

THE THEOLOGY OF JESUS IN THE NEW TESTAMENT

9.1. Introduction

The New Testament presents Jesus Christ as the central figure of God's redemptive plan for humanity, and the Gospels are the primary source of theological reflection on His person, work, and mission. The four Gospels—Matthew, Mark, Luke, and John—offer unique yet complementary portraits of Jesus, emphasizing His divinity, humanity, messianic role, and relationship with God the Father. Each Gospel highlights different aspects of Jesus' ministry and role within God's kingdom, contributing to a fuller understanding of His identity and mission. This chapter analyzes the theological significance of Jesus in the Gospels, focusing on His portrayal as the Messiah, the Son of God, the fulfillment of Old Testament prophecy, and the inaugurator of the Kingdom of God.

9.2. Jesus as the Messiah in the Gospels

One of the primary theological roles of Jesus in the Gospels is that of the Messiah, the anointed one sent by God to deliver His people. The concept of the Messiah was deeply rooted in Jewish expectations, and the Gospels present Jesus as the fulfillment of these hopes, albeit in ways that challenged conventional views of what the Messiah would be.

9.2.1. The Messianic Expectations in First-Century Judaism

During the time of Jesus, many Jews expected the Messiah to be a political and military leader who would liberate Israel from Roman rule and restore the kingdom of David. These expectations were shaped by Old Testament prophecies about a future king from David's line who would establish God's reign on earth (Isaiah 9:6-7, Jeremiah 23:5-6).

However, Jesus redefined the nature of messianic kingship, emphasizing His role as a servant and a spiritual liberator rather than a political revolutionary. Throughout the Gospels, Jesus resists the popular desire for a political Messiah and instead points to His mission as one of bringing spiritual salvation and inaugurating the Kingdom of God.

9.2.2. Matthew's Presentation of Jesus as the Fulfillment of Messianic Prophecy

The Gospel of Matthew, in particular, highlights Jesus as the fulfillment of Old Testament prophecy. From the beginning, Matthew's Gospel presents Jesus as the long-awaited Messiah, tracing His genealogy back to David and Abraham (Matthew 1:1-17). Matthew repeatedly uses the phrase "this was to fulfill what was spoken by the prophet" to demonstrate that Jesus' life and ministry fulfill the promises of the Hebrew Scriptures.

Matthew's portrayal of Jesus' messianic role is particularly evident in His triumphal entry into Jerusalem (Matthew 21:1-11), which echoes the prophecy of Zechariah 9:9. Jesus enters the city riding on a donkey, symbolizing His role as a humble and peaceful king. By doing so, He fulfills the messianic expectations but subverts the idea of a conquering warrior-king, emphasizing His mission to bring peace and salvation through sacrifice, not violence.

9.2.3. The Gospel of Mark: The Suffering Messiah

In contrast to the expectation of a triumphant political leader, the Gospel of Mark presents Jesus as the suffering Messiah, whose path to kingship involves rejection, suffering, and death. Mark's Gospel emphasizes the paradox of Jesus' messianic identity: while He is the Messiah, He must suffer and die to fulfill His mission.

Jesus' identity as the Messiah is a central theme in Mark, particularly in Peter's confession at Caesarea Philippi, where he declares, "You are the Messiah" (Mark 8:29). However, immediately after this confession, Jesus begins to teach His disciples that "the Son of Man must suffer many things and be rejected by the elders, the chief priests and the teachers of the law, and that he must be killed and after three days rise again" (Mark 8:31). This teaching shocks the disciples, as it contradicts their expectations of a victorious, political Messiah.

Mark's emphasis on the suffering Messiah culminates in the crucifixion, where Jesus is mocked as "the King of the Jews" (Mark 15:26). Paradoxically, it is through His suffering and death that Jesus accomplishes His messianic mission of salvation. For Mark, Jesus' kingship is revealed not in earthly power but in His willingness to suffer and die for the sake of humanity.

9.3. Jesus as the Son of God

Another central theme in the theology of the Gospels is Jesus' identity as the Son of God. This title emphasizes both Jesus' unique relationship with God the Father and His divine nature. The Gospels present Jesus as more than a human prophet or teacher; He is the incarnate Son of God, who shares in the divine nature and reveals God to humanity.

9.3.1. The Divine Sonship in the Gospel of John

The Gospel of John places a particular emphasis on Jesus' divine sonship, presenting Him as the eternal Word who was with God and was God (John 1:1). John's Gospel opens with a profound theological statement about Jesus' divinity: "The Word became flesh and made his dwelling among us. We have seen his glory, the glory of the one and only Son, who came from the Father, full of grace and truth" (John 1:14).

Throughout the Gospel, Jesus refers to God as His Father, emphasizing His intimate relationship with God.

Jesus' divine sonship is also affirmed by miraculous signs, such as turning water into wine (John 2:1-11), raising Lazarus from the dead (John 11:1-44), and His own resurrection. These miracles serve as proof that Jesus is the Son of God, sent by the Father to bring life and light to the world.

One of the clearest expressions of Jesus' divine sonship in John's Gospel is found in His statement, "I and the Father are one" (John 10:30). This claim of unity with God highlights Jesus' divine authority and His unique role in revealing God's nature to humanity.

9.3.2. The Baptism of Jesus and the Affirmation of Divine Sonship

In all four Gospels, Jesus' baptism marks a key moment in affirming His identity as the Son of God. At His baptism, the heavens open, the Holy Spirit descends upon Him, and a voice from heaven declares, "This is my Son, whom I love; with him I am well pleased" (Matthew 3:17, Mark 1:11, Luke 3:22). This divine proclamation affirms Jesus' unique relationship with the Father and sets the stage for His public ministry.

The baptism scene also connects Jesus' sonship with His mission of redemption. As the beloved Son, Jesus is sent to accomplish the Father's will, which involves bringing salvation to humanity through His life, death, and resurrection.

9.4. Jesus and the Kingdom of God

One of the central themes of Jesus' teaching in the Gospels is the Kingdom of God. Jesus announces the arrival of God's reign and calls people to repentance, faith, and discipleship. His miracles, parables, and actions all point to the presence of the Kingdom and the need for people to respond to it.

9.4.1. The Kingdom of God in the Synoptic Gospels

In the Synoptic Gospels (Matthew, Mark, and Luke), Jesus consistently proclaims the nearness of the Kingdom of God. Mark opens his Gospel with Jesus' declaration, "The time has come... The kingdom of God has come near. Repent and believe the good news!" (Mark 1:15). This message signals that in Jesus, God's long-awaited reign is breaking into history.

The Kingdom of God, as Jesus teaches it, is both a present reality and a future hope. In His ministry, Jesus demonstrates the power of the Kingdom by healing the sick, casting out demons, and raising the dead. These miracles reveal that God's reign is already at work, bringing liberation and restoration to a broken world.

At the same time, Jesus teaches that the fullness of the Kingdom is yet to come. His parables, such as the parable of the mustard seed (Matthew 13:31-32) and the parable of the wheat and the tares (Matthew 13:24-30), illustrate that the Kingdom grows gradually and will reach its final consummation at the end of the age. Until then, Jesus calls His followers to live as citizens of the Kingdom, embodying its values of love, justice, and mercy.

9.4.2. Jesus as the Inaugurator of the Kingdom

In the Gospels, Jesus is not only the proclaimer of the Kingdom but also its inaugurator. Through His actions and teachings, He reveals that the Kingdom is centered on His person and work. His miracles, especially His casting out of demons, are seen as signs that He is bringing God's reign to bear on the forces of evil (Matthew 12:28). Jesus' ministry inaugurates the Kingdom by confronting the powers of sin, death, and Satan, and by offering forgiveness, healing, and new life.

The Kingdom of God reaches its climax in Jesus' death and resurrection. By dying on the cross, Jesus defeats the power of sin and death, making possible the reconciliation of humanity with God. His resurrection is the firstfruits of the new creation, signaling the ultimate victory of God's reign over death and evil. Through His resurrection, Jesus establishes the Kingdom in its fullest sense, offering eternal life to all who believe in Him.

9.5. Conclusion

The Gospels present a rich and multifaceted portrait of Jesus, emphasizing His role as the Messiah, the Son of God, and the inaugurator of the Kingdom of God. In these narratives, Jesus fulfills the hopes of Israel while also redefining what it means to be the Messiah and the Son of God. His ministry, teachings, and actions reveal the nature of God's reign and call people to respond to the good news of salvation.

The theology of Jesus in the Gospels lays the foundation for Christian belief in His divine and human natures, His role as the Savior of humanity, and His ongoing reign as Lord. As both the fulfillment of Old Testament prophecy and the inaugurator of the new covenant, Jesus stands at the center of God's redemptive plan, offering forgiveness, life, and the hope of the Kingdom to all who follow Him. Through the Gospels, believers are invited to encounter Jesus anew and to live in the light of His saving work.

The Portrayal of Jesus in the Epistles and Revelation

9.1. Introduction

While the Gospels provide the foundational narrative of Jesus' life, ministry, death, and resurrection, the Epistles and the Book of Revelation offer a deeper theological reflection on His identity, significance, and ongoing role in the life of the Church and in God's cosmic plan. The Epistles—written primarily by Paul, Peter, James, and John—focus on the implications of Jesus' death and resurrection for salvation, Christian living, and the Church. The Book of Revelation, meanwhile, offers an apocalyptic vision of Jesus as the exalted Lord and triumphant King, revealing His ultimate victory over evil and His role in the end of history. This chapter examines how Jesus is portrayed in the Epistles and Revelation, focusing on His divinity, His role as the mediator of salvation, His relationship with the Church, and His eschatological reign.

9.2. Jesus in the Pauline Epistles

Paul's letters (the Pauline Epistles) provide some of the earliest theological reflections on Jesus and His role in salvation. Paul presents a highly developed Christology, emphasizing Jesus as the risen Lord, the head of the Church, and the means of salvation for all who believe.

9.2.1. Jesus as the Risen Lord

For Paul, the resurrection of Jesus is central to His identity as Lord and Savior. In his letters, Paul frequently proclaims that Jesus' resurrection is proof of His divinity and His victory over sin and death. In Romans 1:4, Paul declares that Jesus "was declared to be the Son of God in power according to the Spirit of holiness by his resurrection from the dead." The resurrection confirms Jesus' status as the Son of God and establishes His authority as Lord over all creation.

Paul's emphasis on the resurrection goes hand in hand with his teaching that Jesus is the exalted Lord who reigns at the right hand of God. In Philippians 2:9-11, Paul writes that "God exalted him to the highest place and gave him the name that is above every name, that at the name of Jesus every knee should bow, in heaven and on earth and under the earth, and every tongue acknowledge that Jesus Christ is Lord, to the glory of God the Father." This passage, often referred to as the "Christ Hymn," highlights Jesus' exaltation as a result of

His obedience and self-sacrifice, confirming His divine authority and His future reign over all creation.

9.2.2. Jesus as the Mediator of Salvation

One of the most important themes in Paul's letters is Jesus' role as the mediator of salvation. For Paul, Jesus' death and resurrection are the means by which humanity is reconciled to God. In Romans 5:1, Paul writes, "Therefore, since we have been justified through faith, we have peace with God through our Lord Jesus Christ." Paul's theology of justification teaches that through faith in Jesus, believers are forgiven of their sins and declared righteous before God.

In 1 Timothy 2:5, Paul further emphasizes Jesus' mediatorial role, stating, "For there is one God and one mediator between God and mankind, the man Christ Jesus." As both fully divine and fully human, Jesus serves as the perfect mediator who bridges the gap between a holy God and sinful humanity. His sacrificial death on the cross satisfies God's justice, making possible the forgiveness of sins and the reconciliation of humanity to God.

Paul also describes Jesus as the second Adam, drawing a parallel between Adam's role in bringing sin into the world and Jesus' role in bringing salvation. In 1 Corinthians 15:22,

Paul writes, "For as in Adam all die, so in Christ all will be made alive." This comparison highlights Jesus' redemptive work, which reverses the effects of Adam's disobedience and brings new life to those who are united with Him through faith.

9.2.3. Jesus as the Head of the Church

Another key theme in the Pauline Epistles is Jesus' relationship to the Church. Paul describes Jesus as the head of the Church, which he frequently refers to as the "body of Christ." In Colossians 1:18, Paul writes, "And he is the head of the body, the church; he is the beginning and the firstborn from among the dead, so that in everything he might have the supremacy." Jesus' role as the head of the Church emphasizes His authority over believers and His intimate connection with them as their source of life and guidance.

For Paul, the Church is the visible manifestation of Jesus' ongoing presence in the world. Believers are called to live in unity, following the example of Christ, and to serve as His representatives in the world. Through the Church, Jesus continues His mission of bringing reconciliation, healing, and salvation to humanity.

9.3. Jesus in the General Epistles

The General Epistles, which include the letters of Peter, James, and John, also offer important theological insights into the person and work of Jesus. These letters focus on Jesus' role as the Savior, His example for Christian living, and His return as the righteous Judge.

9.3.1. Jesus as the Suffering Savior in 1 Peter

The First Epistle of Peter emphasizes Jesus' suffering and death as central to His mission of salvation. Peter presents Jesus as the suffering servant who willingly endured suffering and death to bring about redemption. In 1 Peter 2:24, Peter writes, "He himself bore our sins in his body on the cross, so that we might die to sins and live for righteousness; by his wounds you have been healed." This echoes the language of Isaiah 53, which portrays the suffering servant who takes upon himself the sins of the people.

Peter encourages believers to follow Jesus' example of endurance in the face of suffering, reminding them that Christ's suffering was the means by which He brought salvation. Jesus' willingness to suffer for the sake of others becomes a model for how Christians are called to endure persecution and hardship with patience and faith.

9.3.2. Jesus as the Perfect High Priest in Hebrews

The Epistle to the Hebrews presents a unique Christology by emphasizing Jesus as the perfect high priest who mediates between God and humanity. In the Jewish tradition, the high priest was responsible for offering sacrifices on behalf of the people to atone for their sins. Hebrews builds on this image by describing Jesus as the ultimate high priest who offers Himself as the perfect sacrifice for sin.

In Hebrews 4:14-16, the author writes, "Therefore, since we have a great high priest who has ascended into heaven, Jesus the Son of God, let us hold firmly to the faith we profess. For we do not have a high priest who is unable to empathize with our weaknesses, but we have one who has been tempted in every way, just as we are—yet he did not sin." Jesus' role as high priest emphasizes both His divinity and His humanity, as He is able to fully represent humanity before God while also being sinless and divine.

Hebrews also emphasizes the finality and superiority of Jesus' sacrifice. In Hebrews 10:12-14, the author writes that Jesus "offered for all time one sacrifice for sins" and "by one sacrifice he has made perfect forever those who are being made holy." This view underscores the sufficiency of Jesus' sacrifice and His ongoing role as the mediator of the new covenant between God and humanity.

9.4. Jesus in Revelation: The Triumphant and Exalted Lord

The Book of Revelation presents a dramatic and apocalyptic vision of Jesus as the triumphant and exalted Lord who will bring about the ultimate fulfillment of God's plan for creation. In contrast to the suffering servant image often emphasized in the Gospels, Revelation portrays Jesus as the victorious King who defeats the forces of evil and establishes God's eternal kingdom.

9.4.1. Jesus as the Lamb Who Was Slain

One of the central images of Jesus in Revelation is that of the Lamb who was slain. This image combines both the suffering and victorious aspects of Jesus' identity. In Revelation 5:6, John describes seeing "a Lamb, looking as if it had been slain, standing at the center of the throne." The image of the Lamb signifies Jesus' sacrificial death, which brought about the redemption of humanity, while His position at the throne signifies His exalted status as the one who reigns with God.

Throughout Revelation, the Lamb is worshipped as the one who is worthy to open the scroll of God's judgments and bring history to its fulfillment. In Revelation 5:9-10, the heavenly chorus sings, "You are worthy to take the scroll and to open its seals, because you were slain, and with your blood you purchased for God persons from every tribe and language and people and nation."

9.4.2. Jesus as the Triumphant King

In addition to the image of the Lamb, Revelation also presents Jesus as the triumphant King who will return to judge the living and the dead and establish God's eternal kingdom. In Revelation 19:11-16, John describes a vision of Jesus as a warrior riding on a white horse, whose name is "Faithful and True" and who judges and wages war in righteousness. He wears a robe dipped in blood, and on His robe and thigh is written the title "King of kings and Lord of lords."

This depiction of Jesus emphasizes His authority over all creation and His ultimate victory over the forces of evil. As the conquering King, Jesus will defeat Satan, sin, and death, and establish the new heaven and new earth, where God will dwell with His people forever (Revelation 21:1-4).

9.4.3. Jesus as the Alpha and Omega

Revelation also emphasizes Jesus' eternal nature by referring to Him as the "Alpha and Omega," the first and last letters of the Greek alphabet. In Revelation 22:13, Jesus declares, "I am the Alpha and the Omega, the First and the Last, the Beginning and the End." This title highlights Jesus' role in creation, His ongoing presence in history, and His ultimate reign at the end of time. It affirms that Jesus is the eternal Lord who holds all of history in His hands and who will bring it to its consummation in God's eternal kingdom.

9.5. Conclusion

The portrayal of Jesus in the Epistles and Revelation expands upon the foundational narratives of the Gospels and offers a deeper theological understanding of His identity and significance. In the Epistles, Jesus is presented as the risen Lord, the mediator of salvation, the head of the Church, and the perfect high priest. His death and resurrection are central to the Christian message of salvation, and His example serves as a model for Christian living.

In Revelation, Jesus is portrayed as the triumphant and exalted Lord who will bring about the ultimate fulfillment of God's plan for creation. He is both the Lamb who was slain and the conquering King who will defeat evil and establish God's eternal kingdom. Through these diverse portrayals, the

New Testament provides a comprehensive and rich theological vision of Jesus as the Savior, Lord, and ultimate ruler of all creation.

Comparative Study of the Synoptic Gospels and John's Portrayal of Jesus

9.1. Introduction

The New Testament offers four distinct portraits of Jesus Christ through the Gospels: Matthew, Mark, Luke, and John. While the first three Gospels—often referred to as the Synoptic Gospels—share many similarities in their accounts of Jesus' life, teachings, miracles, and death, the Gospel of John presents a unique theological perspective. The Synoptic Gospels focus more on Jesus' humanity, His ethical teachings, and His role as the Messiah who fulfills Jewish expectations, while John emphasizes His divinity and eternal nature as the incarnate Word of God. This chapter explores the key similarities and differences in how the Synoptic Gospels and John portray Jesus, comparing their depictions of His identity, ministry, and the theological themes that emerge from their narratives.

9.2. Jesus in the Synoptic Gospels: Matthew, Mark, and Luke

The Synoptic Gospels share a common structure, many of the same stories, and a unified focus on Jesus' ministry in Galilee, His journey to Jerusalem, and His crucifixion. However, each Gospel also highlights specific theological emphases and distinct aspects of Jesus' identity.

9.2.1. Jesus as the Messiah and Fulfillment of Prophecy

One of the central themes of the Synoptic Gospels is Jesus' identity as the Messiah, the anointed one sent by God to save Israel and bring about the Kingdom of God. In Matthew, Jesus is particularly portrayed as the fulfillment of Old Testament prophecy, with the author often quoting Scripture to demonstrate how Jesus fulfills the expectations of the Messiah. For example, Matthew 1:22-23 points out that Jesus' virgin birth fulfills Isaiah 7:14, emphasizing that His life is the fulfillment of God's plan for Israel.

Mark, the earliest of the Gospels, portrays Jesus as a mysterious and somewhat secretive Messiah. Throughout Mark, Jesus repeatedly instructs those He heals to keep quiet about His identity (Mark 1:34, 8:30), a motif known as the "Messianic secret." Mark emphasizes Jesus' role as the suffering Messiah, whose path to kingship involves rejection, suffering, and death on the cross. This portrayal challenges the conventional Jewish expectations of a conquering political Messiah.

Luke's Gospel emphasizes Jesus as the Savior of all people, not just Israel. Luke's genealogy traces Jesus' lineage back to Adam, emphasizing His connection to all humanity, and throughout the Gospel, Jesus is shown extending God's salvation to the marginalized and the outcast, including Gentiles, women, and sinners. In Luke, Jesus is the compassionate and universal Savior, who brings healing and restoration to the entire world.

9.2.2. The Kingdom of God

In the Synoptic Gospels, Jesus' primary message centers on the Kingdom of God. He proclaims that the Kingdom is near and calls people to repentance, faith, and discipleship (Mark 1:15, Matthew 4:17, Luke 4:43). The Kingdom of God is both a present reality and a future hope, with Jesus' miracles and teachings serving as signs of its arrival.

The parables in the Synoptic Gospels, especially in Matthew and Luke, often illustrate the nature of the Kingdom of God. For example, the parable of the mustard seed (Matthew 13:31-32, Mark 4:30-32, Luke 13:18-19) shows that the Kingdom begins small but will grow into something great, while the parable of the lost sheep (Luke 15:1-7) emphasizes God's love for the sinner and His desire to bring people into His Kingdom.

The Synoptic Gospels portray Jesus as the one who inaugurates the Kingdom through His teachings, miracles, and sacrificial death. His healing of the sick, casting out of demons, and raising of the dead are seen as signs that the power of God's Kingdom is breaking into the present world, bringing liberation from the forces of evil, sin, and death.

9.2.3. Jesus' Humanity and Ethical Teachings

The Synoptic Gospels place a strong emphasis on Jesus' humanity. They describe His birth, upbringing, emotions, and experiences, such as His baptism, temptations in the wilderness, and prayers. Jesus is presented as a relatable figure who experiences hunger, fatigue, compassion, and sorrow (Mark 6:34, Luke 19:41). These human characteristics emphasize His role as the perfect representative of humanity and the one who fully identifies with the struggles and sufferings of His people.

The ethical teachings of Jesus, particularly in the Sermon on the Mount (Matthew 5–7) and the Sermon on the

Plain (Luke 6:17-49), are central to the Synoptic Gospels' portrayal of Him. Jesus teaches about love, mercy, forgiveness, and justice, calling His followers to live according to the values of God's Kingdom. He challenges the religious authorities of His day, offering a radical reinterpretation of the Law and placing love of God and neighbor at the center of His ethical vision.

9.3. Jesus in the Gospel of John

The Gospel of John differs significantly from the Synoptic Gospels in both content and structure. John emphasizes the divinity of Jesus from the very beginning, presenting Him as the pre-existent Word of God who became flesh to reveal God's glory. John's Gospel focuses on Jesus' identity as the incarnate Son of God and His role in offering eternal life to those who believe in Him.

9.3.1. Jesus as the Eternal Word and Divine Son

John opens with the profound theological statement, "In the beginning was the Word, and the Word was with God, and the Word was God" (John 1:1). From the outset, John presents Jesus as the eternal Logos (Word) who was with God in the beginning and who participated in the creation of the world (John 1:3). This high Christology contrasts with the Synoptic Gospels, which begin with Jesus' birth or baptism.

For John, Jesus is not just the Messiah; He is the divine Son of God who reveals the Father. In John 1:14, the incarnation is described in striking terms: "The Word became flesh and made his dwelling among us. We have seen his glory, the glory of the one and only Son, who came from the Father, full of grace and truth." Jesus is portrayed as the unique and divine Son who makes God known to humanity (John 1:18).

Throughout the Gospel, Jesus' divinity is emphasized through His "I AM" statements, which echo the divine name revealed to Moses in the burning bush (Exodus 3:14). In these statements, Jesus identifies Himself with God, saying, for example, "I am the bread of life" (John 6:35), "I am the light of the world" (John 8:12), "I am the good shepherd" (John 10:11), and "I am the resurrection and the life" (John 11:25). These declarations highlight Jesus' divine authority and His role as the source of life and salvation.

9.3.2. Jesus as the Source of Eternal Life

A central theme in John's Gospel is Jesus' role in offering eternal life. While the Synoptic Gospels emphasize the Kingdom of God, John focuses on the gift of eternal life that comes through faith in Jesus. In John 3:16, one of the most famous verses in the Bible, Jesus explains His mission: "For God so loved the world that he gave his one and only Son, that whoever believes in him shall not perish but have eternal life."

For John, eternal life is not just a future reality but something that believers experience in the present through their relationship with Jesus. In John 10:10, Jesus declares, "I have come that they may have life, and have it to the full." This fullness of life is found in knowing God and being united with Christ, who offers spiritual nourishment, guidance, and protection.

John also places a strong emphasis on Jesus' role as the "light of the world" who brings spiritual illumination and reveals the truth about God. In John 8:12, Jesus says, "I am the light of the world. Whoever follows me will never walk in darkness, but will have the light of life." This metaphor of light emphasizes the transformative power of Jesus' presence and the new life He offers to those who believe in Him.

9.3.3. The Signs and Glory of Jesus

In John's Gospel, Jesus performs seven "signs" that reveal His divine identity and point to His glory. These signs, which include turning water into wine (John 2:1-11), healing the blind man (John 9:1-12), and raising Lazarus from the dead (John 11:1-44), are presented as evidence that Jesus is the Son of God. Unlike the Synoptic Gospels, which often downplay or conceal Jesus' miracles, John uses these signs to highlight Jesus' divine authority and His power to bring life, healing, and resurrection.

The theme of Jesus' glory is central to John's portrayal. From the opening prologue, John speaks of Jesus' divine glory, which He shares with the Father (John 1:14). Jesus Himself speaks of His upcoming death as the moment when He will be glorified (John 12:23-24), and the crucifixion is presented not as a moment of defeat but as the ultimate revelation of God's love and power.

9.3.4. Jesus' Relationship with the Father

John's Gospel emphasizes the intimate relationship between Jesus and God the Father. Jesus consistently speaks of His unity with the Father, declaring, "I and the Father are one"

(John 10:30) and "Anyone who has seen me has seen the Father" (John 14:9). This close relationship underlines

Jesus' divine mission as the one who reveals the Father to the world and accomplishes His will.

In the Synoptic Gospels, Jesus' relationship with God is also emphasized, particularly in His prayers and obedience to God's will. However, John's Gospel places an even greater emphasis on this relationship, highlighting the unity of the Father and the Son in their shared mission to bring salvation to humanity.

9.4. Key Differences Between the Synoptic Gospels and John

9.4.1. Chronology and Structure

One of the most noticeable differences between the Synoptic Gospels and John is their chronology and structure. The Synoptics generally follow a similar timeline, focusing on Jesus' Galilean ministry, followed by His journey to Jerusalem and His crucifixion. In contrast, John's Gospel includes several trips to Jerusalem and a different sequence of events.

For example, in the Synoptic Gospels, Jesus cleanses the temple toward the end of His ministry (Matthew 21:12-17, Mark 11:15-19, Luke 19:45-48), whereas in John, this event occurs at the beginning (John 2:13-22). Similarly, John's Gospel does not include certain key elements of the

Synoptics, such as the institution of the Last Supper, but it provides a lengthy farewell discourse (John 13–17) in which Jesus prepares His disciples for His departure and the coming of the Holy Spirit.

9.4.2. Emphasis on Jesus' Divinity

While the Synoptic Gospels emphasize Jesus' role as the Messiah and the Son of Man, John places a much greater emphasis on Jesus' divinity. From the opening verse, John portrays Jesus as the eternal Word who existed with God from the beginning and who is Himself God (John 1:1). The Synoptics, by contrast, gradually reveal Jesus' divine identity through His actions and teachings, leading up to Peter's confession of Jesus as the Messiah (Mark 8:29) and the centurion's recognition of Jesus as the Son of God at the crucifixion (Matthew 27:54, Mark 15:39).

9.4.3. The Focus on Eternal Life

In the Synoptic Gospels, Jesus' primary message centers on the Kingdom of God, and His teachings focus on ethical living, justice, and the coming reign of God. In contrast, John's Gospel focuses more on the concept of eternal life, which is offered through belief in Jesus. While the Synoptics emphasize repentance and preparation for the

Kingdom, John stresses faith in Jesus as the source of eternal life (John 3:16, John 10:10).

9.5. Conclusion

The Synoptic Gospels and the Gospel of John present complementary but distinct portraits of Jesus Christ. The Synoptics focus on Jesus as the Messiah who fulfills Jewish expectations, emphasizes the Kingdom of God, and reveals the ethical and compassionate dimensions of His mission. John, on the other hand, places greater emphasis on Jesus' divinity, His role as the pre-existent Word of God, and the offer of eternal life through faith in Him.

While each Gospel offers a unique perspective, together they provide a rich and multifaceted understanding of Jesus' identity and mission. Through the Synoptic Gospels, believers encounter Jesus as the compassionate teacher and suffering Messiah who calls people to live out the values of God's Kingdom. In John, they encounter Jesus as the divine Son who reveals God's glory and offers eternal life to all who believe. These diverse yet harmonious portraits of Jesus invite believers to experience the fullness of His love, grace, and transformative power.

CHAPTER 10

JESUS IN EARLY CHRISTIAN THOUGHT: PATRISTIC VIEWS ON JESUS DIVINITY AND HUMANITY

10.1. Introduction

The early centuries of Christianity were marked by intense theological reflection on the nature of Jesus Christ. Central to these debates was the question of how to understand Jesus' divinity and humanity, a mystery that lies at the heart of the Christian faith. The early Church Fathers, known as the patristic theologians, played a crucial role in shaping the doctrine of Jesus Christ (Christology) through their writings, sermons, and participation in ecumenical councils. Their reflections helped the Church define its orthodox understanding of Jesus as both fully divine and fully human. This chapter explores the key patristic views on Jesus' divinity and humanity, focusing on the contributions of key figures such as Ignatius of Antioch, Justin Martyr, Athanasius, and the Cappadocian Fathers, and the theological developments that culminated in the ecumenical councils of Nicaea (325 AD) and Chalcedon (451 AD).

10.2. Early Reflections on Jesus' Divinity and Humanity

From its earliest days, the Christian community wrestled with the question of how to reconcile Jesus' humanity with His divinity. The New Testament affirms that Jesus is both the Son of God and the Son of Man, but early Christians sought to understand how these two natures were united in the person of Christ.

10.2.1. Ignatius of Antioch: Jesus as Fully Divine and Fully Human

Ignatius of Antioch, an early Christian bishop and martyr (d. 108 AD), was one of the first Church Fathers to articulate a clear understanding of Jesus' dual nature. In his letters written to various Christian communities while on his way to martyrdom, Ignatius affirmed both the divinity and humanity of Jesus in response to early heresies that either denied Jesus' divinity (such as adoptionism) or downplayed His humanity (such as docetism).

In his letter to the Smyrnaeans, Ignatius emphasizes that Jesus Christ is "truly of the race of David according to the flesh, and the Son of God according to the will and power of God" (Smyrnaeans 1:1). Ignatius' emphasis on the reality of Jesus' humanity is particularly important in light of the docetic heresy, which claimed that Jesus only appeared to be human and did not truly suffer or die. Ignatius insists that Jesus truly experienced suffering, death, and resurrection, affirming that His humanity was as real as His divinity.

Ignatius' reflections on Jesus set the stage for later theological developments, emphasizing that the fullness of both divinity and humanity are essential to understanding Jesus' person and work.

10.2.2. Justin Martyr: Jesus as the Logos

Justin Martyr (100–165 AD), one of the earliest Christian apologists, played a key role in developing a

Christology that emphasized Jesus as the pre-existent divine Logos (Word). Drawing on the prologue of the Gospel of John, Justin described Jesus as the Logos through whom God created the world and who became incarnate for the salvation of humanity.

In his First Apology, Justin explains that Jesus, the Logos, is both distinct from the Father and yet fully divine: "We have been taught that Christ is the first-born of God, and we have declared that he is the Word, of whom every race of men were partakers" (First Apology, 46). Justin's use of Greek philosophical categories to explain the relationship between the Father and the Son helped to lay the foundation for later discussions on the Trinity and the nature of Christ.

Justin also emphasized the full humanity of Jesus, arguing that the Logos took on human flesh and experienced the same sufferings as other human beings. By doing so, Jesus was able to serve as the mediator between God and humanity. Justin's writings highlight the early Church's commitment to affirming both the divinity and humanity of Jesus as essential to His role as Savior.

10.3. The Arian Controversy and the Council of Nicaea

As Christianity spread throughout the Roman Empire, debates about Jesus' divinity and humanity became more pronounced, leading to the rise of various Christological heresies. One of the most significant of these was Arianism, a theological position that denied the full divinity of Jesus. The Arian controversy, which dominated the early fourth century, ultimately led to the convening of the First Ecumenical Council at Nicaea in 325 AD.

10.3.1. Arius and the Denial of Christ's Full Divinity

Arius, a priest from Alexandria, taught that Jesus was not co-eternal with God the Father but was a created being, subordinate to the Father. According to Arius, Jesus was the highest of all created beings, but He was not of the same substance (homoousios) as the Father. Arius' teaching raised serious concerns among many early Christians, who saw it as a denial of Jesus' true divinity and, therefore, His ability to save humanity.

Arius' views led to a major theological crisis, as it called into question the very nature of the Christian faith. If Jesus was not fully divine, how could He be worshiped as Lord? How could He truly reconcile humanity to God if He was Himself a created being?

10.3.2. Athanasius and the Defense of Christ's Divinity

Athanasius, the bishop of Alexandria, emerged as the most vocal opponent of Arianism. In his writings, particularly On the Incarnation, Athanasius argued that only a fully divine Christ could bring salvation. He insisted that Jesus, the Son of God, is of the same substance (homoousios) as the Father, meaning that He shares the same divine essence and is co-eternal with the Father.

Athanasius emphasized the importance of the Incarnation for salvation, arguing that Jesus had to be fully divine in order to defeat sin and death. "The Word was made man so that we might be made divine," Athanasius wrote, encapsulating his belief that the divine nature of Christ is what enables humanity to be restored to a right relationship with God.

10.3.3. The Council of Nicaea and the Nicene Creed

In response to the Arian controversy, Emperor Constantine convened the First Council of Nicaea in 325 AD. The council brought together bishops from across the Christian world to settle the debate over Jesus' divinity. Under the leadership of figures like Athanasius, the council condemned Arianism and affirmed that Jesus is "begotten, not made, being of one substance (homoousios) with the Father." This declaration became the basis for the Nicene Creed, which remains one of the foundational statements of Christian belief.

The Nicene Creed affirmed both the full divinity and full humanity of Jesus, stating that He is "true God from true God" who "for us and for our salvation came down from heaven and was incarnate by the Holy Spirit and the Virgin Mary, and was made man." This creed laid the groundwork for orthodox Christology and set the stage for future theological debates about the nature of Christ.

10.4. The Council of Chalcedon and the Definition of Christ's Two Natures

The resolution of the Arian controversy did not end the debates over Jesus' divinity and humanity. In the years following Nicaea, new controversies arose, particularly concerning how Jesus' divine and human natures were related. This led to the Council of Chalcedon in 451 AD, which produced one of the most definitive statements on Christology in Christian history.

10.4.1. The Nestorian Controversy

One of the key debates leading up to Chalcedon was the Nestorian controversy, which centered on the teachings of Nestorius, the Patriarch of Constantinople. Nestorius emphasized the distinction between Christ's divine and human natures to the point that it seemed as though he was dividing Christ into two persons—one divine and one human. This raised concerns that Nestorius' teachings undermined the unity of Christ's person and the effectiveness of His redemptive work.

The Council of Ephesus in 431 AD condemned Nestorianism and affirmed that Christ is one person with two natures—divine and human—that are united in a single person. This laid the groundwork for the Chalcedonian definition that would follow two decades later.

10.4.2. The Chalcedonian Definition

The Council of Chalcedon, convened in 451 AD, sought to clarify the relationship between Christ's divine and human natures. The council produced the Chalcedonian Definition, which affirmed that Jesus Christ is "one and the same Son, our Lord Jesus Christ, perfect in divinity and perfect in humanity, truly God and truly man... acknowledged in two natures, without confusion, without change, without division, without separation."

This definition rejected both Nestorianism (which divided Christ into two persons) and Monophysitism (which claimed that Christ had only one nature after the Incarnation). Instead, it upheld the belief that Christ is one person with two distinct but united natures—fully divine and fully human. The Chalcedonian Definition became the standard of orthodox Christology and remains foundational to Christian belief about the nature of Christ.

10.5. The Cappadocian Fathers and the Development of Trinitarian and Christological Thought

The Cappadocian Fathers—Basil the Great, Gregory of Nyssa, and Gregory of Nazianzus—played a significant role in the development of early Christian thought, particularly in relation to the doctrine of the Trinity and Christology. Their contributions helped to clarify the Church's understanding of the relationship between the Father,

Son, and Holy Spirit, as well as the nature of Jesus Christ.

10.5.1. Basil the Great and Gregory of Nyssa

Basil the Great (330–379 AD) and his brother Gregory of Nyssa (335–395 AD) were instrumental in defending the Nicene Creed and articulating the doctrine of the Trinity. They emphasized the unity of the divine essence shared by the Father, Son, and Holy Spirit, while also affirming the distinct persons within the Godhead.

In terms of Christology, Basil and Gregory defended the full divinity of Christ and insisted that His humanity did not diminish His divinity. Gregory of Nyssa, in particular, emphasized the mystery of the Incarnation, arguing that Christ's divine and human natures were united in a way that preserved both natures without confusion or separation.

10.5.2. Gregory of Nazianzus: "What is not assumed is not healed"

Gregory of Nazianzus (329–390 AD) is perhaps best known for his contribution to Christological thought through his famous statement, "What is not assumed is not healed." Gregory argued that for humanity to be fully redeemed, Christ had to assume the fullness of human nature—body, soul, and spirit. This meant that Jesus had to be fully human in every respect, not merely appearing human or possessing a limited form of humanity.

Gregory's insights were crucial in affirming that Jesus' full humanity was essential to the work of salvation. His writings helped to shape the Church's understanding of the Incarnation and the significance of Christ's dual nature.

10.6. Conclusion

The early Christian reflection on Jesus' divinity and humanity was marked by intense theological debate and development. The patristic theologians, through their writings and participation in councils, helped the Church navigate these complex questions and articulate a coherent Christology. From the early affirmations of Jesus as both fully divine and fully human in the writings of Ignatius of Antioch and Justin Martyr, to the theological battles over Arianism and Nestorianism, the Church ultimately arrived at the Chalcedonian Definition, which remains the cornerstone of orthodox Christian belief about the person of Christ.

The work of the early Church Fathers continues to shape Christian theology today, offering profound insights into the mystery of the Incarnation and the redemptive work of Jesus Christ. By affirming both Jesus' divinity and humanity, the early Church safeguarded the essential truths of the Christian faith, ensuring that believers could worship Christ as both Lord and Savior, fully God and fully man.

The Development of Christology in Early Christian Writings

10.1. Introduction

The development of Christology—the study of the person and work of Jesus Christ—was one of the central theological endeavors of the early Christian Church. As Christianity spread throughout the Roman Empire, early Christian thinkers and leaders grappled with the question of who Jesus was in relation to God and humanity. How could Jesus be both divine and human? How did His death and resurrection accomplish salvation? These questions led to a rich body of early Christian writings that shaped the Church's understanding of Jesus Christ. This chapter explores the key developments in Christology from the Apostolic Fathers to the great ecumenical councils, examining how early Christian writers articulated their beliefs about Jesus' divinity, humanity, and role as Savior.

10.2. Early Christological Reflections: The Apostolic Fathers

The earliest Christian writings after the New Testament come from the Apostolic Fathers, who were leaders in the early Church and were either direct disciples of the Apostles or closely connected to them. Their writings reflect the foundational elements of Christology that emerged in the first century and were meant to defend the faith, correct errors, and instruct believers.

10.2.1. Ignatius of Antioch: Jesus as Fully Divine and Fully Human

One of the most important early Christian writers was Ignatius of Antioch (d. 108 AD), a bishop and martyr who wrote several letters on his way to Rome, where he was executed. Ignatius' writings reveal a deep concern with affirming both the divinity and humanity of Jesus, particularly in response to early heresies such as docetism, which claimed that Jesus only appeared to be human.

In his letter to the Ephesians, Ignatius writes, "There is one physician, who is both flesh and spirit, born and unborn, God in man, true life in death, both of Mary and of God, first passible and then impassible, Jesus Christ our Lord" (Ephesians 7:2). Here, Ignatius affirms the reality of Jesus' incarnation, His full divinity, and His full humanity. For Ignatius, Jesus' humanity is essential to His redemptive work, as only by becoming truly human could He suffer and die for the sins of the world.

10.2.2. The Christology of the Didache and Clement of Rome

Other early Christian writings, such as the Didache (a first-century Christian teaching manual) and the letters of Clement of Rome, also reflect an emerging Christology. The Didache emphasizes Jesus as the expected Messiah and the ethical teachings of Jesus, while Clement's letters stress Jesus' role as the high priest and mediator who reconciles humanity to God.

These writings, while not highly speculative, lay the groundwork for later theological reflection by affirming Jesus as the divine Son of God and the Savior of humanity. They also reveal an early understanding of Jesus' role as the one who inaugurates God's kingdom and provides the model for Christian living.

10.3. Apologists and the Logos Christology: Justin Martyr and Irenaeus

As Christianity expanded in the second century, it faced increasing scrutiny and opposition from both the Roman authorities and various philosophical schools. In response, Christian apologists sought to defend the faith, often drawing on philosophical categories to explain Jesus' divinity and His relationship to God. One of the most significant developments during this period was the emergence of Logos Christology, which emphasized Jesus as the divine Logos (Word) who existed from eternity and became incarnate to bring salvation.

10.3.1. Justin Martyr: Jesus as the Logos

Justin Martyr (100–165 AD) was one of the earliest and most influential Christian apologists. He sought to explain the Christian faith to the pagan world, using the language of Greek philosophy to articulate the Church's beliefs. In his First Apology and Dialogue with Trypho, Justin presents Jesus as the divine Logos, the rational principle through which God created the world and who took on human flesh for the sake of humanity.

Justin's Logos Christology is rooted in the prologue of the Gospel of John, where Jesus is described as the Word (Logos) who "was with God" and "was God" (John 1:1). For Justin, the Logos is not a created being but is fully divine and eternally pre-existent with the Father. At the same time, Justin emphasizes the full humanity of Jesus, particularly in response to docetic views that denied Jesus' human nature.

In his dialogue with the Jewish philosopher Trypho, Justin argues that the Logos became incarnate to fulfill the Old Testament prophecies and bring salvation to both Jews and Gentiles. By presenting Jesus as the Logos, Justin helped to bridge the gap between Jewish messianic expectations and Greek philosophical thought, laying the foundation for later Christological developments.

10.3.2. Irenaeus of Lyons: Recapitulation and the Role of the Incarnation

Irenaeus of Lyons (130–202 AD) was another key figure in the development of early Christology. Writing in response to Gnostic teachings that claimed Jesus was a lesser divine being and denied the value of the material world, Irenaeus emphasized the importance of Jesus' incarnation and His role as the one who "recapitulates" humanity.

In his work Against Heresies, Irenaeus explains that Jesus, as the new Adam, recapitulates or sums up all of human history. By becoming fully human, Jesus reverses the disobedience of Adam and restores humanity's relationship with God. Irenaeus famously writes, "He became what we are, that He might bring us to be even what He is Himself" (Against Heresies 5. Preface).

For Irenaeus, the incarnation is not merely a means to an end (i.e., the cross), but an essential part of God's redemptive plan. Jesus' humanity is the key to the healing of human nature, and His divinity is what allows Him to effect this transformation. This idea of recapitulation would become a central theme in later theological discussions on the nature of Christ's work.

10.4. The Arian Controversy and the Nicene Response

By the early fourth century, debates over Jesus' divinity reached a critical point with the rise of Arianism, a theological movement that denied the full divinity of Christ. The Arian controversy led to the First Council of Nicaea (325 AD), where the Church definitively rejected Arianism and articulated a clear understanding of Jesus' divine nature.

10.4.1. Arius and the Denial of Jesus' Divinity

Arius, a priest from Alexandria, taught that Jesus was not co-eternal with God the Father but was a created being, subordinate to the Father. Arius argued that Jesus, while divine in some sense, was not of the same essence (homoousios) as the Father but was instead of a similar essence (homoiousios). This view gained significant support and led to a major theological crisis in the Church.

Arius' Christology raised serious questions about the nature of salvation and worship. If Jesus was a created being, could He truly bring salvation to humanity? Could He be worshiped as God? These questions led to intense debates throughout the Christian world.

10.4.2. The Council of Nicaea and the Nicene Creed

The First Council of Nicaea, convened by Emperor Constantine in 325 AD, brought together bishops from across the Christian world to settle the Arian controversy. Led by figures such as Athanasius of Alexandria, the council condemned Arianism and affirmed that Jesus is "begotten, not made, being of one substance (homoousios) with the Father."

The resulting Nicene Creed became one of the most important statements of Christian belief, affirming that Jesus is fully divine and co-eternal with the Father. The creed declared that Jesus is "true God from true God" and that His incarnation, death, and resurrection are central to God's plan of salvation.

The Council of Nicaea marked a turning point in the development of Christology, as it solidified the Church's commitment to the belief that Jesus is both fully God and fully human. However, debates over the precise nature of Christ's divinity and humanity would continue in the following centuries.

10.5. The Christological Controversies of the Fourth and Fifth Centuries

Following the Council of Nicaea, further theological debates arose concerning how to understand the relationship between Jesus' divine and human natures. These debates culminated in the ecumenical councils of Ephesus (431 AD) and Chalcedon (451 AD), where the Church defined its Christology in response to heresies such as Nestorianism and Monophysitism.

10.5.1. Nestorianism and the Council of Ephesus

Nestorius, the Patriarch of Constantinople, taught that Jesus had two separate natures—one divine and one human—and that these natures were not fully united in one person. Nestorius rejected the use of the term Theotokos (God-bearer) for Mary, arguing that she only gave birth to Christ's human nature, not His divine nature.

The Council of Ephesus in 431 AD condemned Nestorianism and affirmed that Jesus is one person with two natures, fully divine and fully human, united in a single person. The council also affirmed that Mary could rightly be called Theotokos, as she bore the one person of Jesus Christ, who is both God and man.

10.5.2. The Chalcedonian Definition

The Council of Chalcedon in 451 AD was convened to address the rise of Monophysitism, which claimed that Jesus had only one nature after the Incarnation, with His human nature being absorbed into His divine nature. The council rejected Monophysitism and issued the Chalcedonian Definition, which declared that Jesus is "one and the same Son, our Lord Jesus Christ, perfect in divinity and perfect in humanity, truly God and truly man... acknowledged in two natures, without confusion, without change, without division, without separation."

The Chalcedonian Definition became the standard for orthodox Christology, affirming that Jesus' divine and human natures are united in one person and that both natures retain their full integrity. This formulation allowed the Church to uphold the mystery of the Incarnation while safeguarding the essential truths of Jesus' divinity and humanity.

10.6. Conclusion

The development of Christology in early Christian writings was a complex and dynamic process, shaped by theological debates, heresies, and councils. From the early reflections of the Apostolic Fathers to the theological debates of the fourth and fifth centuries, the Church gradually articulated a clearer understanding of Jesus as both fully divine and fully human. The emergence of Logos Christology, the response to Arianism, and the definitions provided by the councils of Nicaea, Ephesus, and Chalcedon all played a crucial role in shaping the Church's Christological doctrine.

The early Church's commitment to affirming both the divinity and humanity of Jesus was not merely a theoretical exercise; it was essential to understanding the nature of salvation and the Christian faith. By upholding the belief that Jesus is both God and man, the early Church laid the foundation for Christian theology, ensuring that the mystery of the Incarnation would continue to be a source of worship, reflection, and transformation for generations to come.

Influences of Early Heresies on the Understanding of Jesus

10.1. Introduction

The early Christian Church's understanding of Jesus Christ was shaped not only by faithful theological reflection but also by the challenges posed by various heresies. These early heresies questioned and sometimes distorted key aspects of Christian belief about Jesus' identity, particularly His divinity, humanity, and role in salvation. However, in responding to these heresies, the Church was forced to clarify, articulate, and refine its Christology. This chapter explores how early heresies such as docetism, Gnosticism, Arianism, Nestorianism, and Monophysitism influenced the development of orthodox Christology and the Church's understanding of Jesus as both fully divine and fully human.

10.2. Docetism: Challenging Jesus' Humanity

One of the earliest heresies to confront the Christian Church was docetism, which emerged in the first and second centuries. Docetism denied the reality of Jesus' human nature, claiming instead that Jesus only appeared to be human. The term "docetism" comes from the Greek word dokein, meaning "to seem." According to docetic thought, Jesus' physical body was an illusion, and His sufferings and death on the cross were not real.

10.2.1. Origins and Beliefs

Docetism arose from a dualistic worldview that saw the material world as inherently corrupt or evil, and thus incompatible with divine perfection. For docetists, it was unthinkable that the divine Son of God could truly take on human flesh, suffer, and die. This view was influenced by early forms of Gnosticism, which held that salvation came through secret knowledge (gnosis) rather than through the incarnation and death of Christ.

10.2.2. Response to Docetism

The early Church strongly rejected docetism because it undermined the core Christian belief in the incarnation and the redemptive value of Jesus' suffering and death. Ignatius of Antioch, writing in the early second century, was one of the most vocal opponents of docetism. In his letter to the Smyrnaeans, Ignatius insisted on the reality of Jesus' humanity and His physical suffering, stating, "He was truly born, ate and drank, was truly persecuted under Pontius Pilate, was truly crucified and died, in the sight of beings in heaven, on earth, and under the earth" (Smyrnaeans 2:1).

The Church's response to docetism helped solidify the belief in Jesus' full humanity. By affirming that Jesus was both truly God and truly human, the early Christians emphasized the importance of the incarnation for salvation. If Jesus had not truly taken on human flesh, He could not have truly experienced death and resurrection, which are essential to the Christian understanding of redemption.

10.3. Gnosticism: Distorting the Incarnation

Gnosticism was another significant early heresy that influenced Christian thought about Jesus. Gnosticism was not a single, unified system but a diverse movement that combined elements of Greek philosophy, mysticism, and esoteric knowledge. Gnostic teachings often drew a sharp distinction between the spiritual and material worlds, viewing the material world as the creation of a lesser, evil god (the Demiurge) and the spiritual realm as the domain of the true God.

10.3.1. Gnostic Christology

In Gnostic thought, Jesus was often seen as a purely spiritual being who came to deliver secret knowledge to help humanity escape the material world and return to the divine realm. Gnostic texts, such as those found in the Nag Hammadi library, often depict Jesus as a revealer of hidden truths rather than as a savior who redeems humanity through His death and resurrection.

One common Gnostic belief was that Jesus' physical body was either an illusion (as in docetism) or that the divine Christ inhabited the human Jesus temporarily, departing before His crucifixion. This idea, known as Christological dualism, was based on the belief that the divine Christ could not truly suffer or die in the corrupt material world.

10.3.2. Irenaeus and the Defense of the Incarnation

The early Church strongly opposed Gnostic teachings, particularly because they denied the true significance of the incarnation. Irenaeus of Lyons (130–202 AD) was one of the most important early Christian writers to combat Gnosticism. In his work Against Heresies, Irenaeus argued that Jesus' incarnation, death, and resurrection were central to God's plan for the redemption of humanity. He insisted that Jesus was both fully divine and fully human, and that His death on the cross was a real, historical event that brought about the salvation of humanity.

Irenaeus developed the idea of recapitulation, arguing that Jesus, as the new Adam, recapitulated or "summed up" the history of humanity in Himself. By becoming fully human, Jesus reversed the disobedience of Adam and restored humanity's relationship with God. Irenaeus' emphasis on the incarnation as the means of salvation was a direct response to Gnostic claims that minimized or denied Jesus' humanity.

10.4. Arianism: Denying Jesus' Full Divinity

The most significant Christological controversy of the early Church was the rise of Arianism in the early fourth century. Arianism, named after its founder Arius, a priest from Alexandria, denied the full divinity of Jesus Christ. This heresy became a major theological crisis for the Church and ultimately led to the convening of the First Council of Nicaea in 325 AD.

10.4.1. Arian Beliefs

Arius taught that Jesus, while divine, was a created being and not co-eternal with God the Father. According to Arius, Jesus was the highest of all created beings, but He was not of the same essence (homoousios) as the Father. Arius famously declared, "There was a time when the Son was not," implying that Jesus had a beginning in time and was therefore subordinate to the Father. For Arians, Jesus was not equal to the Father in His divinity but was instead a distinct, lesser being.

10.4.2. The Nicene Response

Arianism posed a serious threat to the Church's understanding of Jesus because it called into question His ability to fully reveal God and provide salvation. If Jesus were merely a created being, He could not be worshiped as God, and His death and resurrection would lose their saving power. The response to Arianism came at the First Council of Nicaea, where bishops from across the Christian world gathered to address the controversy.

Led by figures such as Athanasius of Alexandria, the council condemned Arianism and affirmed that Jesus is "begotten, not made, being of one substance (homoousios) with the Father." The resulting Nicene Creed declared that Jesus is "true God from true God," co-eternal with the Father, and that His incarnation, death, and resurrection are central to the Christian faith.

The Council of Nicaea was a turning point in the development of Christology. By affirming that Jesus is fully divine and of the same essence as the Father, the Church safeguarded the doctrine of the Trinity and preserved the belief that Jesus' redemptive work was fully efficacious because of His divine nature.

10.5. Nestorianism: Dividing Christ's Natures

In the early fifth century, a new Christological controversy arose with the teachings of Nestorius, the Patriarch of Constantinople. Nestorianism emphasized the distinction between Jesus' divine and human natures to such an extent that it seemed to divide Christ into two persons—one divine and one human. This view was rejected by the Church because it undermined the unity of Christ's person.

10.5.1. Nestorius and the Title "Theotokos"

Nestorius is best known for his objection to the use of the title Theotokos ("God-bearer") for Mary, the mother of Jesus. Nestorius argued that Mary should be called Christotokos ("Christ-bearer") instead, claiming that she gave birth to Jesus' human nature, not His divine nature. Nestorius' teachings suggested that Jesus' divine and human natures were separate, with the divine nature residing in the human Jesus like in a temple, rather than being fully united in one person.

10.5.2. The Council of Ephesus and the Reaffirmation of Christ's Unity

The Council of Ephesus in 431 AD condemned Nestorianism and affirmed that Jesus is one person with two distinct but united natures—divine and human. The council also affirmed that Mary could rightly be called Theotokos, as she bore the one person of Jesus Christ, who is both fully God and fully human.

The rejection of Nestorianism was crucial for the Church's Christology because it preserved the belief that Jesus is one person with two natures that are fully united. This unity is essential for understanding how Jesus' divine nature works in conjunction with His human nature to bring about salvation. If the natures were too sharply divided, it would call into question the integrity of the incarnation and Jesus' ability to reconcile humanity to God.

10.6. Monophysitism: Denying Christ's Two Natures

In response to Nestorianism, another heresy emerged known as Monophysitism. Monophysitism, from the Greek words mono (one) and physis (nature), taught that Jesus had only one nature after the incarnation. According to Monophysites, Jesus' divine nature absorbed His human nature, resulting in a single, divine nature. This view was an overreaction to Nestorianism and was ultimately rejected by the Church.

10.6.1. Eutychianism and the Rise of Monophysitism

Eutyches, a monk from Constantinople, was one of the leading proponents of Monophysitism. He taught that after the incarnation, Jesus' human nature was "dissolved" into His divine nature, much like a drop of water is absorbed into the sea. This view denied the full humanity of Jesus, effectively reducing His human nature to something that was no longer operative.

10.6.2. The Council of Chalcedon and the Definition of Two Natures

The Church responded to Monophysitism at the Council of Chalcedon in 451 AD. The council affirmed that Jesus is "one person in two natures," fully divine and fully human, without confusion, change, division, or separation. This statement, known as the Chalcedonian Definition, became the standard for orthodox Christology and remains one of the most important Christological formulations in Christian history.

By affirming that Jesus' two natures—divine and human—are fully united in one person, the Council of Chalcedon preserved the mystery of the incarnation. Jesus is both fully God and fully man, and His two natures work together in perfect harmony to bring about the salvation of humanity.

10.7. Conclusion

he early heresies that challenged the Church's understanding of Jesus played a significant role in shaping the development of Christology. From docetism and Gnosticism, which denied Jesus' humanity, to Arianism, which denied His full divinity, and Nestorianism and Monophysitism, which distorted the relationship between His two natures, each heresy forced the Church to confront key theological questions and clarify its beliefs.

Through the writings of early Church Fathers like Ignatius, Irenaeus, and Athanasius, and through the decisions of the ecumenical councils, the Church ultimately articulated a clear and coherent Christology. The affirmation that Jesus is both fully divine and fully human, united in one person, remains the cornerstone of Christian belief. In responding to early heresies, the Church preserved the essential truths of the incarnation and ensured that the mystery of Jesus' person and work would continue to be the foundation of Christian faith and worship for centuries to come.

CONTEMPORARY THEOLOGICAL PERSPECTIVES: MODERN INTERPRETATIONS OF JESUS IN DIFFERENT THEOLOGICAL FRAMEWORKS

11.1. Introduction

The figure of Jesus Christ continues to be central to Christian theology, but modern and contemporary theological frameworks have introduced new interpretations and understandings of Jesus' identity, significance, and role in the world. These diverse perspectives reflect the evolving contexts of theology, shaped by historical events, cultural shifts, philosophical developments, and global challenges. Contemporary interpretations of Jesus often engage with issues such as liberation, justice, cultural identity, postcolonialism, and interfaith dialogue. This chapter explores key modern interpretations of Jesus in various theological frameworks, including liberation theology, feminist theology, black theology, postcolonial theology, and interreligious Christology, highlighting how these perspectives offer fresh insights into the meaning of Jesus for today's world.

11.2. Liberation Theology: Jesus as the Liberator

One of the most influential contemporary theological frameworks is liberation theology, which emerged in Latin America in the 20th century. Liberation theology views Jesus primarily as a liberator, emphasizing His concern for the poor, the oppressed, and the marginalized. It interprets the Christian faith through the lens of social justice, calling for political and economic liberation as an essential expression of Christian discipleship.

11.2.1. Origins and Key Thinkers

Liberation theology began in the 1960s and 1970s in the context of widespread poverty and social injustice in Latin America. It was influenced by Marxist critiques of capitalism and sought to bring the Christian faith into dialogue with the struggles of the oppressed. Key figures in this movement include Gustavo Gutiérrez, author of A Theology of Liberation, Leonardo Boff, and Jon Sobrino. These theologians called for the Church to prioritize the needs of the poor and to see the Gospel as a call to transform unjust social structures.

11.2.2. Jesus as the Liberator of the Oppressed

In liberation theology, Jesus is seen as the liberator who identifies with the poor and oppressed. His life and ministry are interpreted as a radical challenge to systems of domination and exploitation. The Gospel stories of Jesus healing the sick, feeding the hungry, and proclaiming the Kingdom of God are viewed as concrete actions of liberation that confront social and political oppression.

Liberation theologians emphasize that Jesus' crucifixion was a political act—He was executed by the Roman Empire as a threat to the established order. His resurrection, therefore, is seen not only as a victory over death but also as a sign of God's commitment to liberating humanity from all forms of oppression.

Jon Sobrino, for example, describes Jesus as "the crucified people," reflecting the idea that Jesus' suffering on the cross is mirrored in the suffering of the oppressed. Jesus' resurrection offers hope and empowerment for the marginalized, showing that God's love is on the side of the poor.

11.2.3. Implications for Christian Discipleship

Liberation theology emphasizes that following Jesus means actively participating in the struggle for justice. The concept of the "preferential option for the poor" is central to this theology, calling Christians to prioritize the needs and concerns of the poor and marginalized in their spiritual and social lives. Liberation theologians argue that the Kingdom of God is not merely a future reality but something that must be actively realized through justice, solidarity, and resistance to oppression.

11.3. Feminist Theology: Jesus and Gender Justice

Feminist theology seeks to reinterpret Christian theology from the perspective of women's experiences and struggles for gender justice. Feminist theologians critique traditional portrayals of Jesus and the Church's teachings on gender, often highlighting the ways in which patriarchal structures have distorted the message of the Gospel.

11.3.1. Jesus as the Champion of Women

Feminist theologians, such as Rosemary Radford Ruether and Elizabeth A. Johnson, emphasize that Jesus' ministry included a radical challenge to the patriarchal norms of His time. In the Gospels, Jesus is shown interacting with women in ways that break social and cultural barriers. He speaks with women, heals them, and includes them as followers and disciples, even in contexts where women were marginalized or excluded from religious leadership.

For feminist theologians, Jesus' inclusion of women as part of His community of followers is a model for gender equality within the Church. Jesus' actions demonstrate that He was committed to challenging oppressive gender norms and restoring the full dignity and humanity of women.

11.3.2. Reinterpreting the Maleness of Jesus

Feminist theology often grapples with the issue of Jesus' maleness and its implications for women's experiences in the Church. Some feminist theologians argue that while Jesus was historically male, His message and mission transcend gender. Elizabeth A. Johnson, in her book She Who Is, argues that Jesus' maleness should not be used to justify male-dominated leadership in the Church. Instead, the focus should be on His message of liberation and inclusion, which applies to all people, regardless of gender.

Other feminist theologians call for a reimagining of divine imagery to include feminine aspects. They argue that limiting God to exclusively male imagery reinforces patriarchal power structures. Feminist theologians advocate for the use of inclusive language and imagery in worship and theology, reflecting the belief that both men and women are created in the image of God.

11.3.3. Jesus and the Struggle for Gender Justice

Feminist theologians emphasize that Jesus' teachings about love, justice, and equality have direct implications for the struggle for gender justice. Following Jesus means working to dismantle systems of patriarchy and promoting the full inclusion and participation of women in all areas of life, including the Church. Feminist theology calls for a reformation of Christian theology and practice to better reflect the liberating message of Jesus for all people, regardless of gender.

11.4. Black Theology: Jesus and the Struggle for Racial Justice

Black theology, which emerged in the United States during the Civil Rights Movement, focuses on the experience of African Americans and the struggle for racial justice. It views Jesus as a liberator who identifies with the oppressed and stands against racial injustice. Black theology critiques the ways in which traditional Christian theology has been complicit in systems of racial oppression and seeks to reclaim Jesus as a figure of resistance and empowerment for Black communities.

11.4.1. The Origins of Black Theology

Black theology developed in the 1960s and 1970s in the context of the African American struggle for civil rights and against systemic racism. Influenced by the broader liberation theology movement and the writings of Black intellectuals such as James H. Cone, Black theology articulated a distinctly Christian response to the realities of racism in America.

Cone's seminal work, Black Theology and Black Power, argues that Jesus is a figure of liberation who stands with the oppressed, and in the context of the United States, this means that Jesus stands with Black people against white supremacy. Cone famously stated, "Jesus is Black," meaning that Jesus identifies with the suffering of African Americans and all people of color who face racial injustice.

11.4.2. Jesus as the Liberator from Racial Oppression

In Black theology, Jesus is portrayed as the ultimate liberator, not only from sin but also from racial oppression. His life, death, and resurrection are seen as God's act of solidarity with the oppressed. For Black theologians, the cross is a symbol of both suffering and resistance, and Jesus' crucifixion represents God's identification with those who are marginalized and oppressed by racist systems.

Jesus' resurrection, according to Black theology, symbolizes the victory of life and liberation over the forces of death and oppression. The hope of resurrection empowers Black communities to continue the struggle for justice, freedom, and equality, even in the face of ongoing racial discrimination and violence.

11.4.3. Black Theology and the Call for Justice

Black theology calls for an active engagement in the fight for racial justice as a central expression of Christian faith. This theological framework critiques the ways in which traditional Christianity has often been complicit in the perpetuation of racism and challenges the Church to take a stand against all forms of racial injustice. In this sense, following Jesus means participating in the struggle for racial equality and the dismantling of systems of oppression.

11.5. Postcolonial Theology: Jesus and the Colonial Legacy

Postcolonial theology examines how the legacy of colonialism has shaped Christian theology and seeks to reinterpret the message of Jesus in ways that challenge colonial power structures. This theological framework engages with the experiences of people in formerly colonized regions, particularly in Africa, Asia, and Latin America, and critiques the ways in which Christianity has been used to justify imperialism and oppression.

11.5.1. Jesus and Colonialism

In postcolonial theology, Jesus is often portrayed as a figure who stands against empire and colonial domination. The historical context of Jesus' life under Roman occupation is seen as a parallel to the experiences of colonized peoples. Jesus' message of the Kingdom of God is interpreted as a radical challenge to the imperial powers of His time, and His crucifixion is seen as a consequence of His resistance to empire.

Postcolonial theologians, such as Kwok Pui-lan and R. S. Sugirtharajah, argue that Western Christianity often distorted the message of Jesus by aligning itself with colonial powers and justifying the subjugation of indigenous peoples. Postcolonial theology seeks to recover the liberating message of Jesus and reinterpret it in ways that empower marginalized communities in postcolonial contexts.

11.5.2. Jesus as a Figure of Decolonization

Postcolonial theology emphasizes that Jesus' message calls for the decolonization of theology and practice. This means rejecting the Eurocentric interpretations of Christianity that were often used to justify colonial rule and instead embracing a theology that affirms the dignity and agency of colonized peoples.

Jesus is seen as a figure who identifies with the oppressed and calls for the dismantling of systems of exploitation and domination. His teachings about justice, mercy, and love are interpreted as a challenge to both the colonial powers of the past and the ongoing effects of neocolonialism in the present.

11.5.3. Reimagining Jesus in Postcolonial Contexts

Postcolonial theologians emphasize the importance of reimagining Jesus in ways that resonate with the cultural, social, and political realities of postcolonial societies. This involves reinterpreting the Gospel in ways that affirm the identity and dignity of indigenous peoples and challenge the lingering effects of colonialism, such as economic inequality, cultural erasure, and political oppression.

11.6. Interreligious Christology: Jesus in Dialogue with Other Religions

In the increasingly pluralistic world of the 21st century, interreligious Christology seeks to reinterpret Jesus in dialogue with other religious traditions. This theological framework engages with the question of how Jesus is understood in the context of diverse faiths and what His significance might be for people of other religious backgrounds.

11.6.1. Jesus and Religious Pluralism

Interreligious Christology is concerned with how Christians understand the uniqueness of Jesus in a world where multiple religious traditions offer different paths to the divine. Theologians such as Paul Knitter and John Hick have explored ways of understanding Jesus that allow for meaningful dialogue between Christianity and other faiths while affirming the distinctiveness of Jesus within the Christian tradition.

For some interreligious theologians, Jesus is seen as a unique but not exclusive revelation of God. In this view, Jesus reveals God's love and salvation, but other religious traditions may also offer valid paths to the divine. This approach seeks to balance the Christian claim that Jesus is the way, the truth, and the life (John 14:6) with the recognition that God is at work in all cultures and religions.

11.6.2. Jesus as a Universal Savior

Some interreligious theologians emphasize the idea of Jesus as a universal Savior who transcends the boundaries of any one religious tradition. This view sees Jesus not only as the fulfillment of Christian hopes but also as a figure who can speak to the deepest spiritual aspirations of people from all religious backgrounds.

In dialogue with Buddhism, for example, Jesus is sometimes interpreted as a bodhisattva figure—one who, out of compassion, seeks the liberation of all beings from suffering. In dialogue with Islam, Jesus is recognized as a prophet who plays an important role in the spiritual history of humanity, even as Christians affirm His unique status as the Son of God.

11.6.3. Theological Challenges and Opportunities

Interreligious Christology faces the challenge of maintaining the uniqueness of Jesus while remaining open to dialogue with other religious traditions. Some theologians argue that the Christian claim about Jesus' divinity and salvific role must be upheld, while others advocate for a more inclusive approach that acknowledges the possibility of multiple paths to God.

This theological framework offers opportunities for Christians to engage deeply with the beliefs of others while exploring how Jesus' message of love, compassion, and reconciliation can speak to the diverse religious landscape of the modern world.

11.7. Conclusion

Contemporary theological perspectives on Jesus reflect the rich diversity of modern thought and the complex challenges of interpreting the Gospel in new and evolving contexts. Whether seen as a liberator of the oppressed, a champion of gender justice, a symbol of racial liberation, or a figure of decolonization, Jesus continues to inspire and challenge theologians and believers alike. These modern interpretations invite Christians to engage with Jesus' message in ways that address the pressing issues of justice, inclusion, and reconciliation in the contemporary world.

By engaging with different theological frameworks—liberation, feminist, black, postcolonial, and interreligious—the contemporary Church is able to explore new dimensions of Jesus' identity and significance, offering fresh insights into the ongoing relevance of His life, death, and resurrection for the modern world. These diverse perspectives underscore the richness of the Christian tradition and the enduring power of Jesus' message to transform individuals and societies across time and cultures.

Feminist, Liberation, and Post-Colonial Perspectives on Jesus

11.1. Introduction

In the modern era, feminist, liberation, and post-colonial perspectives on Jesus have emerged as critical theological frameworks that seek to reinterpret the figure of Jesus in light of issues related to gender, social justice, and the legacy of colonialism. These perspectives challenge traditional Christological formulations by emphasizing Jesus' role as a liberator, His solidarity with the oppressed, and the need to rethink Christian theology through the lens of contemporary experiences of injustice. This chapter explores how feminist, liberation, and post-colonial theologians reinterpret the life, ministry, and significance of Jesus Christ in ways that resonate with their respective concerns for justice, equality, and liberation.

11.2. Feminist Perspectives on Jesus

Feminist theology, which emerged in the mid-20th century, seeks to reinterpret Christian theology, including Christology, through the lens of women's experiences and struggles for gender equality. Feminist theologians critique the ways in which traditional Christian teachings have reinforced patriarchal structures and excluded women from positions of power and influence within the Church. Central to feminist theology is the reinterpretation of Jesus' life and teachings as a source of liberation for women.

11.2.1. Jesus as a Champion of Women

Feminist theologians such as Rosemary Radford Ruether and Elizabeth A. Johnson emphasize that Jesus' life and ministry challenged the gender norms of His time. The Gospels depict Jesus engaging with women in ways that broke social and cultural boundaries. He spoke to women in public (John 4:7-26), healed them (Luke 8:1-3), and even entrusted women with significant roles in His ministry, such as Mary Magdalene, who was the first to witness His resurrection

(John 20:1-18). These stories reveal Jesus' inclusion of women as equal participants in the Kingdom of God.

For feminist theologians, Jesus' interactions with women demonstrate His commitment to challenging the patriarchal systems that devalue and marginalize women. His teachings about the Kingdom of God, with its emphasis on justice, love, and equality, provide a theological foundation for feminist critiques of gender inequality in both the Church and society.

11.2.2. Reimagining the Maleness of Jesus

One of the key challenges for feminist theologians is the maleness of Jesus and its implications for the role of women in the Church. Some feminists argue that the historical maleness of Jesus has been used to justify the exclusion of women from leadership roles in the Church. However, feminist theologians like Elizabeth A. Johnson argue that Jesus' maleness should not be seen as theologically determinative. Instead, the focus should be on His message of liberation and inclusion, which transcends gender.

In her book She Who Is, Johnson reimagines the Christian understanding of God and Jesus by emphasizing inclusive language and feminine imagery. She argues that both men and women are created in the image of God and that God's saving work in Jesus is for all people, regardless of gender. This approach challenges the patriarchal structures that have dominated Christian theology and calls for a more inclusive vision of Christology.

11.2.3. Jesus and Gender Justice

Feminist theologians argue that Jesus' life and teachings provide a basis for advocating gender justice in the Church and society. They see Jesus as a model for challenging systems of oppression, including patriarchy, and promoting the full participation of women in all areas of life. Feminist theologians call for the Church to embrace the radical inclusivity of Jesus' message and to work toward gender equality in both its leadership structures and theological frameworks.

11.3. Liberation Theology: Jesus as the Liberator of the Oppressed

Liberation theology, which emerged in Latin America in the 1960s and 1970s, views Jesus as a liberator who identifies with the poor and oppressed. This theological framework arose in response to widespread poverty, inequality, and political oppression in Latin America, and it emphasizes that the Christian faith must be lived out through solidarity with the marginalized and active participation in the struggle for social justice.

11.3.1. The Origins of Liberation Theology

Liberation theology was shaped by the social and political context of Latin America, where poverty and oppression were rampant, and the Church often aligned itself with the powerful rather than the powerless. Influenced by Marxist critiques of capitalism and inspired by the radical social justice teachings of the Gospel, theologians such as Gustavo Gutiérrez, Leonardo Boff, and Jon Sobrino developed a theology that emphasized the preferential option for the poor and the need for structural change to address systemic injustice.

11.3.2. Jesus as the Liberator

Liberation theologians interpret the life and ministry of Jesus as a model of liberation. They emphasize that Jesus' teachings and actions consistently sided with the poor, the marginalized, and the oppressed. The Gospels depict Jesus healing the sick, feeding the hungry, and calling for justice for the oppressed (Luke 4:18-19). His message of the Kingdom of God is understood as a call to transform unjust social, political, and economic structures.

Liberation theology also views Jesus' death on the cross as a political act of resistance. Jesus was executed by the Roman authorities as a threat to the established social order, and His crucifixion is seen as a symbol of solidarity with all who suffer under oppression. His resurrection, then, is a sign of hope and liberation, demonstrating that God's power can overcome even the most entrenched systems of oppression.

11.3.3. The Preferential Option for the Poor

One of the central tenets of liberation theology is the preferential option for the poor—the belief that God is especially concerned with the plight of the poor and that Christians are called to prioritize the needs of the marginalized in their faith and practice. Liberation theologians argue that following Jesus means actively working to address the root causes of poverty, inequality, and oppression. This involves not only acts of charity but also efforts to bring about systemic change.

In this view, Jesus' call to discipleship is not just a call to personal holiness but a call to social action. Liberation theology challenges the Church to take a stand against injustice and to align itself with the poor and oppressed in the struggle for liberation.

11.4. Post-Colonial Theology: Jesus and the Colonial Legacy

Post-colonial theology critiques the ways in which Christian theology has been complicit in colonialism and seeks to reinterpret the message of Jesus in ways that challenge the legacy of colonialism. Post-colonial theologians emphasize that Jesus' message of liberation and justice must be understood in the context of the oppression and exploitation experienced by colonized peoples.

11.4.1. Christianity and Colonialism

For many centuries, Christianity was deeply intertwined with the expansion of European empires and colonial rule. Christian missionaries often accompanied colonial forces and played a role in the subjugation of indigenous peoples, while Christian theology was used to justify colonial domination. This legacy has left deep scars in many formerly colonized nations, where Christianity is often seen as a tool of cultural imperialism.

11.4.2. Reinterpreting Jesus in Post-Colonial Contexts

Post-colonial theologians, such as Kwok Pui-lan, R. S. Sugirtharajah, and Musa Dube, seek to reinterpret Jesus in ways that resonate with the experiences of colonized and oppressed peoples. They argue that Jesus' life and teachings can be understood as a critique of imperial power and a call for liberation from all forms of domination.

In post-colonial theology, Jesus is often portrayed as a figure of resistance to empire. His life under Roman occupation is seen as a model for contemporary struggles against colonialism and neocolonialism. Jesus' proclamation of the Kingdom of God is interpreted as a radical rejection of the imperial powers of His time and a call for the establishment of a just and equitable society.

11.4.3. Decolonizing Theology

Post-colonial theologians argue that Christian theology must be decolonized—that is, freed from the Eurocentric interpretations that have historically dominated it. This involves rethinking traditional Christological formulations that have been shaped by colonial power dynamics and reimagining Jesus in ways that affirm the dignity, agency, and identity of indigenous peoples.

For example, post-colonial theologians emphasize the need to recover the voices and experiences of marginalized communities that have been silenced by colonialism. They argue that the message of Jesus can be a source of empowerment for colonized peoples, offering a vision of justice, liberation, and reconciliation that speaks to their unique historical and cultural experiences.

11.5. Conclusion

Feminist, liberation, and post-colonial perspectives on Jesus offer powerful re-interpretations of His life, ministry, and significance in ways that address contemporary issues of gender, social justice, and colonialism. These theological frameworks challenge traditional Christological interpretations that have often been shaped by patriarchal, hierarchical, and imperialistic assumptions.

Feminist theology emphasizes Jesus' radical inclusion of women and His challenge to patriarchal norms, calling for a re-imagining of Christology that affirms gender justice. Liberation theology presents Jesus as a liberator who stands in solidarity with the poor and oppressed, calling Christians to work for social, political, and economic justice. Post-colonial theology critiques the ways in which Christianity has been complicit in colonialism and seeks to reclaim Jesus as a figure of resistance to imperial power.

Together, these perspectives enrich the Christian understanding of Jesus, offering new insights into how His message can inspire and guide efforts to address the pressing social, political, and cultural challenges of the modern world. Through these diverse lenses, Jesus remains a source of hope, liberation, and transformation for individuals and communities facing injustice and oppression today.

The Relevance of Jesus' Theology in Contemporary Christian Life

11.1. Introduction

The theology of Jesus Christ—the understanding of His person, His teachings, His mission, and His role in salvation—remains the foundation of Christian belief and practice. However, the question of how Jesus' theology is relevant in contemporary Christian life continues to invite reflection. In a world facing new social, moral, and political challenges, believers seek to apply the message of Jesus to issues such as social justice, personal discipleship, ethical behavior, and communal life. This chapter explores how the theology of Jesus continues to be relevant in shaping contemporary Christian life, guiding individuals and communities in their faith journeys, and influencing broader social and cultural contexts.

11.2. The Personal Relevance of Jesus' Theology: Discipleship and Transformation

At the heart of Jesus' theology is the call to discipleship, which remains central to contemporary Christian life. Following Jesus is not merely about adherence to doctrine but about a transformative relationship with Christ that shapes every aspect of life. Jesus' call to "take up your cross and follow me" (Matthew 16:24) speaks directly to personal discipleship, challenging individuals to live in alignment with His teachings and example.

11.2.1. The Call to Holiness and Righteousness

In contemporary Christian life, Jesus' call to holiness and righteousness is as relevant as ever. His teachings on the Sermon on the Mount (Matthew 5–7), where He outlines the ethical standards of the Kingdom of God, challenge believers to live lives marked by humility, compassion, and moral integrity. The beatitudes, which bless the poor in spirit, the merciful, and the peacemakers, continue to serve as a guide for Christian character and conduct.

Jesus' emphasis on inward transformation rather than mere outward religious observance speaks directly to the modern quest for authenticity. In an era where many people are disillusioned with hypocrisy in religious institutions, Jesus' teachings call Christians to cultivate a genuine relationship with God that is reflected in their actions and attitudes. The relevance of Jesus' theology is evident in the way it calls individuals to a holistic transformation—one that encompasses spiritual, moral, and relational dimensions of life.

11.2.2. Love as the Foundation of Christian Life

Jesus' command to "love one another as I have loved you" (John 13:34) remains the cornerstone of Christian ethics and personal discipleship. In a contemporary world marked by division, polarization, and hostility, Jesus' radical call to love one's neighbor—even one's enemies—challenges believers to live out a countercultural ethic of love and reconciliation.

This call to love is not limited to personal relationships but extends to societal engagement. Jesus' parable of the Good Samaritan (Luke 10:25-37), where He redefines the concept of "neighbor" as anyone in need, challenges Christians today to extend compassion and care beyond their immediate communities. In an era of global interconnectedness, the relevance of Jesus' command to love calls believers to embrace a wider sense of responsibility toward the suffering and marginalized.

11.3. The Social Relevance of Jesus' Theology: Justice, Compassion, and Community

Jesus' theology has always had a social dimension, and its relevance in the contemporary world is especially evident in the areas of justice, compassion, and community. Throughout His ministry, Jesus consistently reached out to the marginalized, the poor, and the oppressed, embodying God's love for all people. His message of the Kingdom of God is not only a personal invitation but a call to transform society in accordance with divine justice and peace.

11.3.1. Social Justice and the Kingdom of God

In the Gospels, Jesus speaks of the Kingdom of God as both a present reality and a future hope. He inaugurates this Kingdom through acts of healing, liberation, and forgiveness, and He invites His followers to participate in its unfolding. For contemporary Christians, Jesus' vision of the Kingdom provides a framework for social justice, calling believers to work toward a world where God's justice reigns.

Jesus' concern for the poor, the outcast, and the oppressed is central to His ministry and remains a powerful challenge for Christians today. In the face of global poverty, inequality, and systemic injustice, Jesus' theology calls the Church to advocate for the marginalized and to seek justice in economic, political, and social systems. The preferential option for the poor, a concept drawn from liberation theology and rooted in Jesus' teachings, calls Christians to prioritize the needs of the most vulnerable in society, recognizing that how we treat "the least of these" is how we treat Christ (Matthew 25:40).

11.3.2. Compassion and Service

Jesus' acts of compassion—healing the sick, feeding the hungry, and comforting the grieving—continue to inspire Christians to live lives of service. In a contemporary world facing humanitarian crises, environmental degradation, and widespread suffering, the relevance of Jesus' compassionate ministry is more pressing than ever.

Contemporary Christians are called to embody Jesus' compassion in both personal and collective ways. This might include involvement in charitable work, advocacy for refugees and migrants, or participation in movements for racial and social justice. Jesus' theology of compassion calls believers not only to feel empathy but to take action on behalf of those who suffer, following His example of selfless service and sacrificial love.

11.3.3. Building Communities of Peace and Reconciliation

Jesus' teachings emphasize the importance of reconciliation, forgiveness, and peacemaking. His beatitude "Blessed are the peacemakers, for they will be called children of God" (Matthew 5:9) remains a guiding principle for Christians seeking to navigate the conflicts and divisions of the contemporary world.

In a time when societies are deeply divided along political, ethnic, and religious lines, the relevance of Jesus' call to build communities of peace and reconciliation is profound. Jesus' theology invites Christians to be agents of reconciliation, both within their own communities and in the wider world. This may involve fostering dialogue across differences, addressing the wounds of historical injustices, or working to heal broken relationships in families, churches, and nations.

11.4. The Global Relevance of Jesus' Theology: Engaging a Pluralistic World

As Christianity has expanded across the globe, the relevance of Jesus' theology has taken on new dimensions in diverse cultural contexts. In a pluralistic world where multiple religions and belief systems coexist, the message of Jesus continues to resonate, offering a vision of hope, love, and salvation that transcends cultural and national boundaries.

11.4.1. Jesus and Religious Pluralism

In an increasingly interconnected world, Christians are called to engage with people of other faiths in ways that are respectful, open, and dialogical. Jesus' example of engaging with people from different cultural and religious backgrounds—such as His encounter with the Samaritan woman (John 4:1-26)—provides a model for interfaith dialogue. His message of love, compassion, and inclusion speaks to the universal longing for peace and justice, offering common ground for engagement with people of other faiths.

For contemporary Christians, the theology of Jesus calls for a respectful and open-hearted approach to religious pluralism. This does not mean abandoning the core beliefs of Christianity but finding ways to communicate the message of Jesus in ways that resonate with the experiences and concerns of people from other religious traditions.

11.4.2. The Global Church and Inculturation

As Christianity continues to grow in regions such as Africa, Asia, and Latin America, the relevance of Jesus' theology is being reinterpreted in light of diverse cultural experiences. The process of inculturation, which involves expressing the Christian faith in ways that are meaningful to specific cultural contexts, highlights the adaptability and universality of Jesus' message.

In contemporary global Christianity, Jesus is understood not only as a figure from first-century Palestine but as a Savior who speaks to the unique struggles and hopes of people from every culture and nation. His theology is being rearticulated in ways that address issues such as post-colonialism, indigenous rights, economic inequality, and environmental stewardship.

11.5. The Relevance of Jesus' Theology in Ethical and Moral Decision-Making

The teachings of Jesus continue to provide a moral compass for Christians facing complex ethical issues in contemporary society. Whether in matters of personal morality or broader societal concerns, Jesus' theology offers principles of love, justice, truth, and mercy that guide ethical decision-making.

11.5.1. Jesus' Ethics of Love and Justice

Jesus' command to love God and love one's neighbor (Matthew 22:37-40) is foundational for Christian ethics. In contemporary life, this ethic of love guides how Christians approach moral questions, from personal relationships to issues such as bioethics, environmental sustainability, and economic justice. Jesus' emphasis on love as the fulfillment of the law challenges Christians to prioritize the well-being of others, even in difficult and complex situations.

His teachings on justice, particularly His critique of hypocrisy and exploitation (Matthew 23:23-26), call Christians to act with integrity and fairness in all areas of life. In an era where ethical dilemmas often involve competing values, the relevance of Jesus' theology lies in its call to seek justice with compassion, balancing truth and mercy in moral decision-making.

11.5.2. Jesus and the Ethical Challenges of the 21st Century

Contemporary Christians face a range of ethical challenges that require careful discernment. Issues such as genetic engineering, artificial intelligence, economic inequality, and climate change raise profound moral questions about the value of life, human dignity, and the stewardship of creation. Jesus' teachings on the sanctity of life, the importance of caring for the vulnerable, and the responsibility to steward the earth provide a framework for addressing these challenges in ways that honor God and reflect

His Kingdom values.

The relevance of Jesus' theology in contemporary ethical decision-making lies in its emphasis on the dignity of every person and the responsibility of Christians to act as stewards of God's creation. Whether addressing personal moral choices or societal issues, Jesus' teachings continue to provide guidance for living a life that reflects God's love and justice in the world.

11.6. Conclusion

The theology of Jesus remains deeply relevant in contemporary Christian life, offering both a personal call to discipleship and a framework for addressing social, ethical, and global challenges. Jesus' teachings on love, justice, compassion, and reconciliation continue to inspire and guide believers as they seek to live out their faith in a complex and rapidly changing world.

Through the lens of Jesus' theology, Christians are called to engage with the pressing issues of their time—poverty, inequality, injustice, division, and moral complexity—with the same spirit of love and transformation that characterized Jesus' own ministry. The relevance of Jesus' theology lies in its ability to speak to both the individual and the collective, calling for personal transformation and societal change rooted in the values of the Kingdom of God.

As contemporary Christians navigate the challenges of modern life, the teachings and example of Jesus remain a source of hope, guidance, and inspiration, pointing the way toward a world that more fully reflects God's justice, peace, and love.

CHAPTER 12

JESUS AND INTERFAITH DIALOGUE: HOW JESUS IS PERCEIVED IN OTHER MAJOR WORLD RELIGIONS

12.1. Introduction

Jesus of Nazareth is the central figure of Christianity, but His significance extends beyond the Christian faith. He is also a prominent figure in other major world religions, including Islam, Judaism, Hinduism, and Buddhism, although His role and nature are interpreted differently within each tradition. In an increasingly pluralistic and interconnected world, interfaith dialogue has become essential for fostering understanding, respect, and peace among diverse religious communities. This chapter explores how Jesus is perceived in other major world religions, focusing on Islam and Judaism, and discusses the role of Jesus in interfaith dialogue. These perspectives illuminate both the commonalities and differences in how Jesus is understood across religious boundaries, offering insights into how He can serve as a bridge for interfaith engagement.

12.2. Jesus in Islam

In Islam, Jesus (known as Isa in Arabic) is highly revered as one of the greatest prophets, though His identity and mission are understood differently than in Christianity. The Islamic perspective on Jesus is based primarily on the Quran, which mentions Him in several passages and presents Him as a figure of significant spiritual importance.

12.2.1. Jesus as a Prophet and Messenger

In Islam, Jesus is regarded as a prophet and a messenger of God, one of the five greatest prophets (Ulul Azm) alongside Noah, Abraham, Moses, and Muhammad. The Quran acknowledges that Jesus was born of the Virgin Mary (Maryam) through a miraculous conception (Quran 3:45-47) and that He was chosen by God to deliver His message to the people of Israel.

Islam teaches that Jesus was sent to guide the Children of Israel with a new scripture, the Injil (Gospel), and that He performed miracles by God's permission, such as healing the sick, raising the dead, and creating birds from clay (Quran 3:49). However, unlike Christianity, Islam rejects the belief in Jesus' divinity or that He is the Son of God. Instead, Jesus is seen as a fully human prophet who submitted to the will of God.

12.2.2. The Crucifixion and Ascension in Islam

One of the most significant differences between Christian and Islamic views of Jesus is the understanding of His crucifixion. Islam teaches that Jesus was not crucified, nor did He die on the cross, but that it only appeared so to the people (Quran 4:157). Instead, Muslims believe that God raised Jesus up to Himself, and that He will return at the end of time to fulfill His eschatological role (Quran 4:158).

In Islamic eschatology, Jesus is expected to return to restore justice, defeat the false messiah (Al-Masih ad-Dajjal), and affirm the truth of monotheism. His second coming is seen as a key event in the Islamic understanding of the end times, emphasizing His continued importance in the divine plan.

12.2.3. Jesus and Interfaith Dialogue in Islam

Jesus serves as a significant point of connection between Christianity and Islam in interfaith dialogue. Both religions hold Him in high regard, although their theological interpretations differ. In interfaith discussions, Jesus can be seen as a figure who bridges the gap between the two faiths, providing a foundation for mutual respect and understanding.

Muslim-Christian dialogue often highlights Jesus' role as a moral exemplar and a preacher of compassion, justice, and submission to God. While Christians and Muslims may disagree on Jesus' divine status, His prophetic role and His teachings about ethical living, love, and justice remain areas of potential common ground for collaboration on issues such as social justice, peacebuilding, and humanitarian efforts.

12.3. Jesus in Judaism

The figure of Jesus occupies a complex and often contentious place within Judaism. As a Jew born into a Jewish family and raised within the Jewish tradition, Jesus' teachings and actions were originally directed toward a Jewish audience. However, the development of Christianity as a separate faith and its claims about Jesus as the Messiah and the Son of God have led to divergent views between Judaism and Christianity.

12.3.1. Jesus as a Historical Figure

Within Judaism, Jesus is generally regarded as a historical figure—a Jewish teacher or rabbi who lived in the first century CE. However, He is not accepted as the Messiah or as divine. Traditional Jewish teachings reject the Christian claim that Jesus is the fulfillment of Messianic prophecies, arguing that Jesus did not fulfill the key expectations of the Jewish Messiah, such as bringing lasting peace to the world, rebuilding the Temple in Jerusalem, or gathering all Jews back to Israel.

The Jewish concept of the Messiah focuses on a future anointed leader who will restore Israel, bring justice to the world, and usher in an era of peace. Since Jesus' life did not result in the realization of these goals, Judaism does not accept Him as the Messiah.

12.3.2. Jewish Perspectives on Jesus' Teachings

Although Judaism does not accept the divinity or messianic claims about Jesus, there is recognition among some Jewish scholars that Jesus' ethical teachings align in many ways with Jewish values. The emphasis on love, justice, mercy, and adherence to the law found in Jesus' teachings has parallels in Jewish scripture and rabbinic tradition.

For example, Jesus' teaching to "love your neighbor as yourself" (Mark 12:31) reflects the commandment found in Leviticus 19:18, and His focus on mercy and justice resonates with the teachings of the Jewish prophets. However, Judaism interprets these teachings through the lens of the Torah and Jewish tradition, rather than through the framework of Christian theology.

12.3.3. Jesus and Interfaith Dialogue in Judaism

Jesus' Jewish identity offers a starting point for interfaith dialogue between Christians and Jews. While Jewish and Christian understandings of Jesus differ significantly, particularly concerning His messianic role, there is potential for dialogue on His teachings about ethics, justice, and spirituality. In recent decades, Jewish-Christian dialogue has focused on building bridges of understanding, overcoming historical tensions, and fostering mutual respect.

Many contemporary Jewish scholars and theologians engage in dialogue with Christians, acknowledging the historical significance of Jesus within Judaism while also addressing the theological differences that separate the two faiths. This dialogue is often framed around shared values, such as the pursuit of peace, justice, and the well-being of humanity.

12.4. Jesus in Other Religious Traditions

Beyond Islam and Judaism, Jesus is also acknowledged in other world religions, though often in different ways. While these interpretations do not align with the Christian understanding of Jesus as the Son of God and the Savior, they reflect the widespread impact of His teachings and moral example.

12.4.1. Jesus in Hinduism

In Hinduism, Jesus is sometimes regarded as a wise teacher, a spiritual guru, or even a divine figure who embodies qualities such as compassion, love, and self-sacrifice. Some Hindus see Jesus as a manifestation of the divine, akin to an avatar (an incarnation of a deity) who came to guide humanity toward spiritual enlightenment.

Prominent Hindu thinkers like Mahatma Gandhi admired Jesus' teachings, particularly His Sermon on the Mount, which Gandhi saw as a profound expression of nonviolence (ahimsa) and love. Although Hinduism does not accept Jesus in the same theological sense as Christianity, His message of love, humility, and service resonates with many aspects of Hindu spirituality.

12.4.2. Jesus in Buddhism

In Buddhism, Jesus is often viewed as a wise and enlightened teacher whose life exemplified compassion, nonviolence, and ethical living. Some Buddhist thinkers have drawn parallels between Jesus' teachings and the ethical and spiritual values of Buddhism, such as the emphasis on compassion (karuna), loving-kindness (metta), and renunciation of worldly attachments.

While Buddhism does not share the belief in a personal God or Savior, the ethical teachings of Jesus, particularly His call to love others and care for the suffering, align with core Buddhist principles. Interfaith dialogue between Buddhists and Christians often centers on shared values of peace, compassion, and the alleviation of suffering.

12.5. Jesus as a Bridge for Interfaith Dialogue

The diverse perceptions of Jesus across religious traditions offer both challenges and opportunities for interfaith dialogue. While each religion interprets Jesus in its own way, often leading to significant theological differences, His moral teachings and spiritual example provide a common ground for engagement.

12.5.1. Common Ethical Values

One of the key areas where Jesus can serve as a bridge in interfaith dialogue is in the realm of ethics. Across different religions, Jesus is often recognized for His teachings on love, justice, compassion, and humility. These ethical values resonate with the moral principles found in many world religions, offering opportunities for collaboration on issues such as social justice, peacebuilding, and humanitarian efforts.

For example, Christian, Muslim, and Jewish communities can work together on projects that address poverty, inequality, and injustice, drawing inspiration from their respective religious teachings about caring for the marginalized. In such contexts, Jesus' call to love and serve others can inspire joint efforts to create a more just and compassionate world.

12.5.2. Respecting Theological Differences

At the same time, interfaith dialogue around Jesus must acknowledge and respect the significant theological differences that exist between religions. Christians understand Jesus as the incarnate Son of God and the Savior of humanity, a belief that is central to Christian faith but is not shared by other religions. Interfaith dialogue should not seek to diminish or erase these differences but to foster mutual understanding and respect.

By recognizing the unique role that Jesus plays in each religious tradition, interfaith dialogue can create space for respectful conversations about faith, identity, and spirituality. Such dialogue can help build bridges between communities, reduce misunderstandings, and promote peaceful coexistence.

12.6. Conclusion

Jesus is a figure of profound significance not only in Christianity but also in other major world religions. In Islam, He is revered as a prophet and a sign of God's power. In Judaism, He is acknowledged as a historical figure, though not as the Messiah. In Hinduism and Buddhism, He is often seen as a wise teacher and a moral exemplar. These diverse perceptions of Jesus offer both challenges and opportunities for interfaith dialogue.

Through shared ethical values and a commitment to justice, compassion, and peace, Jesus can serve as a bridge for interfaith engagement. While theological differences between religions remain, Jesus' teachings provide a common ground for collaboration on pressing global issues. In an increasingly pluralistic world, understanding how Jesus is perceived across religious traditions is essential for fostering dialogue, mutual respect, and a deeper appreciation of the diverse ways in which humanity seeks to understand the divine.

Theological Implications of Interfaith Understandings of Jesus

12.1. Introduction

As a central figure in Christianity, Jesus Christ's identity, teachings, and role are pivotal for understanding the Christian faith. However, Jesus also holds a significant place in other major world religions such as Islam and Judaism, as well as in traditions like Hinduism and Buddhism. These interfaith understandings of Jesus offer diverse perspectives on His person and message, each grounded in the unique theological frameworks of those traditions. The implications of these varying perspectives have sparked both theological reflection and challenges within Christian discourse. This chapter examines the theological implications of interfaith understandings of Jesus, exploring how these perspectives impact Christian theology, interfaith dialogue, and the global Christian mission.

12.2. Expanding Christological Perspectives

Interfaith understandings of Jesus, particularly from Islam and Judaism, challenge traditional Christian views of Christology. While Christianity proclaims Jesus as the incarnate Son of God, the second person of the Trinity, and the Savior of humanity, other religious traditions offer different interpretations of His role and nature. Engaging with these diverse perspectives forces Christian theologians to reexamine and expand their understanding of Jesus in light of interfaith dialogue.

12.2.1. The Challenge of Religious Pluralism

Religious pluralism—the recognition that multiple religious traditions offer distinct and meaningful paths to the divine—raises important theological questions for Christianity. One key issue is whether Christianity can maintain its traditional claims about Jesus' uniqueness and universality while engaging in respectful dialogue with other faiths. For Christians, Jesus is "the way, the truth, and the life" (John 14:6), a statement that implies the singularity of Jesus' role in salvation. However, in a pluralistic world, how can Christians hold to this belief while also acknowledging the validity of other religious experiences of the divine?

Theological responses to this challenge vary. Exclusivism holds that Jesus is the only way to salvation and that other religions, while they may contain elements of truth, ultimately fall short. Inclusivism, on the other hand, maintains that while Jesus is the definitive means of salvation, God's grace can be at work in other religions, and their adherents may be saved through Christ without explicit knowledge of Him. Pluralism suggests that Jesus is one of many ways to experience God's truth, recognizing multiple valid paths to the divine.

The presence of Jesus in multiple religious traditions highlights the need for Christians to reflect on the theological implications of religious pluralism. Can Jesus be understood as a universal figure who transcends religious boundaries? Or must Christians affirm His exclusive role in salvation while remaining open to dialogue with those of other faiths?

12.2.2. Reexamining the Universality of Christ

One of the key theological implications of interfaith understandings of Jesus is the question of His universality. From a Christian perspective, Jesus is often understood as the Savior of all humanity, whose life, death, and resurrection provide salvation not only for Christians but for the entire world. The Apostle Paul writes, "In Christ, God was reconciling the world to himself" (2 Corinthians 5:19), which speaks to the universal scope of Jesus' mission.

However, interfaith perspectives on Jesus, particularly from Islam and Judaism, challenge the idea that Jesus' salvific role is universally recognized or accepted. In Islam, Jesus is revered as a prophet but not as the Son of God or the Savior. In Judaism, Jesus is not seen as the Messiah or divine. These differing views call into question the extent to which Christian claims about Jesus' universality can be reconciled with the perspectives of other faiths.

Engaging with these perspectives may lead Christians to explore the concept of cosmic Christology, in which Christ is understood as the universal, transcendent presence of God at work in the world, even in ways that may not align with traditional Christian formulations. This understanding allows for a broader view of Jesus' significance across cultures and religions while affirming His central role in Christian faith.

12.3. Theological Dialogue and Mutual Enrichment

Interfaith understandings of Jesus provide opportunities for theological dialogue and mutual enrichment between religious traditions. While theological differences between Christianity and other faiths are significant, engaging with how others perceive Jesus can deepen Christian reflection on His person and mission. This dialogue can lead to a more nuanced and richer understanding of Christology, as well as greater appreciation for the religious insights of other faiths.

12.3.1. Islam: Prophet and Eschatological Figure

In Islam, Jesus (Isa) is seen as a prophet who delivered God's message to the Children of Israel and performed miracles by God's permission. While Islam rejects the Christian belief in Jesus' divinity, His virgin birth and role as a prophet are highly revered. Moreover, Jesus is an important figure in Islamic eschatology, where He is expected to return at the end of time to restore justice and defeat the false messiah (Dajjal).

The theological implications of this understanding for Christians are multifaceted. On the one hand, it challenges the Christian doctrine of the Incarnation, as Islam denies that God could take on human form. On the other hand, the Islamic reverence for Jesus opens up possibilities for dialogue about His ethical teachings, His role as a moral exemplar, and the shared hope in His future return. Engaging with the Islamic understanding of Jesus encourages Christians to reflect more deeply on the significance of Jesus' prophetic role and His relationship to God the Father.

12.3.2. Judaism: Historical Figure and Teacher

Judaism, while not recognizing Jesus as the Messiah or the Son of God, acknowledges Him as a historical figure—a

Jewish teacher whose ethical teachings have parallels with Jewish values. The rejection of Jesus as the Messiah in Judaism is based on the belief that He did not fulfill the Messianic prophecies found in the Hebrew Scriptures, such as establishing world peace or rebuilding the Temple in Jerusalem.

For Christians, engaging with Jewish perspectives on Jesus can lead to a deeper appreciation of His Jewish identity and the context in which He lived and taught. Theological dialogue with Judaism can enrich Christian understanding of Jesus' teachings, particularly His emphasis on the Law, justice, and compassion, all of which are rooted in the Jewish prophetic tradition.

12.3.3. Hinduism and Buddhism: Teacher and Moral Exemplar

In Hinduism and Buddhism, Jesus is often viewed as a spiritual teacher or moral exemplar whose life reflects compassion, selflessness, and wisdom. Some Hindu thinkers, such as Mahatma Gandhi, admired Jesus for His teachings on nonviolence, seeing parallels between Jesus' ethics and Hindu principles like ahimsa (non-harm). Similarly, in Buddhism, Jesus is seen as an enlightened teacher whose emphasis on love and compassion aligns with key Buddhist values.

While these interpretations differ from the Christian understanding of Jesus as the incarnate Son of God, they highlight the universal appeal of Jesus' moral teachings. For Christians, dialogue with Hindu and Buddhist perspectives can offer fresh insights into the ethical dimensions of Jesus' life and message, encouraging a broader reflection on how His teachings resonate with people across different religious traditions.

12.4. The Role of Jesus in Global Mission and Witness

The theological implications of interfaith understandings of Jesus also have an impact on the Christian mission and witness in a global, pluralistic context. As Christians seek to share the message of Jesus with people from diverse religious backgrounds, they must consider how to communicate their faith in ways that are respectful, open to dialogue, and sensitive to the beliefs of others.

12.4.1. Witnessing in a Pluralistic World

Christian mission in a pluralistic world involves proclaiming the message of Jesus while acknowledging and respecting the religious traditions of others. Engaging with interfaith perspectives on Jesus requires humility and a willingness to listen, recognizing that other faiths offer their own understandings of Jesus' significance. This approach emphasizes dialogical mission, where the goal is not to impose Christian beliefs but to enter into a mutual exchange of ideas, seeking common ground while remaining faithful to the core tenets of Christianity.

In this context, Christian mission must be guided by Jesus' own teachings of love, humility, and respect for others. Theological reflection on interfaith understandings of Jesus can help shape a mission that is both faithful to the Gospel and responsive to the complexities of religious pluralism.

12.4.2. The Cosmic Christ and Global Christianity

The concept of the Cosmic Christ—the idea that Christ is present and active throughout creation—offers a theological framework for understanding Jesus' universal significance in a globalized and pluralistic world. This perspective, articulated by theologians such as Pierre Teilhard de Chardin and Richard Rohr, sees Christ not only as the Savior of humanity but as the unifying presence of God in all of creation.

For global Christianity, the Cosmic Christ provides a way to affirm the universality of Christ's mission while recognizing that His presence may be experienced differently in various religious and cultural contexts. This understanding encourages Christians to see Jesus as the source of reconciliation and unity, not only within the Church but also across the boundaries of religion, culture, and nation.

12.5. Conclusion

The interfaith understandings of Jesus present both theological challenges and opportunities for Christian theology. Engaging with these diverse perspectives encourages Christians to reflect more deeply on their own beliefs about Jesus, His role in salvation, and His relationship to God the Father. At the same time, interfaith dialogue around Jesus fosters mutual respect, understanding, and the possibility of collaboration on shared ethical and spiritual concerns.

Theological implications of these interfaith understandings include reexamining the universality of Christ, exploring the possibility of the Cosmic Christ, and developing new approaches to Christian mission and witness in a pluralistic world. As Christians engage in dialogue with other faiths, they are invited to reaffirm their faith in Jesus while being open to learning from the diverse ways in which He is understood and revered across the world.

Through these conversations, the figure of Jesus can serve as both a unifying presence and a source of deep theological reflection, guiding believers toward a more inclusive and expansive understanding of His mission in the world.

The Role of Jesus in Promoting Interfaith Dialogue and Understanding

12.1. Introduction

In an increasingly interconnected and pluralistic world, interfaith dialogue has become an essential component of fostering peace, mutual respect, and understanding among people of diverse religious backgrounds. Within this context, Jesus Christ, a central figure in Christianity, also holds significant roles in other major world religions such as Islam, Judaism, and even in certain interpretations of Hinduism and Buddhism. The figure of Jesus offers a unique opportunity for creating common ground in interfaith dialogue, serving as a bridge between different faith traditions. This chapter explores how the person of Jesus, His teachings, and the values He represents play a key role in promoting interfaith dialogue and understanding. By focusing on His shared ethical teachings, the themes of love and compassion, and the commonalities between religious traditions, this chapter highlights how Jesus can inspire conversations that transcend theological differences and foster deeper connections among diverse communities.

12.2. Jesus as a Bridge in Interfaith Dialogue

In many interfaith dialogues, Jesus serves as a point of connection and discussion, especially among the Abrahamic faiths—Christianity, Islam, and Judaism. While each tradition has its own interpretation of Jesus, His life and teachings provide a foundation for meaningful conversation and cooperation.

12.2.1. Jesus in Christianity, Islam, and Judaism

In Christianity, Jesus is the Son of God, the Savior of humanity, and the incarnate Word. However, in Islam, He is revered as Isa, a prophet and messenger of God, born of the Virgin Mary and destined to return at the end of time. In Judaism, while Jesus is not recognized as the Messiah or divine, He is acknowledged as a historical figure and a teacher.

These different understandings create both challenges and opportunities for dialogue. While Christians view Jesus as central to their faith, Muslims see Him as an important prophet in the line of divine messengers, and Jews view Him through the lens of Jewish history and tradition. Despite the theological differences, all three religions respect Jesus and see Him as embodying moral and spiritual values that transcend their specific interpretations.

This common ground can serve as a starting point for dialogue. Focusing on shared reverence for Jesus' teachings about justice, compassion, and care for others allows people from different faiths to find mutual respect and understanding.

12.2.2. Jesus' Role in Building Bridges between Faiths

Jesus' life and teachings provide common ethical and moral ground for interfaith dialogue, especially when focusing on issues such as justice, mercy, and love for others. By emphasizing these shared values, Jesus can serve as a bridge between different faith traditions, encouraging collaboration and mutual understanding.

In particular, His teachings about loving one's neighbor (Matthew 22:39), forgiving enemies (Matthew 5:44), and serving the marginalized resonate across many religious traditions. These principles of love, humility, and service offer universal values that can guide conversations and cooperative efforts between people of diverse religious backgrounds. By focusing on these shared aspects of Jesus' message, interfaith dialogues can transcend doctrinal differences and foster a spirit of mutual respect and cooperation.

12.3. Shared Ethical Teachings: A Common Foundation for Dialogue

One of the most powerful ways Jesus promotes interfaith dialogue is through His ethical teachings, which emphasize values that are universally admired and practiced across religions. Jesus' message of love, compassion, justice, and humility resonates deeply in many faith traditions and can serve as a foundation for conversations about how religious communities can work together to address global challenges.

12.3.1. Love and Compassion

At the heart of Jesus' teachings is the command to love others—both neighbors and enemies. In the Gospels, Jesus repeatedly calls His followers to love unconditionally, to forgive, and to show mercy (Luke 6:27-36). These values are not unique to Christianity; they are also core principles in many other religions.

For instance, in Islam, compassion (rahma) is one of the central attributes of God, and Muslims are encouraged to act with mercy and kindness toward others. The Quran teaches that God is "the Most Compassionate, the Most Merciful" (Quran 1:1), and this divine compassion is reflected in human relationships. Similarly, in Buddhism, the practice of karuna (compassion) and metta (loving-kindness) is foundational to ethical living, urging individuals to care for others and alleviate suffering.

In interfaith dialogue, these shared values of love and compassion can serve as a platform for meaningful conversations about how religious communities can work together to create a more compassionate and just world. By focusing on Jesus' teachings, participants can explore how love for others can be expressed through practical actions, such as charitable work, peacebuilding, and efforts to combat poverty and injustice.

12.3.2. Justice and Service to the Marginalized

Jesus' concern for the marginalized is evident throughout the Gospels. He consistently advocates for the poor, the sick, and the outcast, emphasizing that the Kingdom of God belongs to those who are often overlooked by society (Luke 4:18-19, Matthew 25:35-40). This emphasis on justice, equity, and care for the vulnerable aligns with teachings found in many other religions.

In Judaism, the concept of tzedakah (justice and charity) is a fundamental ethical obligation, calling Jews to care for those in need and to pursue justice in all areas of life. Likewise, in Islam, the principle of zakat (charitable giving) is one of the Five Pillars, requiring Muslims to share their wealth with the poor and to work toward a more just society.

By focusing on Jesus' call to serve the marginalized, interfaith dialogue can foster collaboration between religious communities in addressing issues such as poverty, inequality, and human rights. These shared commitments to justice and service can form the basis for joint initiatives that seek to alleviate suffering and promote the common good.

12.4. Overcoming Theological Differences through Dialogue

While interfaith dialogue must acknowledge theological differences, particularly concerning Jesus' divinity and role in salvation, these differences do not have to be barriers to meaningful conversation and cooperation. Instead, they can offer opportunities for mutual learning and deeper understanding.

12.4.1. Acknowledging Theological Differences

Theological differences between Christianity and other religions, especially in regard to Jesus' identity as the Son of God and the Savior of humanity, are profound. For Christians, Jesus is the incarnate Word of God, whose death and resurrection bring salvation to all who believe. In Islam, Jesus is honored as a prophet but is not divine, and in Judaism, Jesus is not accepted as the Messiah.

Interfaith dialogue does not require participants to agree on these theological points. Instead, it invites individuals from different faiths to explore their own beliefs while remaining open to understanding the beliefs of others. Respectful dialogue allows participants to appreciate the depth of each tradition's understanding of Jesus without forcing a consensus on theological matters.

12.4.2. Emphasizing Shared Values over Doctrinal Disputes

In promoting interfaith dialogue, Jesus' role can shift from being a subject of theological debate to becoming a symbol of shared values and moral principles. While theological differences may remain unresolved, focusing on common ethical teachings—such as love, justice, mercy, and compassion—can create a space for cooperation and mutual respect.

For example, Christian-Muslim dialogue might focus on how both traditions revere Jesus for His teachings on compassion and forgiveness, even if they disagree on His divine status. Similarly, Jewish-Christian dialogue can explore the ways in which Jesus' ethical teachings align with Jewish prophetic traditions, fostering a sense of shared moral purpose.

By emphasizing shared values, interfaith dialogue can move beyond doctrinal disputes and toward practical collaboration on issues such as poverty, conflict resolution, environmental sustainability, and the promotion of human rights.

12.5. Jesus as a Model for Interfaith Engagement

Jesus' interactions with people of different backgrounds, particularly those who were marginalized or viewed as outsiders, provide a model for interfaith engagement today. His encounters with the Samaritan woman (John 4:7-26), the Roman centurion (Matthew 8:5-13), and the Canaanite woman (Matthew 15:21-28) demonstrate His openness to others, even those who were seen as religious or cultural "others."

12.5.1. Jesus' Openness to the "Other"

In the story of the Samaritan woman at the well, Jesus crosses significant religious and cultural boundaries. Samaritans and Jews had longstanding hostilities, yet Jesus engages the Samaritan woman in a meaningful conversation about faith, offering her "living water" and revealing His messianic identity to her. This encounter shows Jesus' willingness to break down barriers and engage with those from different religious backgrounds.

This openness to dialogue and relationship with the "other" is a powerful model for interfaith engagement today. It encourages participants in interfaith dialogue to approach one another with openness, respect, and a genuine desire to understand different perspectives. By following Jesus' example, religious communities can build relationships based on trust and mutual respect, even in the face of significant theological and cultural differences.

12.5.2. Humility and Service in Interfaith Dialogue

Jesus' emphasis on humility and service is another key aspect of His life that is relevant to interfaith dialogue. In His teachings and actions, Jesus consistently elevates humility and self-giving service as core virtues. In John 13, for instance, Jesus washes the feet of His disciples, demonstrating that true leadership is rooted in humility and service to others.

This model of humility is essential in interfaith dialogue, where participants are called to approach conversations with a spirit of openness and a willingness to learn from others. By adopting an attitude of humility, those engaged in dialogue can move beyond defensive or competitive stances and instead work together to find common ground and shared goals.

12.6. Conclusion

Jesus plays a unique and powerful role in promoting interfaith dialogue and understanding. His teachings on love, compassion, justice, and humility resonate across religious traditions, providing common ground for meaningful conversation and cooperation. While theological differences remain significant, particularly concerning His divinity and role in salvation, these differences do not have to be barriers to dialogue. Instead, they can serve as opportunities for mutual learning, respect, and collaboration.

By focusing on shared ethical values and following Jesus' example of openness to the "other," religious communities can engage in interfaith dialogue that fosters peace, understanding, and cooperation. In a world marked by religious diversity and division, Jesus' teachings and example offer a path toward greater unity and collaboration, helping to build bridges of understanding between people of different faiths.

415

CONCLUSION

SUMMARY OF KEY INSIGHTS AND THEOLOGICAL INPLICATIONS

The exploration of Jesus in the context of interfaith dialogue reveals profound insights and theological implications that are essential for understanding His role in promoting mutual respect, collaboration, and deeper reflection across religious boundaries. Throughout this chapter, several key themes have emerged, shedding light on how the figure of Jesus, His teachings, and His example can inspire meaningful interfaith conversations in today's pluralistic world.

Key Insights

1. Jesus as a Bridge between Faith Traditions

One of the most significant insights is that Jesus can serve as a bridge between various religious traditions. While Christianity holds Jesus as the incarnate Son of God and Savior, other religions such as Islam and Judaism also revere Jesus in different ways. In Islam, Jesus is seen as a prophet and a key eschatological figure, while in Judaism, He is recognized as a historical figure and teacher. These shared perspectives offer a foundation for dialogue, allowing different faith communities to connect through their reverence for Jesus, even while maintaining theological distinctions.

2. Common Ethical Teachings of Love, Compassion, and Justice

Across multiple religious traditions, Jesus' ethical teachings—particularly His emphasis on love, compassion, and justice—resonate deeply. These shared values provide fertile ground for interfaith dialogue, as participants from diverse faiths can come together to discuss how these principles can guide actions in the contemporary world. Whether addressing issues of social justice, care for the marginalized, or promoting peace and reconciliation, Jesus' teachings offer a common moral framework that transcends doctrinal differences.

3. The Role of Jesus in Encouraging Openness to the "Other"

Jesus' interactions with people from different cultural, religious, and social backgrounds, such as the Samaritan woman and the Roman centurion, model an openness and inclusivity that is essential for interfaith dialogue. His willingness to engage with those outside His own religious community sets an example for today's interfaith conversations, encouraging participants to approach one another with respect, curiosity, and a desire to build meaningful relationships across religious divides.

4. Humility and Service as Foundations for Dialogue

Jesus' teachings on humility and service, exemplified through His washing of the disciples' feet and His command to love and serve others, provide an important model for interfaith dialogue. Engaging in dialogue requires participants to adopt a posture of humility, recognizing the value of learning from others and being open to different perspectives. This approach allows for deeper understanding and fosters collaboration, as religious communities work together to address common global challenges.

Theological Implications

1. Reexamining Christology in a Pluralistic World

Interfaith understandings of Jesus challenge traditional Christian Christology, particularly the exclusivist claim that Jesus is the only way to salvation. Engaging with perspectives from Islam, Judaism, Hinduism, and Buddhism requires Christian theologians to reexamine the universality of Christ's salvific role while remaining faithful to core Christian beliefs. This engagement may lead to a more expansive understanding of Christ, such as the concept of the Cosmic Christ, which sees Jesus as present and active in all of creation, allowing for a broader recognition of divine truth across religious boundaries.

2. Religious Pluralism and the Uniqueness of Christ

The theological implications of religious pluralism also prompt Christians to reflect on the uniqueness of Christ in relation to other religious traditions. While affirming the central Christian belief in Jesus' divinity and role in salvation, interfaith dialogue invites Christians to consider how God might be at work in other religions. This has led to discussions around inclusivism—the idea that salvation through Christ might extend beyond explicit belief in Him—and dialogical mission, where the goal is mutual understanding and respect rather than conversion.

3. The Ethical Role of Jesus in Global Interfaith Cooperation

The shared ethical teachings of Jesus, particularly His emphasis on justice, compassion, and care for the marginalized, have significant theological implications for how Christians engage with other faiths in addressing global issues. Jesus' call to love one's neighbor and serve the "least of these" (Matthew 25:40) is not confined to intra-Christian relationships but extends to the entire human community. This theological understanding encourages Christians to work alongside people of other faiths in promoting human dignity, alleviating suffering, and building a more just and peaceful world.

4. The Importance of Interfaith Dialogue for Christian Identity

Finally, interfaith dialogue around the figure of Jesus has implications for Christian identity itself. Engaging with how other religions view Jesus allows Christians to deepen their own understanding of His person and work. It also challenges Christians to live out the radical love, humility, and inclusivity that Jesus demonstrated. In a world marked by religious conflict and division, interfaith dialogue grounded in the teachings and example of Jesus offers a way for Christians to embody their faith in a manner that promotes peace, reconciliation, and mutual respect.

In conclusion, the role of Jesus in interfaith dialogue offers profound opportunities for fostering understanding, respect, and collaboration between people of different religious traditions. His life, teachings, and example provide a common ethical foundation that transcends theological differences, enabling meaningful conversations about shared values and global challenges. The theological implications of these interfaith understandings of Jesus invite Christians to reflect more deeply on their own Christology and to engage with the religious diversity of the world in ways that are both faithful to the Gospel and open to learning from others.

As religious communities continue to engage in interfaith dialogue, the figure of Jesus can serve as a unifying presence, offering hope, inspiration, and guidance for building a world marked by compassion, justice, and peace. Through these dialogues, Christians and people of other faiths can work together to address the most pressing moral and ethical issues of our time, drawing on the rich spiritual and moral teachings of Jesus to promote the common good for all of humanity.

The Ongoing Significance of Jesus' Theology for the Church and the World

The theology of Jesus Christ—His teachings, identity, and mission—continues to hold profound significance for both the Church and the world. Rooted in His message of love, justice, reconciliation, and the Kingdom of God, Jesus' theology provides a timeless framework for understanding God's relationship with humanity and the world. However, the significance of Jesus' theology extends beyond the confines of Christian doctrine; it also speaks to pressing contemporary issues such as social justice, interfaith relations, global conflicts, and the moral and ethical challenges facing humanity today. This section reflects on the ongoing relevance of Jesus' theology for the Church and the wider world, exploring how His teachings continue to inspire individual and collective transformation in the modern era.

The Significance of Jesus' Theology for the Church

Jesus' theology remains the cornerstone of the Church's identity, mission, and worship. His teachings, life, death, and resurrection are not only foundational to Christian doctrine but also shape how the Church engages with the world.

1. Jesus' Call to Discipleship: Personal and Communal Transformation

Central to Jesus' theology is the call to discipleship, where believers are invited to follow Him and live according to His teachings. This call extends beyond mere belief in His divinity; it requires a transformation of life, grounded in love, humility, service, and justice. For the Church, this means fostering a community that reflects the values of the Kingdom of God. Through worship, sacramental life, and acts of service, the Church continually seeks to embody the radical love and selflessness that Jesus exemplified.

In the contemporary Church, Jesus' theology challenges believers to reevaluate their own lives in light of His teachings. How do Christians live out the beatitudes in a world of inequality? How do they embody forgiveness and reconciliation in a time of division and conflict? Jesus' call to personal and communal transformation remains vital, reminding the Church that its mission is not just to preach the Gospel but to live it in every aspect of life.

2. The Kingdom of God: Mission and Justice

The concept of the Kingdom of God was central to Jesus' ministry, and it remains a guiding vision for the Church's mission. Jesus proclaimed a Kingdom characterized by justice, peace, and compassion for the oppressed, challenging both religious and political systems that perpetuated inequality and suffering. This theology has ongoing significance as the Church seeks to participate in the realization of God's Kingdom on earth.

Today, Jesus' vision of the Kingdom inspires the Church's commitment to social justice, peacemaking, and the defense of human dignity. In an era marked by global inequality, environmental degradation, and political instability, the Church's mission, informed by Jesus' theology, calls for active engagement in addressing these issues. Whether through charitable work, advocacy for the marginalized, or efforts to foster reconciliation in divided communities, the Church continues to live out the call to advance the Kingdom of God.

3. The Church as a Community of Reconciliation

Another ongoing significance of Jesus' theology is His emphasis on reconciliation. Jesus' death and resurrection are understood by Christians as the ultimate act of reconciling humanity to God, breaking the power of sin and death. For the Church, this reconciliation extends to relationships among individuals, communities, and nations.

In a world fractured by conflict, division, and injustice, Jesus' theology of reconciliation remains a powerful call for the Church to be an agent of healing and unity. This is not just a spiritual reconciliation with God but also a tangible effort to bring peace between divided groups, whether racial, religious, or political. The Church's ongoing role in promoting peace, forgiveness, and reconciliation reflects its mission to follow Jesus' example as a bridge-builder in a broken world.

The Significance of Jesus' Theology for the World

While Jesus' theology is central to the Christian faith, its relevance extends far beyond the Church. His teachings on love, justice, compassion, and human dignity speak to universal moral and ethical challenges and offer insights that can guide the world's approach to pressing social, political, and ethical issues.

1. Social Justice and Human Dignity

Jesus' commitment to the poor, the oppressed, and the marginalized is one of the most enduring aspects of His theology. His teachings consistently emphasize the inherent dignity of every person and the call to care for the "least of these" (Matthew 25:40). This focus on social justice continues to resonate in a world grappling with systemic inequality, poverty, and human rights abuses.

In modern contexts, Jesus' theology challenges governments, institutions, and individuals to advocate for justice, to fight against structures that oppress the vulnerable, and to promote policies that uphold the dignity of every person. His teachings provide a moral framework that calls for equity and the fair treatment of all, particularly the marginalized. The global movements for justice, human rights, and equitable development can find inspiration in Jesus' message, which calls for a world where the last shall be first and the oppressed are lifted up.

2. Global Peace and Reconciliation

Jesus' emphasis on peace, nonviolence, and reconciliation holds profound significance in the context of global conflicts. His command to love one's enemies

(Matthew 5:44) and His vision of peace challenge the cycles of violence and retribution that continue to plague nations and societies.

In a world marked by wars, political instability, and deep-seated divisions, Jesus' theology provides a vision for global peace and reconciliation. Governments, leaders, and activists can draw on His teachings to advocate for peaceful conflict resolution, diplomacy, and restorative justice. The peacemaking efforts of global institutions and movements are aligned with Jesus' call to seek reconciliation rather than perpetuate division. His teachings remind the world that true peace is not merely the absence of conflict but the presence of justice and right relationships between individuals and nations.

3. Ethics and Moral Leadership

In an age of moral uncertainty and ethical complexity, Jesus' teachings continue to offer guidance for personal and societal moral leadership. His insistence on truth, integrity, and the rejection of hypocrisy challenges both individuals and leaders to act with moral clarity and accountability. His famous saying, "Let your 'Yes' be 'Yes,' and your 'No,' 'No'" (Matthew 5:37), calls for honesty and transparency in all dealings.

For the world, particularly in the realms of politics, economics, and business, Jesus' theology underscores the importance of ethical leadership. His rejection of greed, self-interest, and exploitation calls for a reevaluation of systems that prioritize profit over people and power over justice. In a world facing moral crises—whether in terms of climate change, economic inequality, or political corruption—Jesus' teachings encourage a return to principles of humility, service, and care for the common good.

Interfaith Dialogue and the Role of Jesus

As discussed in the context of interfaith dialogue, Jesus plays a unique role in promoting understanding and cooperation across religious boundaries. His teachings of love, justice, and compassion are shared values that resonate with many of the world's religions, offering a common ethical foundation for collaboration and dialogue.

In an increasingly pluralistic world, where religious conflict and misunderstanding often contribute to global tensions, Jesus' message provides a model for building bridges between communities of different faiths. His openness to those outside His own religious and cultural background, exemplified by His encounters with the Samaritan woman and the Roman centurion, offers a path forward for respectful and meaningful interfaith engagement. The ongoing significance of Jesus' theology in this context lies in its ability to inspire mutual respect, peacebuilding, and a shared commitment to justice and the common good across diverse religious traditions.

The theology of Jesus Christ continues to hold immense significance for both the Church and the world, offering a moral and spiritual framework that speaks to the deepest challenges of the modern era. For the Church, Jesus' call to discipleship, His vision of the Kingdom of God, and His message of reconciliation remain central to its identity and mission. For the wider world, Jesus' teachings on social justice, peace, and ethical leadership provide timeless wisdom that can guide efforts toward creating a more just, peaceful, and compassionate global society.

In the face of ongoing conflicts, inequality, and moral uncertainty, the relevance of Jesus' theology endures, calling both Christians and non-Christians alike to live out the values of love, justice, and humility in their personal lives and in the world at large. As humanity continues to grapple with the complexities of modern life, Jesus' message remains a beacon of hope and a call to action for building a world that reflects the values of God's Kingdom—where justice, peace, and love reign supreme.

Final Reflections on the Study of Jesus and Its Impact on Christian Faith

The study of Jesus—His life, teachings, and theological significance—stands at the heart of Christian faith. As the central figure in Christianity, Jesus is not only the foundation upon which the Church is built but also the lens through which Christians understand God, salvation, and their purpose in the world. Engaging deeply with the person of Jesus and His theology brings profound insights that continue to shape individual believers, Christian communities, and the Church as a whole.

This reflection offers final thoughts on the study of Jesus and its transformative impact on Christian faith, focusing on three core areas: personal spiritual growth, the collective mission of the Church, and the relevance of Jesus' message in the modern world.

1. Personal Spiritual Growth: Encountering the Living Christ

At its core, the study of Jesus is not just an intellectual exercise but an invitation to encounter the living Christ. The more Christians reflect on Jesus' life, His words, and His actions, the deeper their relationship with Him becomes. Through the Gospels and personal devotion, believers are drawn into the transformative power of His love, grace, and forgiveness.

1.1. Jesus as the Model for Discipleship

Jesus' call to "follow me" (Matthew 16:24) remains the defining invitation for every Christian. In studying His teachings, believers are challenged to conform their lives to the values of the Kingdom of God, prioritizing love, mercy, humility, and justice. Jesus is the ultimate model for Christian living, offering a pattern for how to engage with the world—loving God with all one's heart, mind, and strength, and loving one's neighbor as oneself.

For individual Christians, the study of Jesus provides a blueprint for spiritual growth. His Sermon on the Mount, parables, and commands offer practical guidance on how to live in a way that reflects the Kingdom of God. By emulating Jesus' compassion, forgiveness, and selflessness, Christians can grow in holiness and develop a deeper connection with God.

1.2. The Transformative Power of Jesus' Grace

The study of Jesus also leads to a profound recognition of the grace He offers. In reflecting on His crucifixion and resurrection, Christians are reminded of the depth of God's love and the lengths to which Jesus went to redeem humanity. This grace is not earned but freely given, and it serves as the foundation for the Christian life.

For many believers, understanding the grace of Jesus has a transformative impact on their identity and sense of purpose. It offers the assurance that despite human weakness, sin, and failure, God's love is unconditional. This understanding empowers Christians to live lives marked by forgiveness—both receiving it from God and extending it to others. As Christians study Jesus and His redemptive work, they are invited to experience the profound freedom that comes from knowing they are fully accepted and loved by God.

2. The Collective Mission of the Church: Continuing Jesus' Ministry

The study of Jesus not only impacts individual believers but also has significant implications for the collective mission of the Church. Jesus' theology provides the framework for the Church's identity, calling, and mission in the world.

2.1. The Church as the Body of Christ

The New Testament describes the Church as the Body of Christ (1 Corinthians 12:27), a powerful image that conveys the Church's ongoing role in continuing Jesus' ministry on earth. By studying Jesus' life, the Church gains a clearer understanding of its mission to embody Christ's love, justice, and compassion in the world. Jesus' focus on serving the poor, healing the broken, and seeking justice for the oppressed shapes the Church's work in addressing the social, economic, and spiritual needs of humanity.

For the Church, studying Jesus' interactions with the marginalized—the sick, the poor, the outcast—reinforces its calling to be a community of hospitality, service, and advocacy for those on the margins. As the Body of Christ, the Church is tasked with embodying His love and care for all people, particularly those who are most vulnerable.

2.2. Proclaiming the Kingdom of God

Jesus' message about the Kingdom of God is central to the Church's mission. Throughout His ministry, Jesus announced the coming of God's reign—a Kingdom characterized by justice, peace, mercy, and love. For the Church, proclaiming this Kingdom remains a central task, both in preaching the Gospel and in working for its realization in the world.

By studying Jesus' teachings on the Kingdom of God, the Church is continually reminded that its mission goes beyond institutional growth or religious ritual. The Church is called to be a sign and foretaste of God's Kingdom, a community where the values of justice, mercy, and reconciliation are lived out in tangible ways. The study of Jesus inspires the Church to engage in transformative work that brings healing, hope, and renewal to the world.

3. The Relevance of Jesus' Message in the Modern World

The study of Jesus is not confined to history; it speaks powerfully to the challenges and complexities of the modern world. His teachings on love, justice, reconciliation, and humility remain relevant in addressing the most pressing issues of our time—whether they be social inequality, racial injustice, environmental degradation, or global conflicts.

3.1. Jesus and Social Justice

Jesus' commitment to justice, particularly His advocacy for the poor and marginalized, offers a compelling framework for engaging with issues of social justice today. His denunciation of hypocrisy and exploitation, as well as His call to care for the least of these, challenges Christians to take a stand against systemic injustice, inequality, and oppression.

In a world where poverty, discrimination, and human rights abuses are widespread, Jesus' teachings offer a moral and ethical foundation for pursuing justice. His vision of the Kingdom of God invites Christians to work for a world where all people are treated with dignity, equity, and compassion. The study of Jesus equips believers with the tools to address these contemporary challenges from a Christ-centered perspective.

3.2. Jesus as a Source of Hope and Reconciliation

In times of division, conflict, and uncertainty, the study of Jesus offers a message of hope and reconciliation. Jesus' teachings on forgiveness, peacemaking, and love for one's enemies provide a pathway for healing fractured relationships, whether between individuals, communities, or nations.

The relevance of Jesus' message is particularly important in a world often marked by hostility, polarization, and violence. His call to love one's enemies and to seek reconciliation offers a countercultural approach to resolving conflict. By studying Jesus' life and teachings, Christians are equipped to become agents of peace, bringing healing and unity to divided communities.

The study of Jesus has a profound and ongoing impact on Christian faith, shaping both individual lives and the collective mission of the Church. As believers reflect on Jesus' teachings, His example, and His redemptive work, they are drawn into a deeper relationship with God and inspired to live out the values of the Kingdom of God in their daily lives.

For the Church, Jesus' theology provides the foundation for its mission of love, justice, and reconciliation in the world. As the Body of Christ, the Church is called to continue Jesus' ministry, proclaiming the good news of God's Kingdom and working to bring healing and transformation to the world.

In the modern world, where social, political, and moral challenges are ever-present, Jesus' teachings offer timeless wisdom and guidance. His message of love, justice, humility, and peace speaks to the deepest longings of the human heart and provides a path forward for addressing the most pressing issues of our time. Through the study of Jesus, Christians are equipped to be a light in the world, embodying the hope and grace that He came to bring.

Appendix 1: Glossary of Theological Terms

Atonement

The reconciliation between God and humanity brought about through the life, death, and resurrection of Jesus Christ. Different theories of atonement include substitutionary atonement, Christus Victor, and moral influence.

Christology

The branch of theology dealing with the identity, nature, and role of Jesus Christ, especially concerning His divinity and humanity.

Cosmic Christ

A theological concept that sees Christ as not only the historical Jesus but also the eternal, universal presence of God, active in all creation.

Discipleship

The process of following Jesus and living according to His teachings. Discipleship involves spiritual growth, transformation, and commitment to the values of the Kingdom of God.

Eschatology

The study of the "last things" or end times, including the return of Christ, the final judgment, and the establishment of the Kingdom of God.

Exclusivism

The theological position that holds Jesus as the only way to salvation, with all other religious paths leading to falsehood or incomplete truth.

Inclusivism

The belief that while Jesus is the definitive means of salvation, God's grace may be at work in other religions, and people may be saved through Christ even without explicit faith in Him.

Incarnation

The Christian doctrine that God became human in the person of Jesus Christ, fully divine and fully human, in order to redeem humanity.

Kingdom of God

A central concept in Jesus' teaching, referring to God's reign of justice, peace, and love, which has been inaugurated through Christ but will be fully realized at the end of time.

Liberation Theology

A theological movement, particularly influential in Latin America, that interprets the Christian faith through the lens of social justice, emphasizing the liberation of the poor and oppressed.

Logos

A Greek term meaning "Word," used in the Gospel of John to describe Jesus as the divine Word through whom all things were created and who became incarnate to bring salvation.

Messiah

In Christian theology, Jesus is understood as the promised Savior and King from the Old Testament who would redeem Israel and bring salvation to the world. In Judaism, the Messiah is a future figure who will establish peace and restore Israel.

Monophysitism

A Christological heresy that teaches that Jesus has only one nature, either divine or a fusion of divine and human, rather than two distinct natures.

Nestorianism

A heretical belief that Jesus has two separate persons—one divine and one human—rather than being one person with two united natures.

Pentecost

The event described in Acts 2, where the Holy Spirit descended upon the apostles, empowering them to proclaim the Gospel and marking the birth of the Church.

Pluralism

The view that there are multiple valid paths to God, with no single religion holding exclusive access to divine truth.

Soteriology

The branch of theology that deals with the doctrine of salvation, examining how Jesus' life, death, and resurrection bring about human redemption.

Theotokos

A Greek term meaning "God-bearer," used to refer to Mary as the mother of Jesus. This title emphasizes the belief that Mary gave birth to Jesus, who is both fully God and fully human.

Trinity

The Christian doctrine that God is one in essence but exists in three persons: Father, Son, and Holy Spirit.

Appendix 2: Recommended Readings and Resources for Further Study

Books on Jesus and Christology

- N.T. Wright, Jesus and the Victory of God

A comprehensive study of the historical Jesus and His mission, examining His life within the context of first-century Judaism.

- Jaroslav Pelikan, Jesus Through the Centuries

This book explores the various ways Jesus has been interpreted throughout history, from the early Church to the modern era.

- Hans Küng, On Being a Christian

A theological reflection on what it means to be a Christian, with a focus on Jesus' identity, message, and mission.

- Richard Bauckham, Jesus: A Very Short Introduction

A concise yet profound overview of the life and significance of Jesus Christ in both historical and theological contexts.

Books on Interfaith Dialogue

- John Hick, The Metaphor of God Incarnate

This work discusses Christology in the context of religious pluralism and explores how Jesus might be understood across different faiths.

- Paul F. Knitter, Jesus and the Other Names: Christian Mission and Global Responsibility

A book that focuses on how Jesus is viewed in other religious traditions and the implications for Christian mission and dialogue.

Books on Christian Theology

- Alister E. McGrath, Christian Theology: An Introduction

A comprehensive textbook that covers all major areas of Christian theology, including Christology, soteriology, and eschatology.

- Jürgen Moltmann, The Crucified God

A significant contribution to theology that explores how the cross of Christ reveals God's solidarity with human suffering and oppression.

- Gustavo Gutiérrez, A Theology of Liberation

A seminal work on liberation theology, emphasizing Jesus' message of freedom for the poor and oppressed.

Online Resources and Journals

- The Journal of Christology

A peer-reviewed journal focusing on the theological study of Christ.

- The Jesus Seminar

A group of scholars dedicated to the historical study of Jesus and early Christian texts, often engaging with contemporary Christological debates.

- The Vatican Website

Contains official Church documents, encyclicals, and papal writings related to the life and theology of Jesus.

Appendix 3: Index of Key Topics and Names

This set of appendices is intended to provide readers with tools for further engagement with the study of Jesus, offering clear definitions, accessible reading material, and a detailed index to guide deeper exploration into the theological themes discussed in the book.

BIBLIOGRAPHY

This bibliography includes a comprehensive list of the sources and references used throughout the book, offering a range of theological, historical, and scholarly works that contributed to the study of Jesus and His theology.

Books on the Historical Jesus and Christology:

Bauckham, Richard. Jesus: A Very Short Introduction. Oxford: Oxford University Press, 2011.

A concise introduction to the person of Jesus, exploring His historical context, identity, and the theological significance of His life and teachings.

Crossan, John Dominic. *Jesus: A Revolutionary Biography.* San Francisco: HarperOne, 1994.

An exploration of Jesus as a social and political figure, emphasizing His role in challenging the social and religious structures of first-century Judea.

Ehrman, Bart D. *How Jesus Became God: The Exaltation of a Jewish Preacher from Galilee.* New York: HarperOne, 2014.

A historical and theological examination of how the early Christian movement came to view Jesus as divine.

Gutiérrez, Gustavo. *A Theology of Liberation: History, Politics, and Salvation.* Maryknoll: Orbis Books, 1973.

A foundational text in liberation theology, examining the intersection of Christian faith and social justice, and emphasizing Jesus' role as liberator of the poor.

Hurtado, Larry W. *Lord Jesus Christ: Devotion to Jesus in Earliest Christianity.* Grand Rapids: Eerdmans, 2003.

An in-depth study of how devotion to Jesus emerged in the early Christian communities and how this shaped the development of Christology.

Johnson, Elizabeth A. Consider Jesus: Waves of Renewal in Christology. New York: Crossroad Publishing, 1992.

A feminist theological exploration of how contemporary understandings of Jesus have evolved and the impact of this renewal on Christian faith and practice.

Küng, Hans. On Being a Christian. New York: Continuum, 1984.

A wide-ranging theological reflection on Christian faith, focusing on the centrality of Jesus Christ and His significance for Christian life and thought.

N.T. Wright. Jesus and the Victory of God. Minneapolis: Fortress Press, 1996.

A thorough historical and theological examination of Jesus within His first-century Jewish context, with a particular focus on His mission and message.

Books on Theology and Doctrine:

Barth, Karl. Church Dogmatics: The Doctrine of Reconciliation, Volume IV. Edinburgh: T&T Clark, 1956.

A monumental work in systematic theology, with a detailed discussion on the doctrine of reconciliation and the role of Jesus Christ in redeeming humanity.

Bonhoeffer, Dietrich. Christ the Center. New York: Harper & Row, 1978.

A Christological study that focuses on Jesus as the center of Christian theology and ethics, exploring the implications of His person and work for the Christian life.

McGrath, Alister E. Christian Theology: An Introduction. 6th ed. Oxford: Wiley-Blackwell, 2016.

A comprehensive introduction to the major themes and figures in Christian theology, including an in-depth discussion of Christology and the person of Jesus.

Moltmann, Jürgen. The Crucified God: The Cross of Christ as the Foundation and Criticism of Christian Theology. Minneapolis: Fortress Press, 1993.

A critical theological work that examines the meaning of the crucifixion and its implications for Christian theology, focusing on the suffering of Jesus and God's solidarity with the oppressed.

Books on Interfaith Dialogue:

Hick, John. The Metaphor of God Incarnate. London: SCM Press, 1993.

A philosophical exploration of the concept of the Incarnation in relation to religious pluralism, engaging with interfaith perspectives on Jesus.

Knitter, Paul F. Jesus and the Other Names: Christian Mission and Global Responsibility. Maryknoll: Orbis Books, 1996.

An examination of how Christians can approach interfaith dialogue and mission in a pluralistic world, with a particular focus on how Jesus is understood in other religious traditions.

Volf, Miroslav. Allah: A Christian Response. New York: HarperOne, 2011.

An exploration of the theological similarities and differences between Christianity and Islam, focusing on the concept of God and the figure of Jesus in both faiths.

Books on Ethics, Justice, and Social Theology:

Cone, James H. The Cross and the Lynching Tree. Maryknoll: Orbis Books, 2011.

A powerful reflection on the intersection of Christian theology, the cross of Jesus, and racial justice in America, drawing on the legacy of the African American experience.

Day, Dorothy. The Long Loneliness: The Autobiography of Dorothy Day. New York: Harper & Row, 1952.

The autobiography of social activist Dorothy Day, exploring how the teachings of Jesus influenced her work for justice and the poor.

Freire, Paulo. Pedagogy of the Oppressed. New York: Bloomsbury, 1970.

A seminal work in critical pedagogy that examines the relationship between education, oppression, and liberation, with significant implications for understanding Jesus' social message.

Journals and Articles:

Bauckham, Richard. "The Son of Man: 'A Man in My Position' or 'Someone'?" Journal for the Study of the New Testament 23, no. 1 (1985): 23-33.

An in-depth study of the meaning and implications of Jesus' use of the title "Son of Man" within the context of first-century Judaism.

Brown, Raymond E. "The Death of the Messiah: From Gethsemane to the Grave." Catholic Biblical Quarterly 56, no. 2 (1994): 334-338.

A scholarly examination of the Passion narratives in the Gospels, analyzing how they present the theological significance of Jesus' death.

Sobrino, Jon. "Jesus the Liberator: A Historical-Theological View." Concilium 4 (1976): 45-62.

An article that highlights the liberating aspects of Jesus' life and theology, focusing on His identification with the poor and marginalized.

Online Resources:

The Vatican. "Catechism of the Catholic Church." Accessed September 2023. www.vatican.va.

The official teachings of the Catholic Church, including sections on Christology, the person of Jesus, and His role in salvation.

The Jesus Seminar. "The Historical Jesus: Search and Discovery." Accessed September 2023. www.westarinstitute.org.

A collection of scholarly resources focused on the historical study of Jesus, particularly the quest for the historical figure behind the Gospels.

This bibliography represents a broad spectrum of theological and scholarly works that contributed to the exploration of Jesus' life, teachings, and ongoing significance for both the Church and the world. These sources offer a range of perspectives, from historical and doctrinal studies to interfaith and social justice-focused reflections, providing a comprehensive foundation for further study and reflection.